Education and Social Media

The John D. and Catherine T. MacArthur Foundation Series on Digital Media and Learning

Education and Social Media

Toward a Digital Future

edited by Christine Greenhow, Julia Sonnevend, and Colin Agur

The MIT Press
Cambridge, Massachusetts
London, England

This book was set in Stone Sans and Stone Serif by Toppan Best-set Premedia Limited. Printed and bound in the United States of America.

Library of Congress Cataloging-in-Publication Data

Names: Greenhow, Christine, editor. | Sonnevend, Julia, editor. | Agur, Colin, editor.
Title: Education and social media : toward a digital future / Christine Greenhow, Julia Sonnevend, and Colin Agur, eds.
Description: Cambridge, MA : The MIT Press, 2016. | Series: John D. and Catherine T. MacArthur Foundation series on digital media and learning | Includes bibliographical references and index.
Identifiers: LCCN 2015039872 | ISBN 9780262034470 (hardcover : alk. paper) | ISBN 9780262529044 (pbk. : alk. paper)
Subjects: LCSH: Internet in education–Social aspects. | Web-based instruction–Social aspects. | Educational technology–Social aspects. | Social media.
Classification: LCC LB1044.87 .E28 2016 | DDC 371.33/44678–dc23 LC record available at http://lccn.loc.gov/2015039872

10 9 8 7 6 5 4 3 2 1

Contents

Series Foreword

In recent years, digital media and networks have become embedded in our everyday lives and are part of broad-based changes to how we engage in knowledge production, communication, and creative expression. Unlike the early years in the development of computers and computer-based media, digital media are now *commonplace* and *pervasive*, having been taken up by a wide range of individuals and institutions in all walks of life. Digital media have escaped the boundaries of professional and formal practice, and of the academic, governmental, and industry homes that initially fostered their development. Now they have been taken up by diverse populations and noninstitutionalized practices, including the peer activities of youth. Although specific forms of technology uptake are highly diverse, a generation is growing up in an era when digital media are part of the taken-for-granted social and cultural fabric of learning, play, and social communication.

This book series is founded upon the working hypothesis that those immersed in new digital tools and networks are engaged in an unprecedented exploration of language, games, social interaction, problem solving, and self-directed activity that leads to diverse forms of learning. These diverse forms of learning are reflected in expressions of identity, in how individuals express independence and creativity, and in their ability to learn, exercise judgment, and think systematically.

The defining frame for this series is not a particular theoretical or disciplinary approach, nor is it a fixed set of topics. Rather, the series revolves around a constellation of topics investigated from multiple disciplinary and practical frames. The series as a whole looks at the relation between youth, learning, and digital media, but each contribution to the series might deal with only a subset of this constellation. Erecting strict topical boundaries would exclude some of the most important work in the field. For example, restricting the content of the series only to people of a certain age would mean artificially reifying an age boundary when the phenomenon demands otherwise. This would become particularly problematic with new forms of online participation where one important outcome is the mixing of participants of different ages. The same goes for digital media, which are increasingly inseparable from analog and earlier media forms.

The series responds to certain changes in our media ecology that have important implications for learning. Specifically, these changes involve new forms of media *literacy* and developments in the modes of media *participation*. Digital media are part of a convergence between interactive media (most notably gaming), online networks, and existing media forms. Navigating this media ecology involves a palette of literacies that are being defined through practice but require more scholarly scrutiny before they can be fully incorporated pervasively into educational initiatives. Media literacy involves not only ways of understanding, interpreting, and critiquing media but also the means for creative and social expression, online search and navigation, and a host of new technical skills. The potential gap in literacies and participation skills creates new challenges for educators who struggle to bridge media engagement inside and outside the classroom.

The John D. and Catherine T. MacArthur Foundation Series on Digital Media and Learning, published by the MIT Press, aims to close these gaps and provide innovative ways of thinking about and using new forms of knowledge production, communication, and creative expression.

Introduction

Christine Greenhow, Julia Sonnevend, and Colin Agur

The past ten years have brought significant growth in access to web technology and in the educational possibilities of social media. These changes challenge previous conceptualizations of education and the classroom and pose practical questions for students, educators, and administrators. Today, the capabilities of social media are influencing learning and teaching in ways previously unseen. Social media are transforming sectors outside education by changing patterns in personal, commercial, and cultural interaction. These changes offer a window into the future of education, with new means of knowledge production and reception and new roles for learners and teachers.[1] Surveying the uses to which social media have been put in these early years, we see a need to revision education for the coming decades. To date, no book has systematically and accessibly examined how the cultural and technological shift of social media is influencing educational practices. With this book, we aim to fill that gap.

This book critically explores the future of education and online social media, convening leading scholars from the fields of education, law, communications, sociology, and cultural studies. We believe that this interdisciplinary collection of essays will appeal to a broad audience of scholars, practitioners, and policymakers who seek to understand the opportunities for learning that exist at the intersection of social media and education. The book examines educational institutions, access and participation, new literacies and competencies, cultural reproduction, international accreditation, intellectual property, privacy and protection, new business models, and technical architectures for digital education.

The book begins with an introduction to digital education and social media (chapter 1), which conceptualizes the digital transformation now taking place in a variety of educational contexts. Following that, Part I explores the new educational possibilities social media offer, with chapters that examine social media usage in a pair of U.S. school districts (chapter 2), online communities of youth (chapter 3), distance-based educational initiatives in developing countries (chapter 4), and social media–based education in news organizations (chapter 5). In Part II, the discussion shifts to the ways that the incorporation of social media is challenging and disrupting existing educational models. This section looks at new norms of knowledge and authority that have emerged with respect to social media (chapter 6), changing notions of privacy and identity among youth (chapter 7), the challenge online educational institutions pose for accreditation and educational assessment (chapter 8), and the tensions between the new ease of sharing and mixing and laws protecting copyright (chapter 9). Part III offers a series of case studies that demonstrate in practice both the possibilities and the challenges social media offer as educational tools. These case studies explore ways to teach about media (chapter 10), technology and the economics of higher education (chapters 11 and 12), massive open online courses (MOOCs) (chapter 13), educating teachers with social media (chapter 14), and participatory play (chapter 15). The book concludes with an assessment of the changes that have taken place as a result of social media use in educational contexts, and a view to the future.

Part and Chapter Descriptions

Chapter 1, "The Digital Transformation of Education," sets the stage for the discussions to follow. Jack Balkin (Knight Professor of Constitutional Law and the First Amendment, Yale Law School) and Julia Sonnevend (assistant professor of communication studies, the University of Michigan) examine the possibilities of hybrid models in education that combine traditional models of teacher-student interaction with one-to-many and many-to-many digital models. In hybrid models of education, many tasks formerly performed by a single teacher—lecturing, leading discussions, supervising work, answering questions, grading—can be broken down into separate tasks and performed by different actors. Those tasks that scale effectively—such as basic lectures, presentations of materials, peer-to-peer interactions and projects that require minimal direct supervision—can be handled by online media. Other, more time-intensive elements of education would still require the direct interaction of students and teachers in real time and space. Although the emerging hybrid model offers new opportunities for educating vast numbers of people more inexpensively, it also transforms the market for teachers, threatens incumbent models of education—particularly in nonprofit institutions—and raises important questions about the nature of education itself.

The first part, "New Opportunities for Education and Social Media," examines the opportunities for revisioning educational goals, access to education, democratic participation, and the means of knowledge production in global educational contexts.

In "Addressing the Social Envelope: Education and the Digital Divide," Mark Warschauer (professor of education and informatics at the University of California, Irvine) considers equity in access, use, and outcomes related to educational technology and new media in diverse U.S. communities. The author draws on two school districts as exemplars, one that focused on equipment and the other that emphasized curricular reform and social support for increasingly ubiquitous personal communication technologies (ICTs) such as mobile phones. His discussion highlights the importance of social and educational context for learning technologies, illuminating the ways in which such devices can create opportunities for broader democratic participation.

In "Do You See What I See? Visibility through Social Media," danah boyd (research scientist at Microsoft Research and a fellow at the Berkman Center for Internet and Society, Harvard Law School) reports on how American youth project identities through social media. Examining three instances in which adults initially missed the point of MySpace content created by teens, boyd comments on the importance of context in interpreting social media posts. She also describes her methods for finding social media content created by users outside her sociocultural network and explores questions about the motivations and moral obligations of members of the social media audience.

In "ICTs and Education in Developing Countries: The Case of India," Colin Agur (Bartlett Fellow for Access to Knowledge, the Information Society Project, Yale Law School) examines how the "digital divide" is expressed in developing countries as ICTs are introduced into educational contexts. Using several ICT programs in India as examples, Agur demonstrates the potential for technology to lift people of lower socioeconomic status in developing countries by providing access to inexpensive, open learning opportunities. Further, Agur argues that ICTs need not act as invasive species in the native educational ecologies of developing countries. Instead, he asserts, ICTs can stimulate a natural evolution in the educational systems of developing countries in ways that respect local customs and tastes.

In "Social Media Education in News Organizations: Experimentation at the BBC," Valerie Belair-Gagnon (executive director and research scholar with the Information Society Project, Yale Law School) explores how one of the world's leading public broadcasters is putting social media to use. In addition to using social media for news production and distribution, the BBC is also integrating social media into training for journalists at all stages of their careers. Belair-Gagnon shows how, after an initial period of uncertainty, the BBC has become a leader in social media–based education for journalists inside and outside the public broadcaster.

Part II, "Challenges and Disruptions," anticipates the ways in which social media pose challenges and repercussions for education as an institution and for modes of teaching and learning, and suggests how these might be overcome.

In "Social Media and Challenges to Traditional Educational Models," Chris Dede (professor of education, Harvard University) describes how educational institutions are disrupted by social media, with parallels to the disruption of journalism and the music industry. Dede argues that social media users are developing new norms about how knowledge is created and shared—and what authorities are used to evaluate learning. These changes in widely accepted educational practice are bound to provoke changes in how institutions of learning operate, Dede states. In his view, this impending shift can catalyze a complete revision of our education system to acknowledge lifelong and lifewide learning.

In "Reframing Privacy and Youth Media Practices," John Palfrey (head of school at Phillips Andover Academy) summarizes perceived threats to privacy and child protection relevant to educational and institutional policy-making. Although many adults believe that young people don't care about privacy, Palfrey points to research showing that many teens have a high degree of interest in privacy without a solid understanding of how to protect it. In this context, the author proposes several policy reforms designed to help young people better manage the information they post in semipublic forums. Palfrey's suggestions include restricting the commercialization of personal data posted by youth in digital spaces controlled by private companies.

In "The Growth of Online Universities: How to Solve the Accreditation Dilemma, Protect Students, and Expand Access to Higher Education," Nicholas Bramble (former lecturer in law at Yale Law School and director of the Law and Media Program, the Information Society Project) and Yite John Lu (intellectual property litigation associate at the Los Angeles office of Irell and Manella LLP) discuss issues of accreditation, reputation, validity, gatekeeping, and quality control. The authors suggest ways in which accreditation organizations might adjust their metrics to evaluate increasingly popular, peer-driven online educational opportunities. Possible approaches include the creation of an international educational agency and switching from the current binary system—either institutions are accredited or they're not—to a rating system that would allow various grades of accreditation.

In "Copyright Reform and Educational Progress," Nicholas Bramble explores ways for educators to reach more learners by expanding the use of copyrighted material. The author suggests several ways in which the ill-defined concept of fair use might be clarified by courts, educators, and copyright holders to allow both students and educators to creatively adapt, reinterpret and share existing information artifacts for non-commercial, learning purposes.

Part III, "Social Media and Education in the Coming Decade," presents scenarios of social media experiments in education.

In "Do We Really Need Media Education 2.0? Teaching Media in the Age of Participatory Culture," David Buckingham (professor of education and director of the Centre for the Study of Children, Youth and Media, University of London) makes the case for what and how we should teach *about* media, in K–12 schools and universities. He takes a measured approach, advocating the teaching of both traditional media criticism as well as Web 2.0 skills related to content creation and participation. Further, Buckingham urges educators to resist what he calls "technofetishism," or celebrating technology in education for its own sake. Nevertheless, he acknowledges that educators who do not participate in new media culture risk losing the so-called "right to teach" by living in a different society from that of their students.

In "University of the People: A Model for International, Tuition-Free, Open Education Powered by Social Media," Shai Reshef (CEO of University of the People) offers his opinion on how a future international education system might unfold supported by freely available social media and lessons learned from the University of the People model. Launched in September, 2009, University of the People operates on the generosity of volunteers, mainly faculty, staff, and graduate students associated with established universities where English is the main language of instruction. The author gives an insider's view of how University of the People works, noting that one early lesson from its operation is that volunteers need some paid backup staff.

In "Technology and the Economics of Education," Daniel Greenwood (professor of law, Hofstra University, and CFO, University of the People) surveys business models for social media education. Noting that the marginal cost for educating one more student online is zero, while the average cost of creating new research products and training a new scholar is quite high, Greenwood suggests that the traditional economic model underpinning universities is unsustainable in a digital world. While holding out University of the People as an example of how wealthy countries can generously distribute knowledge to the rest of the world, Greenwood argues that such endeavors can bankrupt the more complex, face-to-face educational institutions that are needed to drive innovation and develop new faculty. The author discusses several new financial models for "our core institutions" of education. His recommendations include more substantial government subsidy and a revamp of the current patent and copyright systems.

In "Social Media and Education on a Massive Scale: The Case of MOOCs," Minhtuyen Mai (graduate student in Educational Policy, University of Wisconsin–Madison), Adam Poppe (doctoral student in Educational Psychology and Educational Technology, Michigan State University), and Christine Greenhow (assistant professor, the Department of Counseling, Education Psychology, and Special Education, College of Education, Michigan State University) discuss the emergence of different types of MOOCs and the research on and opinions generated by this new teaching method. They also analyze the benefits of and challenges to using MOOCs, and provide a view of the immediate future of massive open classes.

In "Social Media and Teacher Education: the Case of StarTalk," Jiahang Li (assistant professor, the Department of Counseling, Educational Psychology, and Special Education of the College of Education, Michigan State University) discusses the relationship between social media and teacher education. By synthesizing empirical research, this chapter identifies several affordances that social media has with respect to teacher education, including promoting collaborative learning, building a community of practice, and generating content. Furthermore, it provides an exemplar case of foreign language teacher education program, STARTALK, to illustrate the affordances and challenges in relation to social media adoption.

In "Teens' Participatory Play: Digital Media Learning through Civic Engagement," Benjamin Gleason (PhD candidate in the Educational Psychology and Educational Technology program, Michigan State University) discusses an emerging model of civic engagement. He emphasizes the ways in which young people can use the affordances of the Internet in projects that are personally meaningful to learn valuable technological, communicative, and artistic skills and develop professional expertise. He uses two examples, Mouse and World's Fair 2064, of how digital media can support teenagers' individual competences while also developing the capacity of the community to respond to its pressing needs.

In the conclusion, Ri Pierce-Grove (PhD candidate in Communications, Columbia University, and visiting fellow, the Information Society Project,

Yale Law School) brings together key themes from the preceding chapters and offers thoughts on the changing state of play with respect to social media in education.

Key Themes of This Book

The chapters in this book highlight significant changes taking place in education as a result of the arrival of social media.

Several chapters discuss changes in the ways that knowledge is being produced and consumed. In a variety of educational contexts—traditional classrooms, distance-based learning, continuing education for professionals, and elsewhere—social media enable different types of pedagogy, based on new interactions among a wider set of participants. These interactions also allow for new ways of creating, sharing, displaying, and manipulating knowledge for educational purposes.

Another theme of the book is the appearance of structural change in traditional educational models. Digital education offers new possibilities for the agency of learners as seekers, creators, sharers, and consumers of knowledge. At the same time, this agency has blurred the lines of what is "inside" and "outside" the learning environment and made the classroom part of a connected and "always on" world of information. The structure of educational models is also being challenged by new power dynamics, with old and new actors jostling for control of complex systems of knowledge making and distribution. The debate on social media and education includes not just parents, students, teachers, and administrators but also technology providers, consultants, policy experts, and academic researchers.

Although the book focuses on social media in educational contexts, several chapters hint at wider social changes taking place. These include shifting conceptions of identity and the self, as people make decisions about who they are online and offline, what privacy means to them, and how they relate to those with different digital skills. Another social change is in conceptions of community and belonging. Users of social media can develop links with a much wider network of people than was possible in geographically bound communities such as neighborhoods and schools. These users are able to connect with others—near and far—who share their interests, opinions, experiences, and desires. Social media, in education and in life, allow those who feel alone locally to feel connected to others elsewhere. This has implications for the ways people relate to their neighbors, their classmates, and the institutions that are part of their lives. At the same time, social media can also contribute to alienation, discrimination and inequality in education and in the broader social life. This book shows both the hopeful and the darker implications of digital knowledge distribution in contemporary societies.

Note

1. Christine Greenhow, Beth Robelia, and Joan E. Hughes, Web 2.0 and Classroom Research: What Path Should We Take *Now? Educational Researcher* 38, no. 4 (2009): 246–259.

Bibliography

Greenhow, Christine, Beth Robelia, and Joan E. Hughes. Web 2.0 and Classroom Research: What Path Should We Take *Now? Educational Researcher* 38 (4) (2009): 246–259.

Greenhow, Christine, and Benjamin Gleason. Twitteracy: Tweeting as a New Literacy Practice. *Educational Forum* 76 (2012):463–477.

Greenhow, Christine, and Benjamin Gleason. Social scholarship: Reconsidering Scholarly Practices in the Age of Social Media. *British Journal of Educational Technology* 45 (3) (2014): 392–402.

Greenhow, Christine, and Benjamin Gleason. The Social Scholar: Re-interpreting Scholarship in the Shifting University. *On the Horizon* 23 (4) (2015): 1–8.

1 The Digital Transformation of Education

Jack M. Balkin and Julia Sonnevend

The Internet has transformed many facets of knowledge production and distribution, from journalism to the music industry. Education is also in the early stages of a fundamental reconfiguration. This chapter considers how digital environments will likely shape the content, scope, and practice of education.

1. The Reduction of Spatial and Temporal Limits on Education: Economies of Scale and Superbroadcasting

Traditionally, most education has been spatially fixed and geographically limited. People have gone to schools in buildings in fixed locations. Because students travel to a specific geographic location, they normally have to live within relatively close proximity to their schools or else they have to live within the school itself. In this traditional approach, the number of students is limited by the number of people who can fit into the buildings—and by the number of individual schoolrooms within the buildings. Space puts an upper limit on the number of students any single teacher can teach. Education under these conditions lacks economies of scale. As the student population increases, schools need to increase the number of teachers as well.

The same features of traditional school education make it temporally limited. Teachers cannot teach twenty-four hours per day, nor can students learn. The school day is temporally bounded, and normally is divided into distinct classes that last a certain amount of time. In most schools students attend different classes one after the other; they cannot attend different classes simultaneously. Hence classes must be scheduled so as not to conflict with each other in terms of either space or time. These features make traditional education a bit like a schedule for television networks, with different channels of information packaged into programs that follow one after another in time.

The digitally networked environment frees education from its traditional spatial and temporal limitations. As it does so, however, new constraints and limitations emerge that were always present in the traditional model but now become especially salient.

A traditional model of education is a broadcast model, in which an expert teacher provides instruction to a group of students. The mode of communication is one-to-many. As we shall see, digital networks offer alternatives to this model of one-to-many education; at the same time, they also extend and amplify it. That is because digital networks offer economies of scale for certain forms of education but not for others. When people exploit these economies of scale, the traditional broadcast model becomes a super-broadcast model.

First, using digital networks means that geography no longer places an upper limit on the number of students that a teacher can reach. Students and teachers do not have to be in the same location for the teacher to communicate with the students. Teachers can speak to an indefinite number of students. Conversely, an indefinite number of students can take the same class.

Second, educational institutions do not need to invest in buildings to house additional classes, or offices in which teachers work and plan lessons. Potentially, this lowers cost because fewer and fewer teachers can do the work that previously required many teachers. Moreover, educational institutions do not need to ration space and time as they do in traditional school buildings.

Third, educators do not need to schedule classes like programs on atelevision network. Students can play videos or access websites twenty-four hours a day. They can, at least in theory, experience education at any place and at any time, in any order.

Yet freeing education from traditional limitations of time and space makes other constraints and limitations on education increasingly important and salient. Students can view online materials and videos when their schedule permits but they will enjoy relatively limited direct connection with and feedback from their teachers. A superbroadcast model makes individual student-teacher interactions increasingly difficult if not impossible. Some, but not all, forms of learning may be well suited to such a model.

2. Digital Networks and Peer-to-Peer Education

Problems of scale lead to a second basic model of digital education. Digital networks also facilitate many-to-many or peer-to-peer education. People can learn through using social media such as Facebook, YouTube, and Flickr, and in multiplayer gaming environments. Social media, including gaming environments, provide platforms for intellectual exploration, the exchange of ideas, and the communal construction of projects. Students can get significant feedback from their peers using social media, and they can learn skills by building things together. These media do not require that participants be located in the same geographic space.

Using social media, students can educate themselves and each other. For example, gaming environments, properly designed, can give students opportunities to explore, build, and develop skills without constant input from or intervention by teachers.

To the extent that digital education adopts peer-to-peer methods, the role of the educational professional changes. Increasingly, the roles of teacher and textbook author are joined if not displaced by those of the moderator and the platform designer. The moderator facilitates peer-to-peer interactions, solves technical problems, and resolves conflicts. The platform designer is a sort of educational engineer who sets up the platform (whether a game environment or a social medium), adds appropriate educational content, and designs the space so that it facilitates group interaction and social cooperation and provides maximal educational benefit and exploratory potential. Indeed, there can be multiple levels of platform design, with some designers creating basic social media that can be adapted for educational purposes, some creating interactive tools specifically designed for education, and others adapting these tools to particular educational environments.

Just as some forms of education are more geographically bounded and labor-intensive than others, some forms of education may make better use of social media–based digital education than others. Online environments may be particularly useful in disciplines in which students can work together to solve problems and in situations in which education arises from a repeated process of teamwork, mutual influence, and collaboration. At the opposite end of the spectrum, online environments may be useful in areas where there are clearly defined right and wrong answers and students can mechanically check each other's work. Between these two polar opposites lie disciplines that do not offer clearly correct answers, that emphasize the mastery of a canon of materials and associations, and that require the gradual development of situational sense through professional training.

3. Difficulties of Scale and Hybrid Models

Digital networks facilitate both one-to-many and many-to-many models of digital education. In theory, each of these models might scale well beyond the size of the traditional classroom or lecture hall. But each has its limitations.

What is suitable for some forms of education may prove deficient for others. Some forms of education benefit greatly from students and teachers being in close physical proximity, and from relatively small student-to-teacher ratios. Students may require close supervision in some subjects and interaction and exchange with their teachers. In such situations, teacher expertise and guidance are especially important. These forms of education are labor-intensive; they require relatively small teacher-to-pupil ratios. They do not scale well even when technology eliminates older geographic and temporal limits for education or enables peer-to-peer interactions.

Forms of education that require close supervision and considerable teacher-student interaction may continue to thrive in the digital age precisely because they cannot be effectively duplicated online—assuming, of course, that there is sufficient public and private financial support for them. But that is precisely the problem. One-to-many and many-to-many forms of digital education may crowd out more traditional labor-intensive approaches precisely because economies of scale make the former less expensive.

It is not, however, an either-or proposition. A great advantage of digital networks is that they offer the possibility of hybrid models, combining traditional labor-intensive models of teacher-pupil interaction with one-to-many and many-to-many digital models. Tasks formerly performed by a single teacher—lecturing, leading discussions, supervising work, answering questions, grading—can be broken down into separate tasks and performed by different actors. Those tasks that scale effectively—basic lectures and presentation of materials, and peer-to-peer interactions and projects that do not require much direct supervision—can be handled through online media, even as other elements of education continue to use labor-intensive student-pupil interactions. Both public and private institutions may turn to hybrid models to save costs even if important aspects of education do not scale well.

Long before the arrival of the Internet, research universities had adopted analogous cost-saving methods. Many courses feature lectures by a single professor, assisted by an army of adjuncts and graduate students to teach sections and grade papers and exams. Digital models might allow an even greater extension of these cost-saving approaches. Institutions can pool lectures and lecturers through licensing arrangements, while adjuncts and advanced students can check work and facilitate discussions online.

Some of these hybrid models will improve the educational experience for many students and expand access at lower cost for people who could not otherwise afford an education. At the same time, these hybrid models may produce winner-take-all effects.

To see why, consider the aspects of education that scale most easily and are no longer geographically bounded—lecturing and providing educational materials. Teachers who offer lectures on a particular subject no longer compete solely with teachers in the same geographic area for audiences and employment; they compete in national and even international markets. Therefore fewer lecturers are necessary for any particular subject. This means that a comparatively small number of schools with recognizable brand names might be able to capture an increasingly large share of the market for digital education, with a relatively small group of well-known lecturers attaining higher salaries in the process. Other educators will have to work for less or move to less popular or niche subjects. In the alternative, they will participate in the more labor-intensive aspects of education. Thus, the move to hybrid models may significantly alter labor markets for educators. Fewer educators will be needed to broadcast lectures; more educators will be needed to perform the less well-paid, time-intensive work of grading papers and interacting with students online.

Newspapers offer a partial analogy. Before the Internet, newspaper distribution was geographically limited. People received national and international news from their local paper. Once people could get news from anywhere, however, local newspapers increasingly shed reporters and bureaus covering national and international news and relied increasingly on news services for coverage, while a handful of national newspapers, such as the *New York Times,* the *Wall Street Journal,* and the *Washington Post,* gained the lion's share of traffic for this news. Predictably, the number of well-paying jobs available for reporters covering national and international news has declined.

4. New Limitations

Although digital networks seem to remove limitations on access to education, new limitations on access to education emerge in the digital age, while other limitations, which already existed, become increasingly salient.

The first limitation is Internet access, a special case of the problem of the digital divide. Limited Internet access affects both the number of people who can gain access to digital education and the media that can be used. Cell phone use may be widespread, even in rural areas, but in many places broadband access is both rare and comparatively expensive. To the extent that digital education relies on bandwidth-intensive video and multimedia programming, many students around the world may not have effective access; if they have only low-bandwidth access, they must rely primarily on text-based systems.

A second limitation is language. Language replaces geography as a major barrier to educational access. Schools can reach students all over the world as long as these students understand the language in which instruction is offered. Online enterprises will have to offer versions in different languages to expand their reach in global markets. To lower costs, many enterprises will decide to focus on the most widely spoken languages, such as English, Chinese, Arabic, or Spanish. This may reinforce the dominance of these languages over time. Digital education might also strengthen a single national language at the expense of minority languages.

A third important limitation is control over architectures and standards. Especially when it involves multimedia, online education requires techno-logical standards and platforms for producing and displaying content and facilitating communication and interaction among students and instruc-tors. The design of these platforms and standards raises important ques-tions: whether platforms and standards are freely open for use by others or are closed, whether they are proprietary and require licensing fees, and whether they are interoperable with other platforms and standards. Interop-erable standards mean easy movement of students and materials from one platform to another. If educational platforms are not interoperable, it will be difficult to move educational materials or to exchange information (including homework, collaborative projects, grades, and evaluations) between platforms. This may prevent competitors from free-riding, but it will also promote lock-in. Open standards will encourage third-party appli-cations; closed standards will give online enterprises greater control.

A fourth limitation, already mentioned, is scalability. As we have seen, only some aspects of education are successfully scalable online; other ele-ments are likely to be labor-intensive and costly. The growth of digital edu-cational enterprises will depend on the degree to which they can lower the cost of these labor-intensive elements or avoid responsibility for providing them. If digital enterprises do not have to provide the labor-intensive ele-ments of education, they will shift the responsibility (and the expense) to other actors.

The fifth limitation is control over intellectual property. A vast amount of information is available for free on the Internet or is available for non-commercial purposes under a Creative Commons license. Incumbent institutions already use this material to supplement their courses; conversely, some colleges and universities allow the public access to lectures and teaching materials.

Some digital enterprises will rely extensively on freely available educational materials. But in the long run, intellectual property will be crucial, just as it is in many other areas of knowledge production. Many of the most valuable educational materials will be limited by licenses so that they cannot legally be used by for-profit or nonprofit competitors. In addition, for-profit enterprises will want to create proprietary materials to distinguish themselves and to justify charging tuition. Similarly, publishers of textbooks and other educational materials have developed and will continue to develop online and multimedia versions suitable for digital education. Each of these players will demand intellectual property protection and will use various versions of digital rights management to prevent their materials from being copied and used by competitors and unauthorized end users.

5. Competition with Incumbents, Accreditation, and Government Regulation

State accreditation and regulation will likely prove important factors in the growth and development of digital education. Because the one-to-many and many-to-many models of digital education lower costs, online educational enterprises have sprung up around the world, and more are likely to follow. Some are adjuncts of existing nonprofit educational institutions, while others are for-profit and nonprofit enterprises that offer courses of study tailored to online environments.

To the extent that online enterprises scale and can provide educational services at lower cost, they pose a competitive threat to existing forms of education. A degree or certificate provides not only valuable human capital but also credentials; yet education is often expensive, especially vocational and higher education. People who seek vocational or specialized education may choose less expensive forms of online education. This will put competitive pressure on the market for educational services offered by traditional institutions, which often require considerable investments in tuition and time and force students to assume large amounts of long-term debt. Many students will weigh quality of credentialing and quality of education against cost and debt obligations, just as they already do when choosing among existing educational institutions. Market pressures may lead some incumbent institutions to adopt digital technologies in order to cut costs or provide low-cost alternatives.

Digital alternatives affect both the demand for and the supply of educational services. Traditional educational institutions have high fixed costs, including the costs of maintaining the physical plant and paying administrative and faculty salaries. By dispensing with most of these expenses, online educational enterprises can charge far less for their services per pupil, in return for reduced teacher-student interaction. These enterprises will attract students who would not otherwise have been willing or able to get an education. At the same time, lower costs will put pressure on traditional educational institutions. This pressure will be exacerbated if state governments begin to view online education as an easy way of cutting costs and begin to push state-supported schools to substitute lower-cost online technologies for traditional labor-intensive methods of education.

As we note below, much education in online environments is informal and is not directed to the production of state-approved credentials or degrees, even though internal systems for recognizing achievement may develop within them. Educational organizations that do not seek to issue credentialing degrees and certificates will face a very different path from that taken by for-profit enterprises that seek to issue officially recognized degrees and certificates. That is because the latter compete more directly with incumbent institutions.

For online educational alternatives to succeed, people will have to treat online degrees and certificates as valuable credentials in the same way that they treat degrees and certificates from incumbent institutions. The most obvious path to making these credentials valuable is to have them officially recognized by the state.

This is not the only path, to be sure: businesses can and do award certificates for vocational training, mastery of software, or the development of other skills. A wide range of vocational and technological training exists alongside the education offered by high schools, colleges, and universities. These educational systems offer alternative forms of recognition and credentialing, and in some cases they may be even more important for certain employers. Moreover, even without awarding state-approved diplomas and certificates, online enterprises can produce a wide range of credentials to indicate status and accomplishment. Depending on how these credentials are treated by society at large—and especially by employers—they might create a separate track of educational status and accreditation.

Nevertheless, state accreditation of online degrees and diplomas will greatly accelerate acceptance of online institutions as genuine rivals to incumbents. Therefore we are likely to see repeated controversies and struggles over state accreditation and state regulation of online enterprises.

Online education does more than compete with incumbent educational institutions. It also challenges existing systems of state accreditation, which shape and limit the institutions that participate in the market for educational services. State accreditation systems, like many professional licensing systems, operate simultaneously as a device for ensuring quality and as a means for limiting new entrants.

Because educational systems have traditionally been territorially based, they have fallen within the regulatory competence of territorial governments. Even governments with long-standing protections for freedom of speech have long traditions of regulating education. In the United States, for example, education is subject to regulation at the local, state, and federal levels. In many countries, only accredited educational institutions may satisfy elementary school requirements and grant high school diplomas and university degrees.

Governments generally justify regulation of education on the grounds that education has elements of a public good. The benefits of education do not merely benefit the individual recipient; they are dispersed throughout society. Conversely, a poorly educated population makes society as a whole worse off.

Because education benefits society, and because governments assume that most people who live in a nation will continue to remain there after they are educated, governments traditionally have both subsidized and regulated education. In the United States, most accredited educational institutions are either publicly maintained or receive significant public funding, through government grants or through the tax system. Direct control over public institutions and indirect control of private institutions through government funding and tax policy allows governments to regulate many different aspects of the educational experience. Even with respect to purely privately-funded educational institutions, governments often specify what level of education is required for students, regulate which institutions can be accredited, set requirements on who can teach, and specify the levels of competence that schools must provide. Governments regulate both for quality control and to ensure that appropriate knowledge and values are inculcated.

Online educational programs may fit awkwardly into the assumptions of traditional state educational regulation. Not only do online environments challenge state-accredited educational institutions; in some cases, they may challenge the state's own educational policy goals.

Because online enterprises can provide education in many different jurisdictions simultaneously, they may not conform to the values and policies of territorial governments, including governments' language and cultural policies. Government officials may object that online institutions do not offer education that is adequate or appropriate for their populations. Moreover, in many jurisdictions, governments specify not only the credentials of teachers but also the educational materials used; Internet educators may not always respect these choices. Just as in the case of online speech, online education has the capacity to route around existing regulation and provide educational experiences that differ in content and form from what territorial governments (or incumbent institutions) would like.

Governments are not the only institutions troubled by these end runs. Traditionally, much education has been sponsored by religious institutions, not only for charitable purposes but also to inculcate orthodox views. Online religious education allows multiple perspectives—or heresies, depending on one's view—to be taught and perpetuated. In fact, one of the most likely uses of digital education is religious instruction, especially by groups that lack the resources of more established sects and seek to spread their message.

Some incumbent educational institutions will likely lobby governments to keep new online institutions from gaining official accreditation; failing that, they will try to prevent online institutions from obtaining accreditation on a par with that enjoyed by incumbents. Nevertheless, many incumbents will probably award their own online degrees and certificates in order to expand their influence and market share. In doing so, they will naturally have to consider whether they are undermining their own competitive position or their existing reputation. However, incumbents may reason that if someone is going to offer online education (and especially for a fee), they are the best equipped to do so because of their long experience, professionally trained faculty, and high professional standards.

Incumbents object to accreditation of new online enterprises out of mixed motives. On the one hand, they are concerned about preserving educational quality, maintaining professional values, and preventing newcomers from taking advantage of prospective students, who may be inadequately informed about their choices. On the other hand, incumbents also seek to prevent unwelcome competition that undermines their existing models for financing and providing educational services.

6. The Changing Role of Amateurs and Professionals in Digital Education

Two characteristic features of digital speech—and digital networks gener-ally—are routing around and glomming on. Routing around means that end users do not need to rely on traditional gatekeepers of knowledge pro-duction and distribution; instead, they can use digital media to address fellow audiences (and end users) directly. Glomming on means using exist-ing available content—some created by professionals, some by amateurs—and appropriating, combining, modifying, and sharing it. Digital education features its own characteristic versions of routing around and glomming on, just as we have seen in the cases of journalism, video, and music.

Partly because of these phenomena, digital networks alter the nature of professionalism, as well as the relationships between professionals and nonprofessionals.

First, professional educators reach new audiences. The digitally net-worked environment offers traditional educational institutions the possi-bility of reaching large numbers of people outside the academy. Many educational institutions have begun to place lectures, lecture notes, and outlines online for consumption by the general public. This blurs the tradi-tional boundaries between teaching, public service, and community relations.

Universities and scholars may post educational materials online for an undifferentiated audience rather than exclusively for their students and for fellow academics. This creates the possibility of new conversations between professionals and nonprofessionals, as well as between nonprofessionals. The distinction between teaching enrolled students and engaging in public commentary and public service tends to blur. Interactive media allow knowledge professionals—including professional educators—to be more than merely broadcasters. Professionals may receive increasing amounts of feedback and other information—whether welcome or unwelcome—from their expanded audiences.

Second, and conversely, professional educators face new competition for the attention of and influence over their students. Some of this competi-tion comes from other professionals, whose views and opinions are now more easily accessible to students. Equally important, however, is competi-tion from nonprofessionals for audience attention and influence.

Third, professionalism, generally speaking, involves a form of hierarchy justified by professional conceptions of merit. Competition from nonpro-fessionals for audience attention tends to either flatten or challenge this hierarchy, both for good and for ill. As noted before, accreditation systems are an important means of preserving and enforcing educational standards and thus educational hierarchies. Routing around and glomming on by nonprofessionals undermines these systems.

Fourth, given expanded audience participation, some professional educators and educational organizations will take on a different mix of tasks and functions. One example is more time spent on the curation of knowledge: assembling and organizing materials that others—both professionals and nonprofessionals—can use. Another is the creation and maintenance of platforms for creativity and participation by nonprofessionals. To be sure, professional educators have always performed these functions to some extent. Curating and organizing educational materials have always been parts of teachers' jobs, and good teachers attempt to create opportunities to encourage their students' participation and creativity. Digital education merely places new emphasis on these functions and makes them more important and salient.

Fifth, education and entertainment will tend to merge and become more like each other. There are several different reasons for this convergence: (1) the expanded use of multimedia and visual media, which work best when they are entertaining; (2) the expansion of audiences seeking education; (3) competition from nonprofessionals and for-profit organizations; (4) increasingly scarce audience attention; (5) the widespread diffusion of online gaming and role-playing technologies; and (6) long-term changes spawned by digital networks that tend to merge leisure activity and work. Successful educators have often been good rhetoricians and entertainers, but the merger of digital education and entertainment nevertheless challenges professional values because it changes expectations about how educators should present educational material to their audiences.

Sixth, increased competition will place pressure on professional norms. For-profit enterprises can offer cheaper education using a superbroadcast model, while nonprofessionals can reach (and influence) other people as easily if not more easily than educational professionals can. Indeed, not only must educational professionals compete with nonprofessionals and new online enterprises for audience attention, but the latter can also offer competing educational materials and instruction. Nonprofessionals can also use the wide range of freely available online content create their own versions of educational materials and compete with materials created by professional educators.

These aspects of digital education challenge the professional control—and limits to competition—that traditional educational institutions have enjoyed. Even more than journalism or the music industry, education relies heavily on the authority of professional judgments and professional expertise. The authority of professional educators has been premised on the idea that educational professionals, because of their training and vocation, can be trusted to produce knowledge and convey valuable and truthful information. Digital networks put pressure on these assumptions and allow more people to challenge professional educational hierarchies. Students can seek nontraditional organizations for education. Nontraditional producers of educational materials can compete with traditional textbook companies, and with school boards' choice of educational materials. Threats to professionalism, both real and perceived, will exacerbate political struggles over the recognition and accreditation of online digital enterprises, especially for-profit enterprises.

7. Informal Education, Cultural Memory, and Archives

Digital networks also make increasingly salient informal aspects of education that were always present before the development of the Internet. Professional educators have never been the only source of education. Students have always learned from their peers, relatives, friends, and co-workers. Students and their teachers also influence and educate each other.

Moreover, education does not need to take place in traditional classroom settings or in online universities. It does not need to seek the acquisition of a degree or a professional credential. Instead, much education, perhaps most, is informal. Throughout human history vast amounts of education have occurred outside of schoolrooms and universities. Apprentices and younger workers learn skills from their employers and senior employees. Consumers share information about products and services. Individuals and groups share information and skills over a wide range of practical, moral, and social topics.

Social media make informal peer-to-peer and amateur-to-amateur education increasingly salient. Using social media, everyone—and not merely enrolled students—can share content and identify ideas, information, and skills they believe are particularly relevant and valuable. Just as many people increasingly get their news from Twitter and Facebook, they may get information about every other aspect of their lives from digital platforms. Once again, this is not a new phenomenon. Before digital networks, friends and neighbors educated each other through gossip and ordinary conversations, recommended books and magazines, and offered advice. Digital environments expand these opportunities, allowing new and different groups of digital friends and neighbors to become a source of educational information. And, just as in the predigital era, peers can also be sources of misinformation and miseducation, leading to predictable calls for renewed educational standards, oversight, and accreditation. Efforts at improving schools, however, will not prevent the emergence of these informal methods of education (and miseducation).

Digital environments increase opportunities for informal and peer-to-peer education for four reasons. First, they greatly lower costs. Anyone can put materials online (or link to materials) that might be educational to others. Second, digital technologies increase the number of daily encounters and acts of sharing information. Third, the Internet greatly increases the number of people that individuals can encounter, and thus can learn from. Freed from geographic limitations, and assisted by online platforms and search engines, individuals can learn from virtually anyone in the world with an Internet connection. People thus have access to all of the knowledge, opinion, gossip, and misinformation produced by individuals and groups with a wide range of different interests. Fourth, digital environments tend to mesh education with entertainment and community participation. Platforms like Facebook and Twitter combine social connection with information sharing; platforms like YouTube educate through entertainment.

Facebook, Twitter, and YouTube are examples of platforms that encourage lay expression, and thus enable amateur-to-amateur education. Once again, journalism offers a useful comparison. Compare a traditional twentieth-century newspaper like the *New York Times* with a search engine like Google or a social media platform like Facebook. The *New York Times* hires professionals to decide what content is worth covering and carefully edits it for presentation to its audiences; as its familiar slogan testifies, it offers professional judgments about "All the News That's Fit to Print." Google and Facebook make no such representations. They serve their audiences—now called end users—quite differently. Instead of carefully gathering and editing content, they rely on content from undifferentiated audiences, collate it, arrange it, and make it available to others.

Just as much education is informal, much educational material exists outside educational institutions. Education also occurs through encounters with institutions of social and cultural memory, such as libraries, museums, and archives. Some of these cultural institutions, to be sure, are associated with educational institutions, but many more are not. Just as digital networks challenge professional norms of education, they also challenge professional accumulation of and control over archives, and thus, control over cultural memory itself.

The Internet itself is the world's largest archive, meaning that it is also a crucial repository for social and cultural memory. The Internet greatly lowers the costs of preserving memory and cultural artifacts. It therefore creates new questions about cultural preservation, which are beyond the scope of this chapter. Two issues, however, are worth noting here.

First, on the Internet, cultural memory depends heavily on digital inter-mediaries—examples are search engines like Google or digital sharing plat-forms like Flickr, Instagram, and YouTube. Second, most of these platforms, unlike most museums and libraries, are not nonprofits subsidized by the government. Rather, they are part of privately owned, profit-making enter-prises. The Internet Archive is the most obvious exception, but as a matter of practice, most people access for-profit platforms.

By itself, the fact of private ownership does not raise problems, as long as companies' business models continue to be premised on providing reli-able access for the public. Google, for example, tries to design its search engine to give end users the quickest and most efficient access to what they are looking for. Nevertheless, the business models of for-profit enterprises can change over time. Moreover, history shows that most businesses even-tually go bankrupt, are sold to other enterprises, or sell off valuable assets in order to raise capital. When cultural memory and access to information are privatized, they are subject to the same possibilities. If social media and search engines significantly change their business models to limit access, go bankrupt, or attempt to sell off their holdings, the question of ownership and control over archives becomes quite important.

Conclusion

In this chapter, we have noted the rise of new models of education, chal-lenges to and changes in the nature of professionalism, competition between professional-to-student and amateur-to-amateur education, the flattening of professional hierarchies, the proliferation of informal educa-tion, and the blurring of boundaries between formal and informal educa-tion. Each of these examples points to a more general issue. Before the Internet, it was easier to talk unselfconsciously of an educational system and educational institutions that were more or less distinct from other systems in society. That is because formal education normally occurred in distinct physical spaces and was conducted by a self-policing and self-repro-ducing profession with distinctive norms and practices that justified its control and hierarchical ordering based on conceptions of professional standards and professional merit. Digital networks, however, put into question the boundaries between the educational system and other aspects of the public sphere. This does not mean that professional educational standards will disappear, or that traditional grammar schools and universities will vanish overnight. Nevertheless, digital models of education will inevitably place strong market pressures on the traditional models; they will also encourage cost-cutting pressures from governments that traditionally fund education. Moreover, the boundaries between social practices that we call education and other social practices of knowledge production and communication will increasingly become blurred.

Once again, this does not mean that it becomes impossible to speak of a separate sphere of education; rather, it means that its boundaries will become increasingly permeable, and its end points uncertain. Digital networks merge the social practices of education into other forms of information and knowledge production and distribution, including journalism, political opinion, and entertainment. As these lines continue to blur, we will see ripple effects in professional norms, in the structure of educational institutions, in evolving business models for education, in the hiring and accreditation of educators, and in government regulation and funding of education.

Digital networks do more than alter the practices of educational institutions; they do more than put incumbent institutions into competition with for-profit online enterprises and informal peer-to-peer education; and they do more than blur the boundaries between education and entertainment. Digital networks disaggregate the practices of education into multiple tasks that might be performed by many different actors. They transform professional assumptions and ideals about knowledge production and acquisition, and they reintegrate education into the public sphere. Digital networks, in short, cause us to rethink what education is, how we perform it, who participates in it, and what we want from it.

I   New Opportunities for Education and Social Media

This part shows the wide range of possibilities that social media bring to education, and the variety of experiences that take place in different socio-cultural contexts. The chapters in this section take general claims, such as "new media enhance educational experiences," "new media endanger healthy teenage life," "new media benefit developing countries," and "new media radically alter journalism," and argue that each of these claims has a different meaning, significance, and validity in distinct social, cultural, and economic contexts. The first two chapters map diverse educational and entertainment experiences with social media in the United States, while the third and fourth chapters do the same in global contexts, with a particular interest in India and the UK.

The part begins with chapter 2, by Mark Warschauer (professor of education and informatics at the University of California, Irvine, and associate dean of the School of Education), who shows that is not enough to provide classrooms with new technologies. Digital education programs require careful planning and thorough execution, especially in schools where students lack support structures at home. In chapter 3, danah boyd (principal researcher at Microsoft Research, research assistant professor at New York University, and fellow, Harvard's Berkman Center for Internet and Society) argues that the power dynamics of online visibility deserve a more nuanced scholarly and social understanding. People, including those in power, such as teachers and parents, often assess the online content of others without considering the unique social, cultural, and technological contexts of the shared content. In chapter 4, Colin Agur (Knight Law and Media Fellow, the Information Society Project at Yale Law School) examines the conceptual and practical challenges and opportunities of information and communication technologies (ICTs) for education in developing countries. Like chapter 2, this chapter also highlights that the best ICTs for education programs combine the provision of new technology with the development of human capital. Finally, in chapter 5, Valerie Belair-Gagnon (executive director and research scholar, the Information Society Project at Yale Law School) considers the issues discussed in this part of the book as they pertain to news production. Her chapter shows that the implementation of social media training at a venerable public service broadcaster, the BBC, faces many of the same challenges as the meaningful introduction of new technologies in schools across the globe.

All these chapters highlight numerous ways in which social media provide new opportunities for learning, even as they emphasize that these opportunities are far from universally accessible. The digital divide exists both locally and globally, altering the ways people and institutions benefit from the educational offerings of social media.

Chapter 2: Addressing the Social Envelope: Education and the Digital Divide

Mark Warschauer

As school districts pour greater resources into educational technology, questions arise over the impact this focus may have on social and educational equity. Many hope that the use of technology in schools can help make up for unequal resources in the home environment and thus assist in closing persistent achievement gaps.

To examine this issue, chapter 2 looks at research on access to and the use of new technologies by diverse adolescents in the United States, and the relationship of such use to academic outcomes. It also summarizes a recent case study that compared the deployment of low-cost laptops and open-source software in two school districts. Both the research review and the case study suggest that the main factor benefiting youths is not the presence or absence of technology but rather the support structures in place to ensure the effective use of digital media.

Chapter 3: Do You See What I See? Visibility through Social Media

danah boyd

Social media enable people to share aspects of their lives in unprecedented ways, increasing the visibility of their daily activities. Yet just because a piece of content can be accessed does not mean that it is or that viewers are interpreting it in the context in which it was intended. All too often, people see what they want to see, strive to assert power over others, and use visibility as a justification for violating others' privacy. This chapter explores the dynamics of visibility in social media with an eye toward how visibility can be leveraged to understand, empathize, or help. Collectively shifting our relationship to publicly accessible content is both morally and ethically necessary. The discussion builds on the fieldwork, research, and analysis documented by the author in *It's Complicated: The Social Lives of Networked Teens.*

Chapter 4: ICTs and Education in Developing Countries: The Case of India

Colin Agur

Today, with ICTs proliferating rapidly in developing countries, new questions and debates have emerged over the role ICTs can play in education. For theorists of ICTs and the digital divide in education, developing countries test questions about the universality of technology and usage. For educational practitioners, developing countries offer a complex set of challenges and opportunities for ICTs as educational tools. This chapter examines the conceptual and practical aspects of ICTs in developing countries' educational initiatives. It provides an overview of the socioeconomic features of developing countries and raises the implications for educational technology, followed by a discussion of the digital divide that hampers ICT use in education. The chapter then discusses India as an example of a developing country attempting to overcome the economic, geographic, and social challenges that have thus far limited ICT adoption. It examines a selection of Indian ICT-for-education initiatives and explores the features of these programs that have proved successful. The chapter concludes with a discussion of the importance of networks in educational development, the complex relationship between global ICTs and cultural diversity, and the social and educational possibilities of mass mobile phone usage in India and other developing countries.

Chapter 5: Social Media Education in News Organizations: Experimentation at the BBC

Valerie Belair-Gagnon

Social media prompt a set of questions for news organizations. These questions concern the nature, processes, and consequences of journalism, and focus on changes in the structure, practices, journalistic culture, and beats of reporting. This chapter shows how social media education is becoming more widespread in BBC's norms and practices, and in new educational initiatives designed with social media as a new component in BBC news production and distribution.

2 Addressing the Social Envelope: Education and the Digital Divide

Mark Warschauer

Introduction

The development and diffusion of information and communication technologies (ICTs) is having a profound effect on modern life. As Manuel Castells concludes in *End of Millennium,* based on his socioeconomic analysis of postindustrial capitalism, "information technology, and the ability to use it and adapt it, is the critical factor in generating and accessing wealth, power, and knowledge in our time."[1]

Frank Levy and Richard Murnane's detailed study of occupational patterns in the United States provides empirical support for Castell's claim. Their examination of census data shows that from 1969 to 1999, the demand for jobs in which a computer could substitute for human thought steadily declined, while the demand for jobs in which computers could complement and amplify the creativity and expert thinking of humans steadily expanded.[2]

The large and growing role of new media in the economy and society serves to highlight their important role in education, and especially in promoting educational equity. On the one hand, differential access to new media, broadly defined, can further amplify the already too large educational inequities in American society. On the other hand, the effective deployment and use of technology in schools may help compensate for unequal access to technologies in the home environment, and thus help bridge educational and social gaps.

For these reasons, accurately assessing diverse demographic groups' experiences with technology both in and out of school has been an important priority for advocates of social and economic equality. In this chapter, we examine and discuss studies related to technology and equity for youth in the United States. We begin with *access* as a starting point, but consider not only whether diverse groups of youth have digital media available to them but also how that access is supported or constrained by technological and social factors. From there we go on to the question of *use*, analyzing the ways in which diverse youth demographics deploy new media for education, social interaction, and entertainment. We then move to the question of *outcomes*, considering the academic results achieved by different groups through the use of new media. This analysis points to the key role of social support for technology use. To illustrate this point, we end by comparing two different school districts that have attempted to integrate technology into education, with one program based largely on the distribution of equipment and the other grounded in a socially supported curricular reform effort.

Access

Out-of-School Access
Though there are still substantial differences in access to ICTs at home by race and ethnicity, these differences are narrower among households that have children.[3] A national survey of youth conducted in 2008–2009 by the Kaiser Family Foundation (KFF) found that, among eight- to eighteen-year-olds, 94 percent of whites, 89 percent of blacks, and 92 percent of Hispanics had computers at home. For Internet access, the rates were 88 percent, 78 percent, and 74 percent, respectively.[4] Parental education levels had a somewhat larger impact, with 91 percent of children with college-educated parents reporting Internet access at home, compared to 74 percent of children whose parents had never gone to college.

Conditions of Access
Access to technology is not a binary division between information haves and have-nots; rather, there are differing degrees and types of access.[5] For example, the KFF survey found that, even among families that had Internet access at home, a higher percentage of white youth (65 percent) had home broadband connections as compared to black (62 percent) or Hispanic (57 percent) youth, with, once again, a greater divide between youth with college-educated parents (67 percent had Internet access) and youth whose parents had not gone to college (56 percent). The importance of this disparity is highlighted by research indicating that people who have broadband connections are more likely to use the Internet for research and content production than people who connect to the Internet by dialup devices.[6]

Social factors are likely even more important than technical factors in shaping access. The influence of family members and friends can be critical in deciding whether and how to use computers and the Internet. A study of one thousand people in San Diego found that social contact with other computer users was a key factor correlated with computer access.[7] As the study reports,

Although most respondents stated that they know people who used computers, the digitally detached (those who do not have home personal computers, Internet access, or access to the Internet outside of the home) did not. And when compared with the impact of ethnicity, income, and education level, this sentiment—that they did not know others who used computers—is far more significant.[8]

Youth today are not likely to be "digitally detached." However, with computer mastery depending heavily on social support from both peers[9] and family members,[10] many low-income or immigrant youth will have few friends or relatives who are sophisticated users of digital media. Conditions in the household and neighborhood, such as relatively few computers, the lack of broadband Internet access, fewer people with a college education, and fewer English speakers, are likely to shape the kinds of experience youth have with digital media.

The role of family members in shaping children's experience with technology is illustrated by a study in Philadelphia that examined children's use of the city's libraries before and after computers were introduced in them.[11] The study found that, after the libraries installed computers, children in low-income communities (who typically received little parent mentoring in libraries) spent considerable time either waiting for computers to be free or playing computer-based games with little textual content. Technology thus displaced reading for these children. In contrast, parents in middle-income communities "carefully orchestrated children's activities on the computer, much as they did with books."[12] Children in those communities thus spent more time on print-based computer applications, averaging eleven lines of print per application, compared to 3.9 lines of print for the children in low-income communities. As a result, children in middle-income communities doubled the amount of time spent on reading following the introduction of technology, and the gap in print access between low- and high-income youth increased.

School Access

There have been steady gains in equitable access to technology in schools, but, once again, small gaps persist. A national survey conducted in fall 2008 found that the ratio of instructional computers with Internet access to students in schools with few ethnic minority students was 2.8. In schools that had 50 percent or greater enrollment of ethnic minority students, the ratio was 3.2.[13]

As in home environments, sociotechnical factors support or constrain the use of computers and the Internet in schools, often in ways that heighten educational inequity. A comparative study of school technology use in high- and low-SES communities found that the low-SES neighborhood schools tended to have less stable teaching staff, administrative staff, and IT support staff, which made planning for technology use more difficult.[14] As the study reported, the high-SES schools "tended to invest more in professional development, hiring full-time technical support staff and developing lines of communication among teachers, office staff, media specialists, technical staff, and administration that promoted robust digital networks."[15] This in turn "encouraged more widespread teacher use of new technologies."[16] In comparison, "the low-SES schools had achieved less success in creating the kinds of support networks that made technology workable."[17] Since teachers in low-SES schools were less confident that the equipment they signed up for would actually work, and that if it didn't work they would have available timely technical support, they were more reluctant to rely on technology in their lesson plans.

In addition, even when teachers in low-SES schools had confidence in the hardware and software they were using, the sheer complexity of their instructional environments made it more difficult to use technology well. The challenges they faced included larger numbers of English-language learners and at-risk students, larger numbers of students with limited computer experience, and greater pressure to raise test scores and adhere to policy mandates.[18]

Use

Although black and Hispanic youth have less access to computers and the Internet both at home and at school than do white youth, young people from black and Hispanic groups appear to spend more time online than white youth. According to the KFF's survey of eight- to eighteen-year-olds, the average amount of time spent using a computer on a typical day was one hour and twenty-four minutes for black youth, one hour and forty-nine minutes for Hispanic youth, and one hour and seventeen minutes for white youth. This pattern is consistent with other media trends in the United States, with black and Hispanic youth also spending substantially more time per day than white youth watching TV, listening to music, playing video games, and watching movies—and these gaps in time spent with media by ethnicity growing over the years.[19] In addition, the KFF study found that black teens and Hispanic teens made many more cell phone calls per month than white teens (an average of 210, 150, and 120 calls per month, respectively) and were much more likely to use cell phones to go online (44 percent of black teens and 35 percent of Hispanic teens) than were white teens (22 percent).[20]

Home Use of Digital Media

A 2009 report, based on interviews with and observations of hundreds of middle school– and high school–aged youth, provides an in-depth view of how youth use digital media out of school.[21] Ito and co-workers identified two primary categories of online practice, which they labeled friendship-driven and interest-driven. Friendship-driven practices essentially involve hanging out with peers online and either take the place of or complement other forms of youth socializing, such as hanging out at the mall. The principal tools for hanging out online are social networking sites, such as MySpace and Facebook; instant messaging; and computer and video games. Typical friendship-driven activities include chatting or flirting; uploading, downloading, or discussing music, images, and video clips; updating profiles; and playing or discussing video games. As other studies have underscored, almost all youth participate in these friendship activities, with black and Hispanic youth participating somewhat more than white youth. For example, Victoria Rideout, Ulla G. Foehr, and Donald F. Roberts found that black and Hispanic youth ages eight to eighteen years spend more time per day on social networking sites than do white youth,[22] and Tom Webster found that black and Hispanic youth ages twelve and older are far more likely than white youth to use Twitter.[23]

Most youth do not move beyond friendship-driven activities, but the more creative and adventurous venture into interest-driven genres of media. As with friendship-driven activities, interest-driven activities typically involve communicating, game playing, and sharing of media. But in interest-driven genres, it is the specialized activity, interest, or niche identity that is the driving motivation, rather than merely socializing with local peers. This results in a much deeper and more sophisticated engagement with new media, and also brings participants into communication and collaboration with people of diverse ages and backgrounds around the world, rather than principally with their own local peers. The Digital Youth Project identified two stages of interest-driven participation, which they labeled *messing around* and *geeking out*. Messing around involves early exploration of personal interests, wherein young people "begin to take an interest in and focus on the workings and content of the technology and media themselves, tinkering, exploring, and extending their understanding."[24] Activities in this regard include searching for information online and experimenting with digital media production or more complex forms of gaming. Geeking out is the next stage and involves "an intense commitment to or engagement with media or technology, often one particular media property, genre, or type of technology" and "learning to navigate esoteric domains of knowledge and practice and participating in communities that traffic in these forms of expertise."[25] Examples of geeking out include the creation and sharing of animated films that use computer game engines and footage (machinima); the posting and critiquing of creative writing related to popular culture (fan fiction); the development and publishing of videos based on clips from anime series set to songs (anime music videos); the writing and distribution of subtitles of foreign films or television programs, especially anime, within hours after the films or programs are released (fansubbing); and the creation and posting of short dramatic or humorous films on YouTube (video production).

Learning and media theorists such as James Paul Gee[26] and Henry Jenkins[27] make a compelling case that youth's engagement with new media provides vital learning experiences. However, their writings principally focus on youth who are engaged in interest-driven activities, especially those who geek out. Yet the Ito study found that only a small minority of youth moved on to the geeking-out stage, and also made it evident that access to additional technological and social resources, beyond a simple computer and Internet account, is critical to determining who moves on to these more sophisticated forms of media participation. Because of the nature of geeking-out activities, requisite technological resources include broadband access, relatively new computers with graphics and multimedia capacity, digital production software, and equipment such as digital cameras and camcorders. Requisite social resources include a community that values and enables the sharing of media knowledge and interests, which can be found among family, friends, interest groups, or educational programs such as computer clubs and youth media centers.

Ito's study did not attempt to identify who typically moves on to the geeking-out stage and who does not, but other studies have addressed this issue.[28] One of the most compelling accounts is provided by Paul Attewell and Hella Winston, who spent several months observing and interviewing two groups of computer users at home and school.[29] The first group consisted of African American and Latino children aged eleven to fourteen years who attended public middle school; most came from poor and working-class families, and all scored below grade level in reading. The second group consisted of schoolchildren from more affluent families who attended private schools.

The wealthier youths studied by Attewell and Winston were frequently engaged in interest-driven activities. For example, a white fourth-grade private school student named Zeke was a "political junky at ten years old."[30] He spent his online time reading up on the U.S. presidential inauguration, downloading video clips of politicians, and reading candidates' speeches. He then put this online expertise to use when he decided to run for class president, an office that was not officially sanctioned by the teachers at his school. Zeke found a free website that allowed visitors to construct quizzes and modified it to develop an online voting system. With the cooperation of his rival for office, he told each child in his class to visit the web page for the voting system, both to read the campaign speeches that he and his opponent posted and eventually to vote.

The low-SES group in Attewell and Winston's study also pursued their interests, but in very different ways. Typical was Kadesha, a thirteen-year-old African American girl. Kadesha and her friends spent much of their online time checking out rappers and wrestlers (whom they referred as their "husbands"), downloading their pictures as screensavers, and pasting images into reports.[31] They also went cyber-window shopping together, checking out everything from hot new sneakers to skateboards to Barbie dolls. The authors explained how Kadesha's ability to exploit the Internet was greatly restricted by her limited reading and writing skills:

As image after image flashes by … it becomes noticeable how rarely, how lightly, Kadesha settles on printed text. Like many of her friends, she reads far below grade level. So she energetically pursues images and sounds on the Web, but forgoes even news of her love interest if that requires her to read.[32]

Of course, exploring images and sounds can be an important part of geeking out, but Attewell and Winston's description makes clear that, in the case of Kadesha and many of her friends, engagement with multimedia was limited to consumption, not creation. As exemplified by Zeke, many children in the wealthier communities had greater experience and expertise in creating and publishing online artifacts.

These qualitative findings of discrepancies are backed up by national population survey data analyzed by Matthew DeBell and Chris Chapman.[33] They found that, among children in grades pre-K to twelve who used a computer at home, white youth were more likely than black or Hispanic youth to use word processing, email, multimedia, and spreadsheets or databases. Similarly, children from high-income families or with well-educated or English-speaking parents used such applications more frequently than children from low-income families or whose parents did not graduate from high school or did not speak English. Further statistical evidence comes from a recent study that compared trends in creative computing participation by youth from a high-SES California community and a nearby, low-SES community. Students in the high-SES community had greater home access to diverse digital tools (including computers, the Internet, printers, scanners, handheld devices, digital cameras, and video cameras) and were much more likely to have both depth and breadth of experience in digital media production.[34]

In-School Use of Digital Media

Two major studies on the differential use of technology in U.S. schools by demographic groups were conducted in the 1990s. Both showed sharp disparities by race and SES in how new technologies were deployed for education.

In the first study, Harold Wenglinsky analyzed data from the 1996 National Assessment of Educational Progress (NAEP) to describe the technology use patterns of 6,627 fourth graders and 7,146 eighth graders across the United States.[35] Of all racial groups, African American youth were more likely to use computers at least once a week for mathematics at both the fourth-grade and the eighth-grade level, likely because of the frequent use of remedial computer-based drills in math. Yet a smaller percentage of African American students than any other racial group were taught math by teachers who had had professional training in technology use in the previous five years.

Wenglinsky divided up computer use into two broad categories. The first involved applying concepts or developing simulations to use them, activities that are both thought of as teaching higher-order skills. One example provided was of a teacher who used spreadsheets to help teach algebra. The second involved drill and practice activities, such as doing addition or subtraction problems, which by nature focus on lower-order skills. The study found substantially different trends among teachers' methods, which correlated with differences among students in race or ethnicity, school lunch eligibility, and school type. Most notably, more than three times as many Asian eighth graders as black eighth graders reported their teachers' frequent use of simulations and applications in mathematics instruction, whereas only about half as many Asian eighth graders as black eighth graders reported their teachers primarily using computers for drill and practice.

In the second national study, Henry Becker surveyed a representative sample of four thousand teachers across the United States.[36] His study confirmed the differences found by Wenglinsky and found that they applied more widely than just to mathematics instruction.[37] Specifically, he found that teachers in low-SES schools were more likely to use computers for remediation and mastery of discrete skills, whereas teachers in high-SES schools were more likely to use computers for innovative and constructivist activities involving written expression, analysis of information, and public presentation. This is not surprising, insofar as more low-SES students struggle with discrete skills, but it does indicate why technology use may amplify educational inequality in schools, since low-SES students have fewer opportunities for the kinds of constructivist uses of technology that Wenglinsky found most beneficial for learning.

I have conducted a number of smaller studies that have examined the same issue with a narrower focus. These studies include a comparison of a high-SES private and low-SES public school in Hawaii, both known for good uses of educational technology;[38] a study of twenty mathematics, science, English, and social studies teachers at three high-SES and five low-SES secondary schools in Southern California;[39] and a multisite study of ten diverse schools in Maine and California with one-to-one laptop programs (in which all students in one or more classrooms were provided with an individual computer).[40] Taken as a whole, these studies confirm important discrepancies by student and school SES, while also suggesting that the specific nature of these discrepancies may be evolving over time. For example, the studies found differences not only in constructivist versus rote applications of technology, as suggested by Becker, but also in types of constructivist activity, with those occurring in low-SES schools more typically focused on what Scardamalia and Bereiter call *shallow* as opposed to *deep constructivism*.[41] In these instances, individual or collaborative student-centered work, such as writing newsletters or finding information on web pages, was often carried out with very limited goals, such as the development of the most basic computer skills, rather than the achievement of deeper knowledge, understanding, or analysis through critical inquiry, as more frequently occurred in high-SES schools.

Academic Outcomes

Evidence is mixed as to whether home access to computers brings positive academic outcomes, but there is broad agreement that any benefits gained are strongly mediated by student SES.[42] For example, using National

Longitudinal Youth Survey (NLYS88) data, Paul Attewell and Juan Battle found that, among families with home computers, and controlling for all other possible variables, children from high-SES families compared to low-SES families received more than four and one-half times the benefit in increased math scores and more than two and one-half times the benefit in increased reading scores.[43] Their study also found that white students received significantly greater benefit from home computer use on math and reading outcomes than did black or Hispanic students. Although their data provided no firm evidence as to the potential causes of these differences, they speculate that the discrepant outcomes may be the result of the different technology resources (e.g., educational software) and social resources (scaffolding, modeling, and support from parents) that surround children's use of technology at home—resources that have been referred to by others as the "social envelope" of computing.[44] Attewell and Battle conclude by referring back to a famous children's television show that was touted as beneficial for low-income children but instead proved more helpful for high-income children because of greater support from their parents in watching and discussing the show.[45] As they explain, "Home computing may generate another 'Sesame Street effect' whereby an innovation that held great promise for poorer children to catch up educationally … is in practice increasing the educational gap between affluent and poor … even among those with access to the technology."[46]

Attewell and Battle's study is based on data that are some twenty years old; meanwhile, home computers and their uses have expanded dramatically. However, a 2014 paper by three Duke economists reported similar results from a study in North Carolina, with race and SES strongly mediating the effect on academic achievement of home computer and Internet access.[47] These findings are even more disheartening than Attewell and Battle's, as the Duke study indicates a negative effect of computer and Internet access on math and reading test scores for low-SES and African American students. This, the researchers presume, is to the result of "declines in productivity associated with having a more potent distraction at hand."[48]

Academic Outcomes from School Use of Computers

Studies of academic outcomes from the in-school use of technology are mixed.[49] Many studies are based on very small sample sizes and were conducted in schools or classrooms where individual educators were highly expert in particular uses of technology, and thus their results may not be generalizable to other contexts.

Larger studies, though, suggest that the drill and practice activities more frequently carried out in low-SES schools tend to be ineffective, while the uses of technology typical of high-SES schools achieve positive results. The best evidence of this discrepancy comes from Wenglinsky, who analyzed NEAP data from the years 1996, 1998, and 2000.[50] Overall, Wenglinsky found a consistently negative interaction between frequency of technology use and test score results in mathematics, science, and reading. This appears to reflect the negative effects of the drill and practice activities that are used predominantly in low-SES schools. In contrast, the more constructivist educational technology activities typically used in high-SES schools correlated with higher test scores.

For example, in mathematics, Wenglinsky found that the use of simulations or applications in eighth grade and games in fourth grade positively affected test scores, whereas drill and practice activities negatively affected the scores. In science, game playing, word processing, simulations, and data analysis all positively affected test scores. And in reading, the use of computers for writing activities positively affected test scores, but the use of computers for grammar and punctuation work or for reading activities negatively affected test scores. In each subject area, student SES was the strongest factor predicting whether technology use would be positively or negatively associated with test score results.

Amplifying Access: A Tale of Two Districts

The body of research discussed here strongly suggests that providing the right kind of social support for meaningful learning experiences with technology is far more important than simply providing access to the technology itself. This point is well illustrated by one of my recent studies, on the effects of netbook computers and open-source software in U.S. schools.[51] The study examined three school districts across the country deploying these resources in one-to-one laptop programs. In particular, there was an illuminating contrast between such a program's implementation and the results in two school districts, one in Birmingham, Alabama, the other in Littleton, Colorado.

The Birmingham initiative was based on the model of the One Laptop per Child (OLPC) program, which emphasizes children's independent ability to teach themselves with computers (specifically, the OLPC's XO laptops, which were intended to include child-friendly features and software), and thus deemphasizes curricular reform, professional development, formative evaluation, or development of a technological or social infrastructure to support laptop use by students. As the former mayor of Birmingham, Larry Langford, who initiated the local program, said on the city's website, "If we give them these XOs and get out of their way, they'll be teaching us about the world."[52] Following a six-week pilot program at a single site in spring 2008, laptops were distributed in fall 2008 to all students in first through fifth grades in Birmingham City Schools, a school district of mostly low-SES African American students. No funding was provided to expand the schools' limited Internet access, and only two hours of professional development training was provided to each teacher for implementation of the program. With the program launched by the mayor's office and funded by the city council, the school district had little time, funding, or motivation to develop curricular integration plans.

Observations, interviews, and surveys we conducted all indicated the laptops were little used in school.[53] A large number were broken, and no funding had been provided for repairs; as a result, even in the few classrooms where teachers still wanted to use them, fewer than half the students had functioning laptops on a given day.[54] Without connections from the laptops to servers, printers, or the Internet, teachers had difficulty carrying out even the most common instructional uses of computers, such as asking students to access information online or print and turn in their writing. Many students used the XO computers at home, without any apparent educational benefit. The frequency with which students used computers to conduct research, do homework, or create online content declined following the introduction of the XOs, while the frequency with which they visited chat rooms went up substantially.[55] These results are consistent with the disappointing outcomes found in other settings in which low-SES children gain access to computers without any additional social support for their use.[56]

Despite the use of low-cost XO computers and with little additional money dedicated to social or technical support, the ongoing costs of the Birmingham program are considerable. Since the laptops are given to and owned by the children rather than the schools, a full one-third of the inventory disappears from the program every year, as students either graduate out of the elementary schools or move out of the district. Substantial replacement funding is thus required year after year, with little benefit seen in return. If the city had put the same amount of funding into a better conceived and better organized laptop program—one that focused initially on a few grade levels and provided substantial funding for curriculum development, teacher training, and technological infrastructure—Birmingham City Schools could have had one of the best educational technology programs in the United States, rather than what has been accurately called a "costly lesson."[57]

The laptop program in Littleton Public Schools, on the outskirts of Denver, Colorado, stands in sharp contrast. The school laptop program there was introduced to bolster a well-defined and carefully planned literacy curriculum called Inspired Writing. Low-cost netbook computers using open-source software were gradually deployed over three years for use in all English language arts classes from grades five to ten, beginning with a group of low-performing schools disproportionately located in low-SES and immigrant neighborhoods. This measured rollout allowed the district to evaluate the program as it progressed and fully prepare administrators, teachers, and other stakeholders. The gradual rollout also allowed substantial funding to be raised from state and federal grants and community foundations, further lowering the cost of the already inexpensive program. Though students were not allowed to bring the computers home, almost all student work was done and saved using online sites, such as Google Apps, so that students could continue their work outside school hours on any Internet-connected computer.

Our observations, interviews, and surveys in Littleton indicated that students used their laptops on a regular basis in class to conduct research, write and revise papers, share their work with others, and pursue individualized and differentiated learning activities. The program is highly popular with students, teachers, and administrators and has also gathered some national attention for its innovation and positive impact on test scores.[58] Especially beneficial results have been found at the district's main elementary school for English-language learners, where students spend considerable time every day writing for authentic audiences—including their classmates, students in other classrooms, and adult mentors—through blogs, wikis, and online forums. In the process, students develop both their literacy skills and their identity as writers. Now that the district has established methods for using the computers in the Inspired Writing curriculum, school officials continue to seek ways to expand the program for a broader Inspired Learning initiative in other subject areas.[59]

Conclusion

Over the last two decades, people in the United States and elsewhere have transitioned from using solely expensive desktop computers to using low-cost mobile computing devices for communication and entertainment. It is not surprising that, during these years, access to this wide range of computing devices has steadily grown, and children as well as adults are spending an increasing amount of time using them, most frequently to chat with friends and pursue hobbies. Access to and the use of computers and digital media can bring much more into the lives of young people, but that will usually depend on provision of a broader social envelope of resources surrounding the computer itself. As with earlier experiences with radio, television, and film, those who expect new media to replace teachers or parents in educating children will be disappointed. However, those who seek to amplify effective teaching and learning practices will find Internet-connected computers to be one of the most powerful resources imaginable.

Notes

1. Manuel Castells, *End of Millennium* (Malden, MA: Blackwell, 1998), 92.

2. Frank Levy and Richard J. Murnane, *The New Division of Labor: How Computers Are Creating the Next Job Market* (Princeton, NJ: Princeton University Press, 2004).

3. For a review, see Mark Warschauer and Tina Matuchniak, "New Technology and Digital Worlds: Analyzing Evidence of Equity in Access, Use, and Outcomes," *Review of Research in Education* 34, no. 1 (2010): 179–225.

4. Victoria J. Rideout, Ulla G. Foehr, and Donald F. Roberts, *Generation M2: Media in the Lives of 8- to 18-Year-Olds* (Menlo Park, CA: Kaiser Family Foundation, 2010).

5. See discussion in Mark Warschauer, *Technology and Social Inclusion: Rethinking the Digital Divide* (Cambridge, MA: MIT Press, 2003).

6. John B. Horrigan, *Home Broadband and Adoption 2008,* Pew Internet & American Life Project (Washington, DC: Pew Research Center, July 2008), Error!Hyperlinkrefer encenotvalid.(accessed January 20, 2009).

7. Regional Technology Alliance, *Mapping a Future for Digital Connections: A Study of the Digital Divide in San Diego County,* City of San Diego, 2001, http://files.eric.ed .gov/fulltext/ED463391.pdf (accessed September 28, 2015).

8. Ibid.

9. Jane Margolis et al., *Stuck in the Shallow End: Education, Race, and Computing* (Cambridge, MA: MIT Press, 2008).

10. Brigid Barron et al., "Parents as Learning Partners in the Development of Technological Fluency," *International Journal of Learning and Media* 1, no. 2 (2009): 55–77.

11. Susan B. Neuman and Donna Celano, "The Knowledge Gap: Implications of Leveling the Playing Field for Low-Income and Middle-Income Children," *Reading Research Quarterly* 41, no. 2 (2006): 176–201.

12. Ibid., 193.

13. Lucinda Gray, Nina Thomas, and Laurie Lewis, *Educational Technology in U.S. Public Schools: Fall 2008* (Washington, DC: National Center for Education Statistics, 2010).

14. Mark Warschauer, Michelle Knobel, and Leeann Stone, "Technology and Equity in Schooling: Deconstructing the Digital Divide," *Educational Policy* 18, no. 4 (2004): 562–588.

15. Ibid., 578.

16. Ibid.

17. Ibid.

18. Ibid.

19. Rideout, Foehr, and Roberts, *Generation M2*.

20. Amanda Lenhart et al., "Teens and Mobile Phones," http://www.pewinternet .org/(accessedMay25,2010).

21. Mizuko Ito et al., *Hanging Out, Messing Around, Geeking Out: Living and Learning with New Media.* (Cambridge, MA: MIT Press, 2009).

22. Rideout, Foehr, and Roberts, *Generation M2*.

23. Tom Webster, *Twitter Usage in America: 2010. The Edison Research/Arbitron Internet and Multimedia Study,* http://www.onecommunity.org/wp-content/uploads/2010/ 04/Twitter_Usage_In_America_2010.pdf (accessed May 25, 2010).

24. Mizuko Ito et al., *Living and Learning with New Media: Summary of Findings from the Digital Youth Project,* 2008, The John D. and Catherine T. MacArthur Foundation Reports on Digital Media and Learning (Chicago: MacArthur Foundation, November 2008), https://www.macfound.org/media/article_pdfs/DML_ETHNOG _WHITEPAPER.PDF (accessed September 28, 2015)

25. Ibid., 28.

26. James Paul Gee, *What Video Games Have to Teach Us about Learning and Literacy* (New York: Palgrave Macmillan, 2003). See also James Paul Gee, *Situated Language and Learning: A Critique of Traditional Schooling* (New York: Routledge, 2004).

27. Henry Jenkins, *Confronting the Challenges of Participatory Culture: Media Education for the 21st Century* (Cambridge, MA: MIT Press, 2009), https://mitpress.mit.edu/ sites/default/files/titles/free_download/9780262513623_Confronting_the _Challenges.pdf (accessed September 28, 2015).

28. See discussion in Warschauer and Matuchniak, "New Technology and Digital Worlds."

29. Paul Attewell and Hella Winston, "Children of the Digital Divide," in *Disadvantaged Teens and Computer Technologies,* ed. P. Attewell and N. M. Seel (Münster, Germany: Waxmann, 2003), 117–136.

30. Ibid., 124.

31. Ibid., 117.

32. Ibid.

33. Matthew DeBell and Chris Chapman, *Computer and Internet Use by Students in 2003* (Washington, DC: National Center for Education Statistics, 2006).

34. Brigid Barron, Sarah E. Walter, C. K. Martin, and Colin Schatz, "Predictors of Creative Computing Participation and Profiles of Experience in Two Silicon Valley Middle Schools," *Computers & Education* 54, no. 1 (2010): 178–189.

35. Harold Wenglinsky, "Does It Compute? The Relationship between Educational Technology and Student Achievement in Mathematics," Educational Testing Service, 1998, http://files.eric.ed.gov/fulltext/ED425191.pdf (accessed September 28, 2015)

36. Henry Jay Becker, "Who's Wired and Who's Not: Children's Access to and Use of Computer Technology," *The Future of Children* 10, no. 2 (2000): 44–75.

37. Ibid.

38. Mark Warschauer, "Technology and School Reform: A View from Both Sides of the Track," *Education Policy Analysis Archives* 8, no. 4 (2000), http://epaa.asu.edu/ojs/article/view/395/518 (accessed September 28, 2015)

39. Warschauer, Knobel, and Stone, "Technology and Equity in Schooling."

40. Mark Warschauer, *Laptops and Literacy: Learning in the Wireless Classroom* (New York: Teachers College Press, 2006).

41. Marlene Scardamalia and Carl Bereiter, "Knowledge Building," in *Encyclopedia of Education* (New York: Macmillan Reference, 2003), 1370–1373.

42. See discussion in Warschauer and Matuchniak, "New Technology and Digital Worlds."

43. Paul Attewell and Juan Battle, "Home Computers and School Performance," *Information Society* 15, no. 1 (1990): 1–10.

44. J. B. Giacquinta, J. A. Bauer, and J. E. Levin, *Beyond Technology's Promise: An Examination of Children's Educational Computing at Home* (Cambridge: Cambridge University Press, 1993), 134.

45. See, for example, T. Jordan, *Discriminating Characteristics of Families Watching Sesame Street* (St. Louis, MO: Central Midwestern Regional Educational Lab, 1970).

46. Attewell and Battle, "Home Computers and School Performance," 1.

47. Jacob L. Vigdor, Helen F. Ladd, and Erika Martinez, "Scaling the Digital Divide: Home Computer Technology and Student Achievement," *Economic Inquiry* 52, no. 3 (2014): 1103–1119.

48. Ibid., 1117.

49. See, for example, discussion in J. A. Kulik, *Effects of Using Instructional Technology in Elementary and Secondary Schools: What Controlled Evaluation Studies Say* (Arlington, VA: SRI, 2003).

50. Henry Wenglinsky, *Using Technology Wisely: The Keys to Success in Schools* (New York: Teachers College Press, 2005).

51. Mark Warschauer, Binbin Zheng, Melissa Niiya, Sheila Cotten, and George Farkas, Balancing the One-to-One Equation: Equity and Access in Three Laptop Programs, *Equity & Excellence in Education* 47, no. 1 (2014): 46–62. Also see M. Warschauer, *Learning in the Cloud: How (and Why) to Transform Schools with Digital Media* (New York: Teachers College Press, 2011).

52. Mark Warschauer, Sheila R. Cotten, and Morgan Ames, "One Laptop per Child Birmingham: Case Study of a Radical Reform," *International Journal of Learning and Media* 3, no. 2 (2012): 61–76.

53. Ibid.

54. Ibid., 68.

55. Ibid., 70.

56. See, for example, M. Warschauer and M. Ames, "Can One Laptop per Child Save the World's Poor?," *Journal of International Affairs* 64, no. 1 (2010): 33–51.

57. Christina Crowe, "A Costly Lesson: A Look at Birmingham's Curious Commitment to the XO Laptop," *Black & White,* November 26, 2009, http://www.bwcitypaper.com/Articles-i-2009-11-26-232786.113121_A_Costly_Lesson.html.

58. Anne Rawland Gabriel, "Inspiring Education," EdTech: Focus on K–12, April–May 2010,http://www.edtechmagazine.com/k12/article/2010/04/inspiring-education (accessed September 28, 2015).

59. Mark Warschauer, *Learning in the Cloud: How (and Why) to Transform Schools with Technology* (New York: Teachers College Press, 2006).

Bibliography

Attewell, Paul, and Juan Battle. "Home Computers and School Performance." *Information Society* 15, no. 1 (1999): 1–10.

Attewell, Paul, and Hella Winston. "Children of the Digital Divide." In *Disadvantaged Teens and Computer Technologies*, ed. P. Attewell and N. M. Seel, 117–136. Münster, Germany: Waxmann, 2003.

Barron, Brigid, Caitlin Kennedy Martin, Lori Takeuchi, and Rachel Fithian. "Parents as Learning Partners in the Development of Technological Fluency." *International Journal of Learning and Media* 1, no. 2 (2009): 55–77.

Barron, Brigid, Sarah Walter, Caitlin Kennedy Martin, and Colin Schatz. "Predictors of Creative Computing Participation and Profiles of Experience in Two Silicon Valley Middle Schools." *Computers & Education* 54, no. 1 (2010): 178–189.

Becker, Henry Jay. "Who's Wired and Who's Not: Children's Access to and Use of Computer Technology." *Future of Children* 10, no. 2 (2000): 44–75.

Castells, Manuel. *End of Millennium*. Malden, MA: Blackwell, 1998.

Crowe, Christina. "A Costly Lesson: A Look at Birmingham's Curious Commitment to the XO Laptop." *Black & White*, November 26, 2009. http://www.bwcitypaper.com/Articles-i-2009-11-26-232786.113121_A_Costly_Lesson.html.

DeBell, Matthew, and Chris Chapman. *Computer and Internet Use by Students in 2003*. Washington, DC: National Center for Education Statistics, 2006.

Gee, James Paul. *Situated Language and Learning: A Critique of Traditional Schooling*. New York: Routledge, 2004.

Gee, James Paul. *What Video Games Have to Teach Us about Learning and Literacy*. New York: Palgrave Macmillan, 2003.

Giacquinta, Joseph B., Jo-Anne Bauer, and Jane Levin. *Beyond Technology's Promise: An Examination of Children's Educational Computing at Home*. Cambridge: Cambridge University Press, 1993.

Gray, Lucinda, and Laurie Lewis. *Educational Technology in U.S. Public Schools: Fall 2008*. Washington, DC: National Center for Education Statistics, 2010.

Horrigan, John. *Home Broadband and Adoption 2008*. Pew Internet & American Life Project. Washington, DC: Pew Research Center, July 2008. http://www.pewinternet.org/files/old-media/Files/Reports/2008/PIP_Broadband_2008.pdf (accessed January 29, 2009).

Ito, Mizuko, Sonja Baumer, Matteo Bittanti, danah boyd, Rachel Cody, Becky Herr-Stephenson et al. *Hanging Out, Messing Around, Geeking Out: Living and Learning with New Media*. Cambridge, MA: MIT Press, 2009.

Ito, Mizuko, Heather Horst, and Matteo Bittanti, danah boyd, Becky Herr-Stephenson, Patricia G. Lange, C. J. Pascoe, Laura Robinson. *Living and Learning with New Media: Summary of Findings from the Digital Youth Project*. The John D. and Catherine T. MacArthur Foundation Reports on Digital Media and Learning. Chicago:

MacArthur Foundation, November 2008. http://digitalyouth.ischool.berkeley.edu/files/report/digitalyouth-WhitePaper.pdf (accessed December 22, 2008).

Jenkins, Henry. *Confronting the Challenges of Participatory Culture: Media Education for the 21st Century*. Cambridge, MA: MIT Press, 2009. http://wheatoncollege.edu/president/files/2012/03/Confronting-Challenges-of-Participatory-Culture.pdf (accessed September 28, 2015).

Jordan, Tomas E. *Discriminating Characteristics of Families Watching Sesame Street*. St. Louis, MO: Central Midwestern Regional Educational Lab, 1970.

Kulik, James. A. *Effects of Using Instructional Technology in Elementary and Secondary Schools: What Controlled Evaluation Studies Say*. Arlington, VA: SRI, 2003.

Lenhart, Amanda, Rich Ling, Scott Campbell, and Kristen Purcell. "Teens and Mobile Phones."http://www.pewinternet.org/2010/04/20/teens-and-mobile-phones (accessed September 28, 2015).

Levy, Frank, and Richard J. Murnane. *The New Division of Labor: How Computers Are Creating the Next Job Market*. Princeton, NJ: Princeton University Press, 2004.

Littleton Public Schools. *A Premier Education: Educational Technology and Information Literacy Plan*. Littleton Public Schools, CO, 2009. http://www.littletonpublicschools.net/Portals/0/ITS/Technology/Final-ETIL-Plan-2009-2012.pdf (accessed May 2010).

Margolis, Jane, Rachel Estrella, Joanna Goode, Jennifer Jellison Holme, and Kimberly Nao. *Stuck in the Shallow End: Education, Race, and Computing*. Cambridge, MA: MIT Press, 2008.

Neuman, Susan B., and Donna Celano. "The Knowledge Gap: Implications of Leveling the Playing Field for Low-Income and Middle-Income Children." *Reading Research Quarterly* 41, no. 2 (2006): 176–201.

Regional Technology Alliance. *Mapping a Future for Digital Connections: A Study of the Digital Divide in San Diego County*. City of San Diego, 2001. http://files.eric.ed.gov/fulltext/ED463391.pdf (accessed September 28, 2015).

Rideout, Victoria J., Ulla G. Foehr, and Donald F. Roberts. *Generation M2: Media in the Lives of 8- to 18-Year-Olds*. Menlo Park, CA: Kaiser Family Foundation, 2010.

Scardamalia, Marlene, and Carl Bereiter. "Knowledge Building." In *Encyclopedia of Education*, 1370–1373. New York: Macmillan Reference, 2003.

Vigdor, Jacob L., Helen F. Ladd, and Erika Martinez. 2014. Scaling the Digital Divide: Home Computer Technology and Student Achievement. *Economic Inquiry* 52 (3): 1103–1119.

Warschauer, Mark. *Laptops and Literacy: Learning in the Wireless Classroom*. New York: Teachers College Press, 2006.

Warschauer, Mark. *Learning in the Cloud: How (and Why) to Transform Schools with Digital Media*. New York: Teachers College Press, 2011.

Warschauer, Mark. "Technology and School Reform: A View from Both Sides of the Track." *Education Policy Analysis Archives* 8, no. 4 (2000). http://epaa.asu.edu/ojs/article/view/395 (accessed October 1, 2015).

Warschauer, Mark. *Technology and Social Inclusion: Rethinking the Digital Divide*. Cambridge, MA: MIT Press, 2003.

Warschauer, Mark, Sheila R. Cotten, and Morgan Ames. 2011. One Laptop per Child Birmingham: Case Study of a Radical Reform. *International Journal of Learning and Media* 3 (2): 61–76.

Warschauer, Mark, Michelle Knobel, and Leeann Stone. "Technology and Equity in Schooling: Deconstructing the Digital Divide." *Educational Policy* 18, no. 4 (2004): 562–588.

Warschauer, Mark, and Tina Matuchniak. "New Technology and Digital Worlds: Analyzing Evidence of Equity in Access, Use, and Outcomes." *Review of Research in Education* 34, no. 1 (2010): 179–225.

Warschauer, Mark, Binbin Zheng, Melissa Niiya, Sheila Cotten, and George Farkas. "Balancing the One-to-One Equation: Equity and Access in Three Laptop Programs." *Equity & Excellence in Education* 47, no. 1 (2014): 46–62.

Webster, Tom. *Twitter Usage in America: 2010. The Edison Research/Arbitron Internet and Multimedia Study*. http://www.onecommunity.org/wp-content/uploads/2010/04/Twitter_Usage_In_America_2010.pdf (accessed May 25, 2010).

Wenglinsky, Harold. "Does It Compute? The Relationship between Educational Technology and Student Achievement in Mathematics." Educational Testing Service, 1998. ftp://ftp.ets.org/pub/res/technolog.pdf (accessed February 2, 2006).

Wenglinsky, Harold. *Using Technology Wisely: The Keys to Success in Schools*. New York: Teachers College Press, 2005.

3 Do You See What I See? Visibility through Social Media

danah boyd

Introduction

When you log in to Twitter, Facebook, Instagram, or any social media site, you see a world that you've constructed. You see your "friends," the people with whom you've chosen to connect. (And perhaps some people with whom you've been guilted into connecting.) These people shape your experience of social media and the world that you've constructed there. These people post about things that matter to you, either because you know them personally or because you like the way they think or see.

The people you follow share as you do. Or, more accurately, you share as they do. Your sense of norms is shaped by the people you follow or the content you consume. The audience that you have in your mind is not really the people who follow you but the people whose content you regularly see. You norm-set to the people you follow on Twitter or Instagram, the people who frequently update their content on Facebook and similar sites. Because of this, you're posting for the people you follow even though they may not be the ones who actually consume your content.

Social media present us with countless opportunities to connect with new people in different circles, and yet most people turn to these tools to connect with those whom they already know. In so doing, we collectively reinforce pervasive structural patterns. Your sense of what people do with social media is highly dependent on what you consume, how you consume it, and why you're there in the first place. The world you live in online looks different from the world I live in. And it looks different from the world that an average teen lives in or the world Rihanna lives in. What you experience through social media may be technically similar to what other people experience, but the cultural dynamics differ tremendously. Our worlds are different, even if the interface looks the same.

While we are each living in our own sociotechnical bubble, the potential visibility of our interactions introduces new possibilities and new challenges. Through social media, we have the ability to peek into the lives of so many more people today than ever before. More accurately, we have the ability to see the traces of one aspect of others' lives. Social media like Instagram and Twitter create opportunities for us to see other people in new ways. Regardless of where we are in the world, we can bear witness to the expressions of people who are quite different from us. But who's looking? In what circumstances? For what purposes? Through what lens? And with what intentions?

This chapter explores the complicated nature of visibility in social media. I approach these issues as an ethnographer seeking to map the cultural practices that unfold as people engage with social media as a part of their daily lives. For the last ten years, I have focused primarily on American youth and social media.[1] To do my work, I am constantly examining the public traces that teens leave through their interactions online, but I also regularly traverse the United States to interview teens and their families about their practices. In doing so, I've learned what I can and cannot see and how biased each of our viewpoints is.

Looking Around

People make their social media content publicly accessible for a variety of reasons. Some wish to attract wide audiences to consume their content; others simply want what they post to be easily accessible to the small cohort of friends that they expect will bother looking. Through the power of surfing links, searching, or leveraging open APIs and scripts, much of this data can be easily accessed by any number of people for any number of purposes. Researchers consume data to understand it; hackers scrape data for fun; businesses analyze data for profit. In fact, anyone with an ounce of curiosity can easily start poking around and looking at the content of strangers.

As a researcher trying to map diverse cultural practices, I am always trying to find new ways to access the digital universe and see new patterns. On Twitter, I search for common words like "the," or, better yet, "teh," just to see what will appear. I also look for obscure combinations, cultural references, and names. This practice—common among bored teenagers and researchers alike—creates opportunities to see into different corners of the site. Needless to say, this process is filled with all sorts of biases, and the sample that I obtain is anything but random or representative. Still, this technique allows me to habitually observe practices that are different from my own and that shake up my own understanding of what is common. This is the least sophisticated of my practices but the easiest for anyone to implement.

My observation practices have changed over time. In the early days of MySpace, when user identifiers were sequential numbers, I could simply look up the profile of a person associated with a random number. This allowed me to randomly sample all of MySpace. Facebook, Instagram, and other more recently developed social media sites are too sophisticated to allow this to happen easily, rendering this practice difficult for all but the technical elite.

Participant observation is an essential component of ethnographic work, and, while I'm a regular participant in all the social media I study, the practices of my friends and colleagues are not at all representative. Because these services are segmented and because what we see through everyday use is limited, we must go out of our way to observe difference. I do so as a researcher, while others do so because they are curious about different perspectives.

Most individuals use social media to seek out people they already know. Though the same tools that allow us to narrow in on people we know may also give us opportunities to seek out those whom we don't know, most people do not look beyond their narrow worlds. And when they do, it is typically because they're looking to assert power or make judgments.

Visibility can easily be leveraged for surveillance. Yet just because someone can be seen doesn't mean that that person will be seen: most people are obscure because no one bothers to look for them. Visibility is an odd beast—it's an opportunity for some and a liability for others. Failing to understand visibility can be costly when something not intended for broad consumption is spread widely, or when someone desperately seeking attention fails to obtain it. Visibility can also be deceiving. Taken out of context, publicly accessible data might signal something very different from what was intended. To interrogate the nature of visibility, I present three case studies from the early days of my fieldwork on MySpace. These examples shed light on different issues that are now common across all types of social media.

Case 1.   What Is Truth?

When MySpace was just gaining visibility beyond its early adopters back in 2005, I received a phone call from a college admissions officer at an Ivy

League institution. The school had received an application from a young black man living in South Central, Los Angeles. He had written a heart-wrenching essay about how he wanted to leave his gang-ridden community. When the college went to his MySpace profile, it was aghast. His profile was filled with gang insignia and references to gang activities.

The admissions officer asked me why kids today would bother to lie about their lives when it's possible to see the "truth" online. I was stunned because I doubted that that kid from South Central was lying to the college admissions officer; he was trying to survive in his hometown. Presumably, he walked into his school in South Central every day, where being a part of gang culture is necessary for survival. Quite likely, this young man had family or friends who were involved in gangs, and he might have owed favors. It was clear from his MySpace page that he was posting for his classmates, not for the college admissions officer. Yet the college admissions office had the ability to access his profile and make a judgment from afar. And the admissions officer chose to interpret it based on the college's context rather than try to understand the applicant's.

Content is always produced and interpreted in a context, but the context in which it is created might not be the context in which it is consumed. Just because something is publicly accessible doesn't mean that its meaning or explanation is. In projecting our assumptions of the situation, we often misunderstand the meaning of what we see. And, depending on where we stand, we assert power over people in doing so. Learning how to read information in context is one of the greatest challenges of managing visibility.

Case 2. Where Is Meaning?

The father of a sixteen-year-old was ecstatic when his daughter invited him to be her friend on MySpace. She had kept a private profile because she didn't want strangers peeking in. Her father supported her decision but was also disappointed that he was excluded. When she finally invited him to connect on MySpace, he felt overjoyed—but not for long. When he first visited his daughter's MySpace profile, he found, halfway down the page, a personality quiz called "What drug are you?" His daughter's answer was cocaine. This left the father shocked and unsure of what to do.

Deciding not to rush to judgment, he approached his daughter for an explanation. When he described what he saw, she reacted with laughter and exasperation. This was not what he was expecting, so he looked at her blankly. She went on to explain that it was just a quiz. Quizzes were popular at her school and, from her perspective, they were both fun and meaningless. "What drug are you?" was just the latest quiz circulating among her group of friends. Still puzzled, her father asked her what cocaine had to do with her personality. She explained that it was easy to guess the answer based on the questions provided, and so she was able to answer in a way that allowed her to choose the result. As far as she was concerned, the kids who smoked marijuana at school were lame, and the ones who preferred mushrooms were crazy. But it was the next line that her father could never forget: "Your generation did a lot of coke, and you came out OK."

The father was stunned, speechless, trapped between his desire to keep his daughter away from drugs and his awareness that many of his peers had been heavy drug users. His tattoos were also a signal to his daughter that his past wasn't without blemishes. On shaky ground, and in great fear, he proceeded to ask if she was doing coke. She immediately responded with shock and horror, negating all of his fears.

This father chose to look, but he also chose to see. Rather than misinterpreting what was visible, he made a decision to understand the context. He did not force his daughter to take down what she posted, but he did use it as an opportunity to open a conversation that he's very glad he had with her. Eventually she removed the quiz on her own. Choosing to look is one thing; having the confidence to know that one's interpretation may not be accurate is another. Visibility introduces new opportunities to bear witness, but making meaning out of available content is often harder than it may seem.

Case 3. Who Is Looking?

In 2007, a Colorado girl named Tess killed her mother with the help of a few friends. When the TV news picked it up, they covered the story as "girl with MySpace kills mother." Seeing this news story flash by, I decided to look at Tess's MySpace, which was still publicly accessible. What I saw on the site was heartbreaking. For months, Tess had been documenting her mother's alcoholic rages through her public MySpace blog postings. She detailed how her mother physically abused her, yelled at her, and psychologically tormented her. The reflexive content on her page consisted of emotional outpourings, frustration and rage, depression and confusion. She documented her own decision to start abusing alcohol and her struggle to navigate her mother's moods. She talked about running away to live with a friend and then moving back out of guilt. Her friends had left comments, offering emotional support, but they were in over their heads. None of the comments I read were written by adults.

Reading through Tess's page, I found comments from a close friend of hers. This friend was defending Tess's actions to the people who were criticizing Tess. This friend's page was also publicly accessible, filled with its own breed of heart-wrenching confusion, hurt, and uncertainty. I decided that I couldn't responsibly ignore this girl's pain, so I reached out to her and we began a conversation. She told me that everyone knew Tess's mom beat her, but no one knew what to do. No one was willing to listen. Tess's friend told me that the school had blocked MySpace, and so none of the teachers was able to look at what Tess wrote on her page. When the case went to trial, testimony suggested that social workers had been informed of the abuse from teachers, but nothing was done because there was not enough evidence.

Tess's cries for help went unheard, but I did my best to hear her friend out. She told me that there were no adults Tess could turn to, that no one was willing to listen. She felt as though she too was on trial because she was a friend of Tess's. I advised this young girl to get support from a professional and provided her with information about resources in her community. Even though I know that it's quite common, it pained me to realize that this girl, like her friend Tess, had no adults in her community to turn to for support.

Just because content is visible doesn't mean that anyone is actually looking or taking action. Obscurity can be both a blessing and a curse. It can enable people to build their own safe space, but it can also prevent people from getting help when they most desperately need it. We consistently use technology to search for and examine the presence of people who interest us, but we rarely use these same features to seek out those who are at risk and could use our help. Visibility doesn't guarantee community, support, or help.

Each of these cases raises critical questions to be addressed. The public and networked nature of the Internet creates the potential for visibility. We have the ability to see into the lives of so many people who are different from us, but only when we choose to look. So who is looking? Why are they looking? And in what context are they interpreting what they see?

The Right to Look?

Information is power. And those who are looking are typically those who hold power over the people being observed. Parents look. Teachers look. Employers look. Governments look. Corporations look. These people are often looking to judge or manipulate, even when they justify their actions.

Parents believe that looking constitutes responsible parenting; employers believe that doing so optimizes hiring. Many who look believe they have to right to do so simply because the content they're accessing is available. "But it's public!" is the refrain I hear.

People engage in public activities all the time without wanting to be an object of others' scrutiny. When we walk out into the street, anyone could approach us or stare at us, but most people experience a sense of obscurity in even the most public settings. The sociologist Erving Goffman argues that situations are bearable because of a collective commitment to what he calls "civil inattention."[2] In short, it is possible in public settings to be aware of and acknowledge others while also going out our way to give each other space. This process, most common in urban settings, allows us to maintain a sense of anonymity, but it also relieves us of the burden introduced by attention.

While most people can enter a public space without being ogled, public figures, such as celebrities and politicians, often cannot. Many believe that celebrities' stature means they don't deserve the right to privacy or obscurity when they enter publicly accessible spaces. The same "but it's public!" logic that parents and employers use to justify their actions is also used by paparazzi to justify their practice of circling celebrities like hawks.

Such public scrutiny is often discussed through the lens of surveillance, where people leverage power to observe others. Surveillance has a psychological effect. When we believe we're being watched, we act differently. And when those who are watching hold power over us, their acts of systematic observation function as a mechanism of control. This notion is best described by Michel Foucault, who analogizes Jeremy Bentham's panopticon to describe how prisoners can be controlled through a central tower that makes it difficult for prisoners to know when they are being watched and when they are not.[3] Foucault highlights that even the mere threat of being watched can serve to control people.

Although surveillance is a valuable frame for thinking about certain aspects of online data usage, it is inadequate for framing most issues presented by visibility. People don't feel as though they are being broadly watched because, for the most part, they're not. They contribute to visibility because they feel as though they might gain something and they don't think that the consequences outweigh the benefits. What frustrates them is not the fact that their content is accessible but that those whose attention is unwanted don't have the decency and respect to keep out. Civil inattention is a social contract. No structural limitations prevent a person from staring at another person. In polite society, staring is thought to be rude. Why is it any different online?

Most people are curious about other people. This curiosity drives our desire to gossip and tell stories. Getting access to social information has typically required reciprocity; people share information as a bonding ritual. Likewise, seeing typically requires being seen. This is the foundation for Baudelaire's *flâneur*, who walks the city streets to see and be seen, to be a participant and an observer.[4] While the notion of voyeurism is not new, the Internet makes it easier to watch from afar, to see without being seen. Mutual visibility, social reciprocity, and accountability are all key to civil inattention. Without these, people feel as though they can assert their right to look without being challenged because when they are actively observing, they are invisible. They are only visible when they choose to make themselves so.

Those appalled by people who demand visibility often argue for the right to privacy in public places. People have always carved out privacy in public spaces, whispering and winking and otherwise sharing in ways that could not be understood by everyone present. But what happens through social media is shaped by affordances that are fundamentally different from those we take for granted in unmediated settings. When people demand the right to privacy, they are often demanding the right to understand the context and control the social situation. Because content is persistent, replicable, and searchable online, it can spread beyond the original situation. Privacy in public may be easily manageable in a public park when a person can see everyone who sees her, but it is not that simple online. Achieving privacy in a networked work requires new skills and is constantly complicated by both the technology and the social norms surrounding the technology.[5] Frustrated by their inability to effectively control access to content, people seek to limit access to meaning, all in an attempt to have some semblance of privacy. Thus, even when something is accessible and functionally visible, making sense of what's being shared requires going beyond the content itself.

The Practice of Seeing

Even when engaging in civil inattention, people are peripherally aware of the social dynamics around them. If someone falls, there's a high likelihood that others will turn their attention to helping that person. Although there are highly celebrated cases of public pleas being ignored by large crowds, such as the murder of Kitty Genovese, whose cries for help were heard by many bystanders who did not act, people regularly move from strategic avoidance to active engagement when a situation presents itself. This is marked by Jane Jacobs when she speaks of the importance of "eyes on the street" as a mechanism to achieve safety in urban settings.[6] People are aware of what's happening around them even if they are not actively engaged. Their awareness operates as a subtle form of surveillance, creating control through observation and providing a safety net for those who run into difficulties.

While being observed can be costly, so can being ignored, just as we saw with the story of Tess. The right to privacy and obscurity cannot be used to justify allowing harm to occur, but just as with Genovese's murder, there is often an assumption that, when it's public, it's someone else's responsibility. With new sociotechnical systems, we need new frames for understanding ethical responsibility. Consider that we used to argue for a right to privacy to justify anything that happens in our private homes, including domestic violence. The idea that domestic violence was once acceptable is hard to imagine today, but not that long ago the logic used to be, "She's my wife. It's my home. I can do whatever I want to her." We cannot use a so-called right to privacy to justify a right to abuse people in private. Likewise, we also cannot use privacy to justify not looking when people are hurting or when they're crying out for help.

This forces us to ask, Who should be looking? When should we be looking? And why are we looking? We should not be looking to judge or manipulate but to learn, support, or empower. Consider at-risk youth who are in trouble. Shouldn't we be seeking them out so that we can help them? It breaks my heart that there are youth out there crying out for help, with no one listening.

Looking is not easy. It can be heartbreaking. What is made visible online includes the best and worst of society and everything in between. When one chooses to look, one is forced to see inequity, racism and misogyny, cruelty and violence, pain and anger. It's too easy to see all of this and blame the technology for creating it. Most people who see terrible things taking place because of the visibility made possible through the Internet blame the messenger.

Most people prefer not to look beyond their local worlds. This is not unique to the Internet. Gated communities cropped up when wealthy individuals decided to seek refuge from the poor, most notably those who were black or brown. Self-segregation is pervasive, as people seek to connect only with others like them. These same people are not happy when technology makes visible content that reveals a world different from their own. They seek to keep their children away from people whose values, backgrounds, and tastes are different from their own. And when people are forced to see difference, they often respond negatively.

Twitter's Trending Topics prominently showcase terms that are popular across all of the tweets posted at a given time. While most people consume only a small fraction of the millions of tweets that are posted each minute, this feature often makes diverse segments of the network visible. Shortly after this feature was launched in 2009, the Black Entertainment Television Awards were aired. Enough people were tweeting about the TV coverage that all of the Trending Topics reflected icons of the black community. This made black users quite visible on Twitter. Some users were upset by this unaccustomed visibility and started posting tweets like *"wow!! too many negros in the trending topics for me. I may be done with this whole twitter thing,"* and *"Did anyone see the new trending topics? I don't think this is a very good neighborhood. Lock the car doors kids,"* and *"Why are all the black people on trending topics? Neyo? Beyonce? Tyra? Jamie Foxx? Is it black history month again? LOL."*[7] The racist reaction by Twitter users reflects how people respond to seeing content that is outside their normal purview.

While openness sometimes breeds tolerance, not everyone is willing or able to look with open eyes. Just because something is visible doesn't mean that people are open to hearing or seeing it. And just because they are looking doesn't mean that they know how to interpret what they see or how to act on it. Interpreting visible data requires that we maintain what Helen Nissenbaum calls "contextual integrity."[8] We cannot simply derive meaning from what we see without understanding the context in which it is situated. The failure to properly situate what we see can too easily breeds intolerance. Likewise, the failure to act on what is made visible might also put people in harm's way.

Living with Visibility

Technology will continue to make publicly accessible content available in new ways, aggregating and distributing all sorts of information that participants contribute through their explicit creations or their implicit actions. We will need to learn to live with visibility, both as the people being exposed and as those who have the ability to look and see. Fundamentally, we will need to develop a sense of ethics and social norms around these dynamics. When do we have the right to look? When is it crucial that we look? How do we actively go about looking when there's a need, and actively choose not to look when it's not appropriate?

Social norms concerning visibility will develop over time, but this moment of transition provides a tremendous opportunity to critically interrogate our biases and practices. The right to look—often espoused when referencing publicly accessible content—is not the same as *choosing* to ethically see. To look is to assert power; to see is to respect.

We have an ethical responsibility to see others in the context in which they operate and a moral responsibility to look out for those who are at risk. Most of those who are choosing to look are doing so with punitive intentions, focused on those who violate terms of service, laws, or societal norms. We need to also consider what it means to empower those seeking to help to be able to see, listen, learn, and respond. We need social services to be able to see even as law enforcement chooses to look.

The challenges presented by visibility are complex and intertwined. Just because content is publicly accessible doesn't mean that it's meant to be accessed broadly—but this doesn't mean that public content should be ignored, either. We need to develop the right balance, to provide civil inattention, and to develop eyes on our digital streets with the goal of empowerment, not surveillance. How we manage the challenges presented by visibility will shape the next generation.

Notes

1. danah boyd, *It's Complicated: The Social Lives of Networked Teens* (New Haven, CT: Yale University Press, 2014).

2. Erving Goffman, *Behavior in Public Places: Notes on the Social Organization of Gatherings* (New York: Free Press, 1966).

3. Michel Foucault, *Discipline and Punish: The Birth of the Prison,* trans. A. M. Sheridan-Smith (New York: Vintage, 1977).

4. Charles Baudelaire, *The Painter of Modern Life* (New York: Da Capo Press, 1964 [1863]).

5. Alice Marwick and danah boyd, "Networked Privacy: How Teenagers Negotiate Context in Social Media," *New Media & Society,* 2014. doi:10.1177/1461444814543995.

6. Jane Jacobs, *The Death and Life of Great American Cities* (New York: Vintage, 1992).

7. boyd, *It's Complicated,* 161–162.

8. Helen Nissenbaum, *Privacy in Context: Technology, Policy, and the Integrity of Social Life* (Palo Alto, CA: Stanford Law Books, 2009).

Bibliography

Baudelaire, Charles. *The Painter of Modern Life.* New York: Da Capo Press, 1964 (1863).

boyd, danah. *It's Complicated: The Social Lives of Networked Teens.* New Haven, CT: Yale University Press, 2014.

Foucault, Michel. *Discipline and Punish: The Birth of the Prison.* Trans. A. M. Sheridan-Smith. New York: Vintage, 1977.

Goffman, Erving. *Behavior in Public Places: Notes on the Social Organization of Gatherings.* New York: Free Press, 1966.

Jacobs, Jane. *The Death and Life of Great American Cities.* New York: Vintage, 1992.

Marwick, Alice, and danah boyd. "Networked Privacy: How Teenagers Negotiate Context in Social Media." *New Media & Society*, 2014. doi:.10.1177/1461444814543995

Nissenbaum, Helen. *Privacy in Context: Technology, Policy, and the Integrity of Social Life.* Palo Alto, CA: Stanford Law Books, 2009.

4 ICTs and Education in Developing Countries: The Case of India

Colin Agur

Introduction

Today, with information and communication technologies (ICTs)[1] proliferating rapidly in developing countries,[2] new questions and debates have emerged about the role ICTs might play in education. For theorists of ICTs and the digital divide in education, developing countries test assumptions about the universality of technology and usage. For educational practitioners, developing countries offer a complex set of challenges and opportunities for ICTs as educational tools. This chapter examines the conceptual and practical aspects of ICT use in developing countries' educational initiatives. After looking at developing countries' role in the world, the chapter discusses the digital divide that hampers ICT use in education. It then turns to India as an example of a developing country attempting to overcome the economic, geographic, and social challenges that have thus far limited ICT use, examines a selection of Indian ICT-for-education initiatives, and highlights the features of these programs that have proved successful. The chapter concludes with a discussion of the importance of networks in educational development, the complex relationship between global ICTs and cultural diversity, and the social and educational possibilities of mass mobile phone usage in India and other developing countries.

Developing Countries and the Digital Divide

Developing countries have a special importance with respect to ICTs and education. According to the World Bank, 80 percent of the global population lives in developing countries, and this percentage will grow in the decades to come.[3] Developing countries are also undergoing significant social changes associated with internal migration, urbanization, and industrialization. These changes have placed stress on educational systems' existing infrastructure and personnel and have heightened the challenge of providing education in contexts of economic scarcity: developing countries are home to a majority of the more than 61 million children outside educational systems worldwide.[4] The rapid and uneven distribution of ICTs that has recently taken place in developing countries has exacerbated preexisting social (rich–poor) and geographic (urban–rural) divisions. Today, in a majority of developing countries the income gap between rich and poor is widening.[5]

In the years to come, the question of who gets what technology will have a large effect on the educational and economic potential of citizens in developing countries. In light of these countries' substantial share of the world's population and the well-documented link between education and development, there is a strong case for directing more attention to ICT use in developing countries. Many of the big-picture questions that surround ICT use—for example, whether such technologies will become tools of greater social inclusion and democracy or tools of elite dominance—will be decided in developing countries. Though industrialized countries will continue to develop, export, profit from, and control ICT use through copyright, a fascinating and unpredictable set of narratives will unfold in developing countries, which represent four-fifths of humanity.[6]

As ICT use continues to grow, however unevenly, among populations in developing countries, researchers need to understand the "digital divide" (or, perhaps more accurately, a series of divides) that limits ICT access. Most obviously, the digital divide involves a set of infrastructural deficiencies affecting large swaths of populations in developing countries. Access to the Internet is hindered by lack of access to prerequisite infrastructure such as electricity. Where Internet access does exist in educational institutions, it suffers from inadequate or outdated hardware, limited bandwidth, and frequent service interruptions.[7] Across the developing world, the most reliable (and most popular) point of access to the Internet is a mobile phone connected to a cellular network. The low cost of mobile phone service in many developing countries has brought rapid growth in telephone usage, and in many countries a higher percentage of people have a telephone than have electricity or running water. Although high-end smartphones are typically expensive, there are dozens of competitively priced "semismart" phones that allow users to access the Internet. And in recent years, some popular global sites such as Wikipedia and Facebook have developed "zero-rated" versions that users can access for free, without using up any of their cellular data plans. These developments have brought many individual users into a world of digital content, where they can draw from and contribute to communities of knowledge. But there are limits to participation with mobile phones: preexisting economic constraints mean that the same people who are excluded from other common goods and services are limited in which phone (if any) they can afford, how many minutes they can buy, how easily they can find a place to charge the phone, and how much leisure time they have. Despite the rapid adoption of mobile phones in developing countries, there remain significant barriers to usage by the global poor.

In addition to economics, social factors also play a role in the digital divide. As Manuel Castells has noted, the digital divide often follows preexisting geographic divides: rural and remote areas typically have delayed (and lower-quality) access to ICTs.[8] Cities are home to developing countries' highest concentrations of ICT infrastructure, as well as the majority of users and most content production, but they too have their politics of geography. Slums, even when located in proximity to rich enclaves, suffer from infrastructural deficits, with a lack of reliable electricity the largest technical hindrance to ICT usage. To these infrastructural and geographic challenges we must add perhaps the largest challenge of all: social divisions. Developing countries contain significant internal diversity, with social class, language, and ethnicity or tribal affiliation the most significant differentiators of national subgroups. Thus the digital divide is a multifaceted concept: it refers to a complex set of divisions that exist within developing countries, but it also refers to divisions between the industrialized world (historically the producers of ICTs, and where access is often taken for granted), developing countries (where components of ICTs are often manufactured, and where access is inconsistent), and least developed countries (which depend on technology imports and offer only severely limited ICT usage). These divides mean that in different parts of the world, users enjoy differing levels of affordances in ICT usage.[9] This differential in turn limits the educational and developmental potential of ICTs.[10]

It is easier to understand these abstract challenges and identify solutions to them by discussing ICT use in a major national case study that reflected the economic realities of developing countries. These realities included material constraints, such as strained infrastructure, and the combination of formal structures and informal activity that frequently characterizes developing countries' economies. India's aggregate statistics place it on the lower rung of developing countries. According to the most recent figures from the United Nations Development Program (UNDP), 63 percent of adult Indian citizens are functionally literate, 37 percent have completed secondary education, and 75 percent are satisfied with the quality of education they receive.[11] Among developing countries, India is both typical and an outlier. It is typical in that educational technology initiatives face a set of economic, geographic, and social constraints common to other developing countries. It is also typical in that ICT access and usage are highly differentiated, reflecting the concentration of wealth in the country. Today, India has some of the cheapest basic telephony in the world, and as a result, more than 800 million users have access to basic telephone service.[12] At the same time, value-added telephone services and Internet access are concentrated in urban areas.[13] Among developing countries, India is an outlier in its scale and composition: it is a highly populous country and home to an unusually diverse citizenry. India's size also makes it an outlier in another respect: it offers significant indigenous technological expertise and is a production center for ICT devices.[14] India thus reveals many of the challenges (widespread poverty, low literacy, social marginalization) most developing countries face, as well as the advantages (home-grown talent in IT and the capacity to manufacture specialized technology for educational use) enjoyed by a handful of developing countries.

For those contemplating ICT-for-education initiatives in developing countries, the case of India underscores the complex set of challenges such a program would likely face. From a technological, economic, and social standpoint, the country's urban–rural split is striking: India's urban residents are nearly twice as likely as its rural residents to have a telephone, and several times more likely to have Internet access.[15] Within India's often sprawling cities, intraurban divides mean that some groups have high-speed Internet access and good telephone reception, while others remain largely off the grid. India's social complexity means that any efforts to implement ICTs in educational contexts will encounter the divisions of ethnicity, religion, class, caste, language, and wealth, as well as divergent generational attitudes toward technology and usage. Such efforts will also need to deal with low literacy levels in much of the country. Like many developing countries, India struggles with a strained electrical grid: blackouts last from minutes to hours and occur daily in some parts of the country. India's telecommunications infrastructure is similarly strained, and connection quality is hampered by bottlenecks, poor maintenance, and tampering. The implementation of educational technology is also hampered by the difficulty of training teachers to work with new and often imperfect technology, and the challenge of retaining quality teachers, whose new skills in technology make them attractive candidates for higher-paying jobs.[16] Governments and partner organizations also face technophobia from two groups: teachers, who are wary of having their work replaced by machines, and community elders, who fear a loss of traditional social values. One particular challenge in India is institutional fragmentation: educational policymaking involves multiple levels of government (mainly the center and the states, although some cities, such as Delhi, add a local element to education planning). This can lead to healthy intellectual tension and creative experimentation, but it can also leave unclear what role the state should play and what metrics should be used to assess educational initiatives.

A Case Study in the Digital Divide: ICT-for-Education Initiatives in India

As in many developing countries, India's digital divide involves more than a lack of specific technology: it also involves a lack of educational infrastructure and programming. India's constitution guarantees free and compulsory education for all children under the age of fourteen.[17] But for a variety of economic and social reasons, significant numbers of Indian children do not complete these years of schooling.[18] During the past twenty years, India has experimented with several types of ICT-for-education initiatives. These have included broad policy vision documents, investments in satellite technology for the distribution of content, and a series of programs involving the central and state governments and external partners.

The largest actor in India's ICT-for-education initiatives has been the central government, which has put forward a series of increasingly ambitious national plans. In 1992, the National Policy on Education drew attention to the potential of educational technology to improve access to knowledge among India's poor: "Modern communication technologies have the potential to bypass several stages and sequences in the process of development encountered in earlier decades. Both the constraints of time and distance at once become manageable."[19] Throughout the mid- to late 1990s, the government promoted the National Open School program, which grew dramatically and claimed more than three million total graduates by the end of the decade.[20] In 2004, the central government launched the National Policy on ICT in School Education, with a focus on teaching skill building at the secondary level.[21] In 2005, the Central Advisory Board issued a report on universal secondary education, emphasizing the importance of ICTs.[22] That same year, the central government established the National Knowledge Commission to generate research on education in India and provide policy advice to the government. That commission has since created the National Knowledge Network, an ambitious initiative to provide broadband connectivity throughout the country.[23] In more recent years, these initiatives have become part of a growing governmental effort to make ICTs central features in Indian education. ICTs have received significant attention in the two most recent Five Year Plans. The Eleventh Five Year Plan (2007–2012) provided U.S. $900 million for the Mission on Education through ICTs.[24] The Twelfth Five Year Plan (2012–2017) calls for additional funding of ICTs "to enrich teaching-learning experience, extend and diversify delivery, improve research quality and collaboration by making knowledge and information widely available, and ensure effective governance both at the institutional and systemic level."[25] As a sign of the importance of ICTs in educational policymaking, the Twelfth Five Year Plan has included a series of hackathons.[26]

At the same time as it has issued broad policy recommendations, the Indian government has been the key player in designing new satellite-based distribution systems for educational programs. In 2004 the Indian Space Research Organization launched EDUSAT, India's first education-specific satellite.[444] EDUSAT is designed to facilitate distance-based education, with an emphasis on providing educational content to rural areas of the country. To this end, it now distributes ViCTERS and several dozen other educational TV networks intended for national, regional, and targeted (i.e., girls, scheduled castes, blind students, special needs) audiences. The original mandate of EDUSAT emphasized its broadcast potential. In recent years it has expanded to include interactive TV, video-conferencing, computer conferencing, and web-based lessons.[27] Programs from EDUSAT now reach students in all Indian states, including remote mountain areas (Jammu, Kashmir) and islands (Lakshdweep, Anduman, Nicobar).

EDUSAT is a conduit for programming at multiple levels. Its elementary programming is concentrated in the Hindi, Tamil, Marathi, Oriya, and Telugu languages and is available nationwide. EDUSAT has also become a distributor of content directed at colleges and universities: It provides college-level enrichment courses developed by the University Grants Commission (UGC) and daily lectures offered by the Indira Gandhi National Open University (IGNOU). EDUSAT shows how the central government can contribute financially and technically to ICT-oriented learning programs. And the expanding mandate of EDUSAT shows that once operational, satellite technology can become a conduit for expanding, changing, and differentiated educational content.

The central government has also launched a series of ICT-for-education programs. At the elementary level, Sarva Shiksha Abhiyan (SSA) is the central government's flagship program in its drive to achieve universal elementary education. The mandate of SSA includes more than 190 million children nationwide.[28] SSA has an infrastructural element: it builds schools in areas where they are needed, and seeks to improve infrastructure in existing schools. SSA also has a training element: it trains new teachers and retrains existing teachers, and gives particular attention to girls, members of scheduled castes, and special needs students. SSA has also been a major provider of computers and training for teachers so they can integrate the technology into the curriculum.[29]

To a lesser extent, the central government has also developed ICT-for-education initiatives at the secondary level. The central government manages the National Institute of Open Schooling (NOS), which it calls "the largest open schooling system in the world."[30] The NOS is a collaboration among the central government, UNESCO, and the Commonwealth of Learning. Each year more than 300,000 students, scattered across two dozen states, take secondary, senior secondary, or vocational training courses available online. Students can browse current and past assignments in their courses, conduct research via an online library, and communicate with tutors, who grade their assignments. Recognizing the higher level of technical skills possible at the secondary level and the growing importance of IT skills for tertiary education, these programs focus on ICTs in education rather than education as a whole. Established in 2004, the ICT in Schools program is a joint venture between the central government (which pays the majority of costs) and state governments. It has four components: providing computer-aided education in existing secondary schools, building "smart schools," developing teacher capacities in ICT usage, and creating and distributing e-content.[31]

India has also experimented with ICT-for-education experiments at the state level. In Kerala, ICT@School is a twelve-year-old initiative with two goals: creating an IT-literate community and improving the quality of education by using ICT technology.[32] The program currently involves 120,000 teachers and three million students across the state of Kerala. The project began in 2001 at the elementary level, with a statewide IT awareness campaign and training of instructors and administrators. In 2003, IT became a compulsory subject, with statewide practical exams. From 2005 to 2007, the program took three steps toward open-source software: it developed IT@School Linux, it shifted all textbooks to free software models, and it moved all practical exams to FOSS. In 2008, the project made several ambitious moves: it offered broadband connectivity to all schools in the state, issued laptops to all schools in the state, made ICT@School its primary delivery mechanism for e-governance within the Education Department, and used ICT@School as a model for FOSS implementation across the entire Education Department. In 2009, the ViCTERS[33] educational channel was available on cable networks statewide; the project launched an initiative to provide electricity to all classrooms in Kerala; and ICT@School was expanded to upper primary and higher secondary sections. In subsequent years, ICT@School rolled out the first model smart classrooms, launched school wikis, and offered training for 28,000 new student school IT coordinators.

Several features of ICT@School make it a remarkable project. It has succeeded where others have failed in the material construction of networks: Kerala's schools are now (mostly) electrified and connected be means of broadband, laptops are available to most schools, and in-school hardware clinics repair and upgrade computer technology. The project has succeeded beyond its original mandate: in recent years it has grown into a network for education e-governance, as shown by the use of ICT@School for an open-source redesign of the Education Department. ICT@School has made free and open-source software a central part of its mission, lowering its content-production costs and making software more malleable for the needs of schools.

For these ICT-for-education initiatives to succeed, India's state and central governments will need to make effective use of limited resources and avoid the policy missteps of the past. India's central government has historically given higher funding priority to tertiary education than to secondary education. Sharma argues that this funding differential has created a privileged situation for a minority of privately educated secondary school graduates, who continue on to India's subsidized universities, but has limited the potential for those who struggle in the country's often under-funded secondary schools.[34] The result, Sharma points out, is a small group of white-collar workers in a position to enjoy the fruits of the IT revolution and a much larger disenfranchised majority who lack meaningful access to ICTs and the affluence that accompanies such access. He quotes Abdul Waheed Khan of the Indira Gandhi National Open University, who juxtaposes the government's aspirational targets with the low percentage (6.5 percent) of school graduates who pursue tertiary education in India.[35] In a similar vein, Gulati argues that India's economic progress has masked an inability or unwillingness to deliver effective, widespread ICTs in educational contexts.[36]

The above programs have worked best when they have focused not just on the provision of technology but also—and arguably more important—on the development of human capital. If schools have staff who are competent and confident in using ICTs for education, technology will be put to effective use. Strong technological competence at the local level allows schools to make better use of suboptimal technology; that same competence can help schools overcome neglect by administrators.[37] Conversely, without adequate training, even the best technology is not a solution on its own.

India's ICT-for-education programs have enjoyed success when they have empowered existing teachers. Initially, Kerala's IT@School project used external resources for training, but this proved ineffective: teachers using the technology felt that it undermined their competence and hindered their teaching style. As a report on the project noted, "The 'importing' of specialists in the form of external instructors in schools created a negative impact among the teaching populace."[38] In response to feedback from teachers, the project took a different approach: it solicited volunteers among existing teachers and trained them as master trainers. Once they had completed this training, the master trainers taught their colleagues how to use the technology. This allowed preexisting groups of teachers to define a technology on their collective terms and collaborate in putting that technology to use. Such an approach has two main benefits: it creates a sense of local ownership of the technology and authorship of content, and it generates competence and confidence at the local level, lessening schools' dependence on (often distant) administrators for day-to-day operations.[39] Tian Belawati identifies this as the critical challenge for developing countries—to empower students and teachers so they may put to use new network infrastructure and benefit from the interactivity offered by online learning.[40]

ICT-for-education projects can also empower local administrators and teachers by choosing free and open-source software (FOSS). In India as in much of the developing world, education departments and schools have limited funds to purchase proprietary software. By emphasizing FOSS options, administrators can save money on software and divert the savings to other tasks, such as the electrification of classrooms, the construction of new facilities or the procurement of computer hardware.[41] Beyond economics, FOSS creates educational benefits: by opening up code to changes: FOSS allows states, local boards, and individual schools to experiment and fashion software to the needs of content and users, rather than the other way around. Proprietary software often includes restrictions on sharing content, which can be a major limitation in the effective use of ICT for education. During the early years of a project, FOSS can help education departments create and distribute content without the difficulties of limitations imposed by proprietary software. Within individual schools and classrooms, FOSS enables sharing, copying, and modifying content to suit the needs of students. Over time, as more teachers gain skills in the use of ICTs for education, FOSS can enable more sophisticated, specialized, and interactive uses of ICTs for learning.[42]

In countries with problems of oversight and histories of institutionalized corruption, the procurement process is a major source of worry. Procurement of technology is typically the most costly element in ICT-for-education initiatives.[43] Cost overruns in procurement of technology are common at educational institutions, and large-scale purchases by educational departments present additional opportunities for costs to exceed expectations. Overruns can happen because of poor initial estimates by administrators, changing requirements by the school, or the politicization of procurement by those who are able to benefit from acquisitions. Decisions about hardware and software (especially if it is proprietary) can create a path dependency for schools and entire education departments. If teachers are locked into suboptimal or inadequate technology, the quality of education will suffer and students will fall behind their counterparts at schools with the right technology.

To date, numerous studies have shown that well-designed and well-executed ICT initiatives can improve access and quality of education.[44] But developing countries face a double challenge: First, to achieve absolute gains, they must find ways to integrate ICT use into deficient educational systems. The second challenge, relative gains, is more difficult: developing countries must take advantage of their strengths. Often, a lack of legacy technology can make it easier to adopt new technology and enjoy the benefits of leapfrogging.[45]

One of the largest selling points for ICTs in education—their applicability for open and distance education—is an even larger consideration in developing countries. The urbanization of poor and middle-income countries has been well documented in recent years: many cities have grown rapidly, with corresponding crowding and strain on infrastructure. But what is sometimes forgotten is that in much of the developing world, a majority of inhabitants still live in rural areas. In India, more than 65 percent of the population lives outside cities, and government efforts to provide universal education are hindered by several divisions (geographic, economic, and social), as well as by deficiencies in the infrastructure (transportation, communication, schools) required for education. ICTs offer a means of delivering educational content to this population.

ICTs, particularly mobile phones, offer a low-cost means for the creation and delivery of content, and for interactive learning. In less than twenty years, India has experienced a dramatic transformation in telephone policy and usage. In the early 1990s, India had one of the lowest teledensity[46] rates in the world, a small and weak telephone sector, and a set of regulations derived from nineteenth-century legislation intended to administer the country's telegraph networks. In 2014, India had more than 900 million mobile subscribers; several indigenous telecom champions, including one (Bharti Airtel) of the world's giants; and a sophisticated regulatory regime that has kept mobile costs low for consumers and encouraged universal mobile connectivity. Through a physical network of towers, switches, cables, and phones, users have access to an impressive set of existing and emerging educational programs.

Conclusion

Developing countries are important potential sites for the educational use of ICTs, yet face the challenges of the digital divide in ICT access. The set of ICT-for-education initiatives in India discussed in this chapter show how these programs have attempted to reduce the digital divide. Of particular importance is the potential of ICTs in developing countries to support low-cost, open learning opportunities. For India and other developing countries to narrow the digital divide, they will need ambition, funding, and flexibility in design: when software is open, it allows for experimentation at the local level, and modifications over time as the needs of learners and systems evolve. Developing countries will also need new human capital at the local level. When administrators, teachers, and students are empowered users of ICTs for education, the result is the type of "network of choice" that Manuel Castells and co-workers called for in their seminal study of ICT use.[47]

ICT-for-education initiatives in developing countries provide insight into the wider relationship between culture and technology. While hardware and software may appear to be universal, ICT usage differs widely in different localities. Contrary to expectations that ICTs will undermine local forces, ICTs have been shown to reinforce existing social relations at the local level. At the same time, global forces come into play: for example, administrators, teachers, and parents are concerned about students' easy access to pornography, violence, and other (often externally produced) content that conflicts with traditional social values. In educational contexts in developing countries, ICTs allow for a mix of continuity (reinforcing existing social relations) and change (allowing outside content to enter, and giving young people discreet pathways to communicate with each other). Thus, ICTs do not alter culture but instead allow for new cultural inputs and new pathways of communication within an existing social structure.[48] As the ICT-for-education initiatives discussed in this chapter demonstrate, developing countries can introduce ICTs on their own terms, in ways that address the needs of their learners and respect cultural differences and traditions. And as this chapter has highlighted, the mobile phone will play a major role in the development and delivery of educational content.

Notes

1. The term "information and communication technologies" (ICTs) as used in this chapter refers to the integration of different types of networks (telephone, computer, radio) into a single, usually mobile, device.

2. The World Bank gives the following definition of developing countries: "countries with low or middle levels of GNP per capita as well as five high-income developing economies—Hong Kong (China), Israel, Kuwait, Singapore, and the United Arab Emirates. These five economies are classified as developing despite their high per capita income because of their economic structure or the official opinion of their governments. Several countries with transition economies are sometimes grouped with developing countries based on their low or middle levels of per capita income, and sometimes with developed countries based on their high industrialization. More than 80 percent of the world's population lives in the more than 100 developing countries." See World Bank, *Beyond Economic Growth*, Glossary (Washington, DC: World Bank, 2013), http://www.worldbank.org/depweb/english/beyond/global/glossary.html.

3. Ibid.

4. UNESCO Institute for Statistics, *Reaching Out-of-School Children* (Montreal: UNESCO Institute for Statistics, June 26, 2014), http://www.uis.unesco.org/Education/Pages/reaching-oosc.aspx.

5. The World Bank is matter-of-fact about the tendency for new development to bring concentrated economic gains, and for income levels to initially diverge (even if all income levels are rising in an absolute sense). See World Bank, *World Development Report 2009: Reshaping Economic Geography* (Washington, DC: World Bank, 2009), xxi.

6. The most recent annual report from the International Telecommunications Union emphasizes the importance of developing countries in global ICT figures on usage and pricing. See International Telecommunication Union, *Measuring the Information Society 2012* (Geneva: ITU, 2012), http://www.itu.int/en/ITU-D/Statistics/Documents/publications/mis2012/MIS2012_without_Annex_4.pdf.

7. World Economic Forum, *Global Information Technology Report 2013* (World Economic Forum, 2013), http://www.weforum.org/reports/global-information-technology-report-2013/.

8. Manuel Castells, *The Rise of the Network Society* (Oxford: Blackwell, 1996).

9. The concept of affordances was raised by James J. Gibson in "The Theory of Affordances," in *Perceiving, Acting, and Knowing: Toward an Ecological Psychology*, ed. Robert Shaw and John Bransford (Hillsdale, NJ: Erlbaum, 1977), 67–82. More recently Lucas Graves has made a helpful addition to this concept, identifying the invitational quality of affordances in social media. See his "The Affordances of Blogging: A Case Study in Culture and Technological Effects," *Journal of Communication Inquiry* 31, no 4 (2007): 331–546.

10. See Tahereh Saheb, "ICT, Education and Digital Divide in Developing Countries," *Global Media Journal* 4, no. 7 (2005), http://www.globalmediajournal .com/open-access/ict-education-and-digital-divide-in-developing-countries.pdf; and UNESCO, *ICT Competency Framework for Teachers, Version 2.0*, 2011, http://iite .unesco.org/pics/publications/en/files/3214694.pdf.

11. United Nations Development Program (UNDP), *Human Development Report 2013: The Rise of the South: Human Progress in a Diverse World*, Statistical Annex, 170, http://hdr.undp.org/en/media/HDR2013_EN_Statistics.pdf. India has an unusually high satisfaction rate for a country with its literacy and school completion rate. This raises the question of what satisfaction means in different cultural contexts, and what expectations different countries' learners have of their educational systems.

12. Telecommunications Regulatory Authority of India (TRAI), *A Decadal Profile*, Introduction (TRAI, 2012). http://www.trai.gov.in/WriteReadData/Publication/Docu ment/20130412105240353667SNCAER--Report08june12.pdf.

13. TRAI, *The Indian Telecom Services Performance Indicators, July–September, 2012* (New Delhi: TRAI, January 11, 2013), http://www.trai.gov.in/WriteReadData/ PIRReport/Documents/Indicator%20Reports%20-%20Sep_2012.pdf.

14. P. Sharma, "The Distance in Education and Online Technologies in India," in *Global Perspectives on E-learning: Rhetoric and Reality*, ed. A. A. Carr-Chellman (London: Sage, 2005), 52–66.

15. TRAI, *A Decadal Profile*, Introduction.

16. This has been a long-standing challenge in educational development. See H. D. Perraton, *Open and Distance Learning in the Developing World* (London: Routledge-Falmer, 2000).

17. Constitution of India (1950). 86th Amendment. *The Constitution Act*, 2002. http://indiacode.nic.in/coiweb/amend/amend86.htm.

18. See UNDP, *Human Development Report 2013*, Statistical Annex, 170.

19. Government of India, *Amended National Policy on Education* (New Delhi, 1992), 27. http://www.ncert.nic.in/oth_anoun/npe86.pdf.

20. K. Sujatha, *Distance Education at Secondary Level in India: The National Open School*, report for the UNESCO International Institute for Educational Planning, Paris, Working Document, February 2002, http://unesdoc.unesco.org/images/0012/001262/126210e.pdf.

21. Government of India, Ministry of Human Resource Development, *ICT in Schools*, "Program Overview," 2015, http://mhrd.gov.in/ict_overview.

22. Government of India, Ministry of Human Resource Development, *Report of the Central Advisory Board of Education (CABE) Committee on Autonomy of Higher Education Institutions* (New Delhi, 2005), http://www.teindia.nic.in/Files/Reports/CCR/cabe/Ahei.pdf.

23. Government of India, National Knowledge Network, "Vision," 2013, http://www.nkn.in.

24. Government of India, Planning Commission, *Eleventh Five-Year Plan (2007–2012)*, 2007, http://planningcommission.nic.in/plans/planrel/11thf.htm.

25. Government of India, Planning Commission, *Faster, Sustainable and More Inclusive Growth: An Approach to the Twelfth Five Year Plan* [2012–2017], October 2011, http://planningcommission.gov.in/plans/planrel/12appdrft/appraoch_12plan.pdf.

26. Government of India, Data Portal (2013). See the link to the Five Year Plan Hackathon, http://www.data.gov.in/hackathon.

444. Indian Space Research Organization, Satcom Applications description, 2015. See also the Tele-education description, http://india.gov.in/official-website-indian-space-research-organisation.

27. Ibid.

28. Government of India, Ministry of Human Resource Development, Sarva Shiksha Abhiyan program overview, 2015, http://mhrd.gov.in/sarva-shiksha-abhiyan.

29. Ibid.

30. Government of India, Ministry of Human Resource Development, National Institute of Open Schooling, 2013, program overview, http://www.nios.ac.in.

31. Government of India, Ministry of Human Resource Development (2015). ICT in Schools program overview, http://mhrd.gov.in/ict_overview.

32. Government of India, Ministry of Human Resource Development (2015). See the SSA program description at http://mhrd.gov.in/sarva-shiksha-abhiyan.

33. ViCTERS stands for Virtual Classroom Technology on EDUSAT for Rural Schools.

34. Sharma, "The Distance in Education and Online Technologies in India," 52–66.

35. Ibid., 54.

36. See Shalni Gulati, "Technology-Enhanced Learning in Developing Nations: A Review," *International Review of Research in Open and Distance Learning* 9, no. 1 (2008), http://www.irrodl.org/index.php/irrodl/article/view/477/1012.

37. Ibid.

38. Government of Kerala, Department of General Education, "The Kerala Experience: IT@School Project" (Centre for Innovation in Public Systems, 2010), http://www.cips.org.in/public-sector-systems-government-innovations/documents/IT@School_PPT_cips_hydbad.pdf.

39. See UNESCO, *ICT Competency Framework for Teachers, Version* 2.0.

40. Tian Belawati, "The Impact of Online Tutorials on Course Completion Rates and Student Achievement," *Learning, Media & Technology* 30, no. 1 (2005): 15–25.

41. See C. G. Naidu, "Funding and Costs in Open and Distance Education: A Case Study of India," in *Strategies for Sustainable Open and Distance Learning,* ed. Andrea Hope and Patrick Guiton (Vancouver: Commonwealth of Learning; London: Routledge Falmer, 2005).

42. See Steven Weber, *The Success of Open Source* (Cambridge, MA: Harvard University Press, 2004); Yochai Benkler, *The Wealth of Networks: How Social Production Transforms Markets and Freedom* (New Haven, CT: Yale University Press, 2006); and Clay Shirky, *Here Comes Everybody: The Power of Organizing without Organizations* (New York: Penguin, 2008).

43. See the discussion in Pedro Hepp et al., *Technology in Schools: Education, ICT and the Knowledge Economy* (TIC en Educación, 2004), 30–34, http://www.sca2006.tic-educa.org/archivos/modulo_1/sesion_1/ICT_report_oct04a_Pedro_Hepp.pdf.

44. On the correlative relationship between technological adaption and aggregate economic growth in low income countries, see UNDP *Human Development Report 2001: Making New Technologies Work for Human Development,* chap. 2, "Today's Technological Transformations: Creating the Network Age," 27–64.

45. This is an example of the economic "leapfrogging" concept pioneered by Alexander Gerschenkron in *Economic Backwardness in Historical Perspective: A Book of Essays* (Cambridge, MA: Belknap Press of Harvard University Press, 1962).

46. Teledensity is measured as the number of telephones per one hundred persons in a given jurisdiction.

47. Manuel Castells et al., *Mobile Communication and Society* (Cambridge, MA: MIT Press, 2007), 248–249.

48. See Sirpa Tenhunen, "Mobile Technology in the Village: ICTs, Culture, and Social Logistics in India," *Journal of the Royal Anthropological Institute* 14 (2008): 515–534.

Bibliography

Belawati, Tian. "The Impact of Online Tutorials on Course Completion Rates and Student Achievement." *Learning, Media & Technology* 30, no. 1 (2005): 15–25.

Benkler, Yochai. 2006. *The Wealth of Networks: How Social Production Transforms Markets and Freedom*. New Haven, CT: Yale University Press, 2006.

Castells, Manuel. *The Rise of the Network Society*. Oxford: Blackwell, 1996.

Castells, Manuel, Mireia Fernández-Ardèvol, Jack Linchian Qui, and Araba Sey. *Mobile Communication and Society*. Cambridge, MA: MIT Press, 2007.

Constitution of India (1950). 86th Amendment. *The Constitution Act, 2002*. http://indiacode.nic.in/coiweb/amend/amend86.htm.

Gerschenkron, Alexander. *Economic Backwardness in Historical Perspective: A Book of Essays*. Cambridge, MA: Belknap Press of Harvard University Press, 1962.

Gibson, James J. "The Theory of Affordances." In *Perceiving, Acting, and Knowing: Toward an Ecological Psychology*, ed. R. Shaw and J. Bransford, 67–82. Hillsdale, NJ: Erlbaum, 1977.

Government of India. *Amended National Policy on Education*. New Delhi, 1992. http://www.ncert.nic.in/oth_anoun/npe86.pdf.

Government of India. Data portal, 2013. http://www.data.gov.in.

Government of India, Ministry of Human Resource Development. *Report of the Central Advisory Board of Education (CABE) Committee on Autonomy of Higher Education Institutions*. New Delhi, 2005. http://www.teindia.nic.in/Files/Reports/CCR/cabe/Ahei.pdf.

Government of India, Ministry of Human Resource Development. *ICT in Schools*, "Program Overview." 2015. http://mhrd.gov.in/ict_overview.

Government of India, Ministry of Human Resource Development. Sarva Shiksha Abhiyan program overview. 2015. http://mhrd.gov.in/sarva-shiksha-abhiyan.

Government of India, Ministry of Human Resource Development. National Institute of Open Schooling overview. 2013. http://www.nios.ac.in.

Government of India, National Knowledge Network. "Vision." 2013. http://www.nkn.in/.

Government of India, Planning Commission. *Eleventh Five Year Plan* [2007–2012]. 2007. http://planningcommission.nic.in/plans/planrel/11thf.htm.

Government of India, Planning Commission. *Faster, Sustainable and More Inclusive Growth: An Approach to the Twelfth Five Year Plan* [2012–2017]. October 2011. http://planningcommission.gov.in/plans/planrel/12appdrft/approach_12plan.pdf.

Government of India, Planning Commission. *Twelfth Five Year Plan* [2012–2017]. 2007. http://planningcommission.nic.in/plans/planrel/12thplan/welcome.html.

Government of Kerala, Department of General Education. "The Kerala Experience: IT@School Project." Centre for Innovation in Public Systems, 2010.

Graves, Lucas. 2007. "The Affordances of Blogging: A Case Study in Culture and Technological Effects." *Journal of Communication Inquiry* 31, no. 4: 331–346.

Gulati, Shalni. "Technology-Enhanced Learning in Developing Nations: A Review." *International Review of Research in Open and Distance Learning* 9, no. 1 (2008). http://www.irrodl.org/index.php/irrodl/article/view/477/1012.

Hepp, Pedro, Enrique Hinostroza, Ernesto Laval, and Lucio Rehbein. *Technology in Schools: Education, ICT and the Knowledge Economy.* TIC en Educación, 2004. http://www.sca2006.tic-educa.org/archivos/modulo_1/sesion_1/ICT_report_oct04a_Pedro_Hepp.pdf.

Indian Space Research Organization. "Satcom Applications." ISRO, 2015. http://india.gov.in/official-website-indian-space-research-organisation.

Indian Space Research Organization. "Tele-education." ISRO, 2015. http://india.gov.in/official-website-indian-space-research-organisation.

International Telecommunication Union. *Measuring the Information Society 2012.* Geneva: ITU, 2012. http://www.itu.int/en/ITU-D/Statistics/Documents/publications/mis2012/MIS2012_without_Annex_4.pdf.

Naidu, C. G. "Funding and Costs in Open and Distance Education: A Case Study of India." In *Strategies for Sustainable Open and Distance Learning,* ed. Andrea Hope and Patrick Guiton. World Review of Distance Education and Open Learning 6. Vancouver: Commonwealth of Learning; London: Routledge-Falmer, 2005.

Perraton, Hilary D. *Open and Distance Learning in the Developing World.* London: Routledge-Falmer, 2000.

Saheb, Tahereh. "ICT, Education and Digital Divide in Developing Countries." *Global Media Journal* 4, no. 7 (2005). http://www.globalmediajournal.com/open-access/ict-education-and-digital-divide-in-developing-countries.pdf.

Sharma, Priya. "The Distance in Education and Online Technologies in India." In *Global Perspectives on E-learning: Rhetoric and Reality,* ed. A. A. Carr-Chellman. London: Sage, 2005.

Shirky, Clay. *Here Comes Everybody: The Power of Organizing without Organizations.* New York: Penguin, 2008.

Sujatha, K. *Distance Education at Secondary Level in India: The National Open School.* Report for the UNESCO International Institute for Educational Planning, Paris.

Working Document (UNESCO, February 2002). http://unesdoc.unesco.org/images/0012/001262/126210e.pdf.

Telecommunications Regulatory Authority of India. *A Decadal Profile.* New Delhi: TRAI, 2012. http://www.trai.gov.in/WriteReadData/Publication/Document/2013041 21052403536675NCAER--Report08june12.pdf.

Telecommunications Regulatory Authority of India. *The Indian Telecom Services Performance Indicators, July–September, 2012.* New Delhi: TRAI, January 11, 2013. http://www.trai.gov.in/WriteReadData/PIRReport/Documents/Indicator%20Reports%20-%20Sep_2012.pdf.

Tenhunen, Sirpa. "Mobile Technology in the Village: ICTs, Culture, and Social Logistics in India." *Journal of the Royal Anthropological Institute* 14 (2008): 515–534.

UNESCO. *ICT Competency Framework for Teachers, Version 2.0.* UNESCO, 2011. http://iite.unesco.org/pics/publications/en/files/3214694.pdf.

UNESCO Institute for Statistics. *Reaching Out-of-School Children.* UNESCO, June 26, 2014. http://www.uis.unesco.org/Education/Pages/reaching-oosc.aspx.

United Nations Development Program. *Human Development Report 2001: Making New Technologies Work for Human Development.* UNDP, 2001. http://www.itu.int/net/wsis/docs/background/general/reports/26092001_undp.htm.

United Nations Development Program. *Human Development Report 2013: The Rise of the South: Human Progress in a Diverse World,* Statistical Annex. UNDP, 2013. http://hdr.undp.org/en/media/HDR2013_EN_Statistics.pdf.

Weber, Steven. *The Success of Open Source.* Cambridge, MA: Harvard University Press, 2004.

World Bank. *World Development Report 2009: Reshaping Economic Geography.* Washington, DC: World Bank, 2009. http://www-wds.worldbank.org/external/default/WDSContentServer/WDSP/IB/2008/12/03/000333038_20081203234958/Rendered/PDF/437380REVISED01BLIC1097808213760720.pdf.

World Bank. *Beyond Economic Growth,* Glossary. Washington, DC: World Bank, 2013. http://www.worldbank.org/depweb/english/beyond/global/glossary.html.

World Economic Forum. *Global Information Technology Report 2013.* World Economic Forum, 2013. http://www.weforum.org/reports/global-information-technology-report-2013.

5 Social Media Education in News Organizations: Experimentation at the BBC

Valerie Belair-Gagnon

Introduction

On Thursday, July 7, 2005, during the morning rush hour, terrorists launched a coordinated set of attacks on the London transportation system. These attacks have been referred to as the London bombings, or "7/7," following the nomenclature of the 9/11 attacks on the United States. Trapped in the London underground system, those affected used their mobile phones to record videos and take photographs of the events unfolding before their eyes. Unable to deploy its journalists to the bombing sites, the BBC relied on a variety of sources, from eyewitness accounts to victims' stories. Alexander Chadwick, one of the survivors, snapped a cell phone camera photograph of the evacuation of the Tube at Kings Cross Station. Standing outside on the street, Chadwick emailed the picture to yourpics@bbc.co.uk. Around 11:30 a.m. the picture landed on the desks of BBC editors. It quickly became the signature image of the day's events. Other mainstream news media organizations, including the *Times* of London and the *New York Times*, used that image on their front page. And Chadwick's highly viewed photograph was not an isolated case: as the day progressed, user-generated content became the main source of information for BBC journalists covering the attacks.[1]

The publication of Chadwick's photograph was an important moment in BBC journalism, a manifestation of the increasingly blurred boundary between journalists' and audiences' contributions to news accounts.[2] In the years to follow, the BBC would draw on a set of social media lessons derived from its coverage of the 7/7 attacks in an effort to make effective journalistic use of new devices and new platforms for information sharing.[3] The BBC would also establish social media education as part of its training program.

This chapter suggests that as social media education achieved greater penetration of BBC norms and practices, the temporal and physical aspects of journalism education also changed. Since their emergence in 2005, social media have contributed to a gradual transformation in the nature, processes, and consequences of journalism, affecting everything from the organizational structure, to the practice, to journalistic culture and reporting beats.[4] Of particular interest in this chapter is the effect of social media on journalism education.

The Origins of Social Media Education at the BBC

Traditionally, the BBC did not have a large in-house organization responsible for education, such as today's BBC Academy's College of Journalism. (The BBC Academy, which opened to students in December 2009, trains current and prospective employees in journalism and broadcasting skills; the College of Journalism, now a subsidiary of the Academy but which preceded the formation of the Academy, opened in June 2005 to provide free e-training courses in journalism to all those who pay a license fee.) Since 2005, the BBC's College of Journalism, with Kevin Marsh as executive director, and subsequently the Academy more broadly, have expanded in scope, providing training and education for BBC journalists, techies, senior managers, other media organizations, and members of the public. The institutionalization of journalism education in general, and of social media education in particular, is a recent phenomenon at the BBC. The origins of social media education lie in the BBC's "martini media" approach, meaning that content is made available anytime, anyplace, and anywhere, and in the BBC's development of new organizational structures.

At the BBC, training in the use of social media had its origins in a scandal involving BBC reporting about Iraqi weapons of mass destruction (WMD) during the year before the US-led invasion of Iraq. On September 24, 2002, the UK government published a dossier titled "Iraq Weapons of Mass Destruction: The Assessment of the British Government." On May 22, 2003, the BBC journalist Andrew Gilligan met with Dr. David Kelly, an expert in biological weapons at the British Ministry of Defense and a former UN WMD inspector in Iraq. One week after that meeting, on May 29, 2003, Gilligan broadcast several reports on the *Today* program on BBC Radio 4. Some BBC journalists alleged that then prime minister Tony Blair had ordered that experts "sex up" the dossier and the government's report. Gilligan named Kelly on air as a source. Kelly subsequently committed suicide. After these events, the British government asked Lord Hutton to conduct an investigation into the circumstances of Kelly's death. The BBC was accused of breach of impartiality in the affair. The Hutton inquiry asked hard questions about the ability of the BBC to be impartial.

In response to these circumstances, in 2004 the BBC convened a committee chaired by Ronald Neil, former BBC News and Current Affairs director, and commissioned a report. The ensuing Neil Report recommended several reforms, among them a mechanism to improve journalism education, particularly with regard to training and standards; the upshot was the creation of the College of Journalism, which now provides the BBC Academy's social media curriculum.[5] In a further development, in April 2006 the UK Department of Culture, Media and Sports published a white paper for the BBC's Royal Charter review process and renewal of the license fee, to be published in 2016.[6] The white paper redefined the BBC's new mandate to include playing a leading role in technological development, particularly in "building digital Britain" and "making digital switchover happen," through training and technological research and development. This policy was then translated into the vision and practices of the BBC. In practice, this meant making digital content and services available on a variety of digital platforms and devices; working with the media industry to develop a UK-wide digital television network; supporting the coverage of digital audio broadcasting; supporting the switch from analog to digital broadcasting, which occurred in April 2012; and working with other organizations to acquaint audiences with emerging communication technologies and services during the move to digital broadcasting.[7]

As a second prong of its response to the UK government's white paper, in 2006 the BBC initiated Creative Future, an editorial endeavor designed to deliver more value to BBC's audiences. Creative Future exemplified the BBC's martini media approach to news dissemination, with content made available anywhere, anyplace, and anytime, and it defined audience involvement to mean taking part in, creating, and sharing content. This involved moving resources into providing news coverage continuously on TV, radio, broadband, and mobile platforms. Beginning in 2006, the BBC promoted a new panplatform journalism strategy that focused more on mobile devices and provided 24/7 news coverage on the web, TV, and radio. The BBC website was relaunched with more personalization and richer audiovisual and user-generated content. The earlier shift to Internet Protocol television starting in 1995, which allowed the broadcasting of video-on-demand, catch-up television, and live television online facilitated this process.

To explain its approach to broadcasting and new technologies, the BBC in 2007 published a report on social media use titled *From See-saw to Wagon Wheel: Safeguarding Impartiality in the 21st Century*. That report was the first time the BBC publicly connected the role of social media to its ideal of impartiality. This would have implications for the BBC's social media education. The publication of *From See-saw to Wagon Wheel* signaled a period of integration of social media concerns into BBC journalistic norms and practices, reflecting discussions that had started well before the publication of the report. *From See-saw to Wagon Wheel* addressed issues related to new media, and defined BBC impartiality as a mix of accuracy, balance, context, distance, evenhandedness, fairness, objectivity, open-mindedness, rigor, self-awareness, transparency, and truth. The report indicated that user-generated content would become a new source of information, centralized in the BBC's User-Generated Content (UGC) Hub operations. The changes in operating structure to support education and social media practices in journalism training marked a transitional moment in the institutional history of the BBC.

From 2005 to 2009, the BBC's College of Journalism website remained available only to BBC staff.[8] In December 2009 the BBC Academy was launched as the overarching educational arm of the BBC, part of the organization's response to a recommendation for such made in the Neil Report. Specific changes adopted at the time included (1) making the BBC College of Journalism website available to anyone in the UK and to subscribers outside the UK; (2) collaborating with ITV to improve employability in the media industry, and with Channel 4 to ensure contemporary and culturally diverse programming; and (3) sharing the BBC's training model with other broadcasters, including the broadcasting union (BECTU) and the independent producers trade body (PACT), to enhance the public's understanding of BBC capabilities and practices. The BBC Academy became the organization's center for education, under which are grouped the Colleges of Journalism, Production, Leadership, and Technology.

Opening Moves

The changes in operational structure and in the BBC's charter opened the way to an idiosyncratic social platform education program at the BBC. The program developed in a particular context whose main pillars were the emerging social media, political and journalistic responses to social media, and the BBC's capability of creating a new educational program in the new media ecology.

The trajectory has been deliberate, even slow, however. From 2005 to 2012, the BBC remained inward-looking and reactive in its approach to social media education. From 2009 to 2010, for example, the BBC held social media–oriented courses for only its own journalists, limiting the geography and scope of training journalists. With experience and better knowledge of social media education, it has become more outward-looking.

During the initial phase of the BBC's training program, aspiring journalists underwent one-on-one training sessions with BBC journalists. In November 2009, the BBC developed its first social media course, "Making the Web Work for You." The course trained BBC journalists in the use of social media to find content and build community. The course took a full working day and involved fifteen journalists working together in one room, participating in exercises and following demonstrations on their laptops. "It dealt with Facebook, but it also introduced people to digital tools on the Internet and how to use Google advanced search. The course was about social media, but also it was about Internet tools for journalists and for producers."[9] A social media trainer later remarked that "it was very important that they were actually learning on the Internet as we were going along."[10]

Several characteristics of "Making the Web Work for You" showed the BBC's social media approach of that period. First, training in the journalistic use of social media was offered exclusively to BBC staff. Second, the approach to social media education was more reactive. The courses were offered because a problem had been identified that needed to be solved with education. One journalist described the "solve-this-problem" mentality common at the time:

My boss said to me, I want you to do something on social media. I then investigated and looked around. We hired a freelance person called Claire Wardle, which was a former academic at Cardiff School of Journalism. She developed the content, with me overseeing it, but it was mainly Wardle for the content for the courses.[11]

Other, more senior journalists initially resisted the change. For example, Lyse Doucet, a BBC senior presenter and correspondent, said that she was skeptical about social media for a year after a 2010 speech by Peter Horrocks, director of the BBC's Global News division, urging journalists to use social media for sourcing and news gathering. As social media training gained in importance and techies learned better how to deal with social media, the scope of the content, the means of dissemination, and the temporal and spatial nature of social media education all changed.

New Scope, Spaces, and Temporality of Social Media Education

As social media gained in importance at the BBC, education in using social media underwent a corresponding transformation.

First the scope of training changed, with the BBC's educational offerings demonstrating a blurring of the line dividing traditional journalism and social media inputs. Since 2010, social media use has been integrated into journalism courses offered by the BBC. For instance, in the fall of 2012, the Academy gave a five-day course for the Journalism Foundation. A half day was dedicated to the use of social media tools in reporting, news gathering, and sourcing. The Academy also developed a series of weeklong intensive programs: the new journalists' program, the Editorial Leadership Programme, and the Social Media and Digital Journalism Programme. The Editorial Leadership Programme covers editorial guidance and content. Broadcasters, freelancers, students, and independent media organizations have taken part in the course. The Social Media and Digital Journalism Programme focuses on how to find original stories and content online and gather news, how to verify, how to filter the noise, how to set up news feeds, how to cope with news in real time, how to engage and develop the loyalty of an audience, and how to drive that audience to traditional content such as programs and outputs (e.g., websites, television, and radio). Both courses seek to help reporters manage online noise, set up effective social media tactics while engaging the audience and bringing it back to traditional news content, and foster BBC editorial values. Also in 2012 the BBC launched a UGC editorial standards course to teach editors and independent contractors how to verify content, post, share, engage audiences, analyze site metrics, and evaluate the success rate of social media endeavors.[12]

Since 2011, more courses have focused on adjusting journalism practices and norms to integrate social media content and affordances. The BBC has conducted different types of "how to" social media courses, from editorial (Social Media Overview, for editors and executives who want to know what to put in place for different social media work) to practical (Twitter Basic, Twitter Advanced, Facebook for Producers, Social Media Best Practice, Social Media and Connected Journalism, Making the Web Work for You, which has since morphed into Social Media and Internet Sources, an introduction to social media tools, and a course on how to use LinkedIn to find material and develop case studies). The Academy designed the course New Social Media Tools for journalists who wanted to learn about Twitter's and Facebook's particular uses and shortcomings.[13]

The BBC Academy also provides a five-day intensive course, the Social Media and Digital Journalism Programme, as well as an editorial leadership program. These courses teach social media understanding and strategy to both BBC and non-BBC journalists and news organizations around the world. The BBC also recommends that journalists take the five-day intensive BBC New Journalist Programme, which brings social media into discussions of story finding, storytelling, multimedia practices, ethics and values, and understanding audiences. Through these efforts, the BBC has strived to establish itself as a mediator of offerings from the media industry, using social media training as a tool.

With respect to the dissemination of training, the BBC has expanded its scope here by making educational training available on social media platforms such as YouTube, Facebook, Twitter, and blogs.[14]

In a second major change, as journalists gained knowledge of how to use social media in news gathering and reporting, the BBC expanded its training to activities outside the news organization, in this way changing the temporal-spatial training envelope. This move to a more public, outside-the-walls educator stance helped refocus attention on the BBC's conception of itself as a public service provider. For example, during the Arab Spring, many journalists realized the value of using social media in their daily work.[15] After the Arab Spring uprisings, in 2011, an important change took place in the BBC's social media training. The BBC started providing additional one-on-one training sessions and created a forum for BBC journalists, independent media producers, and social media organizations. On May 19 and 20, 2011, the BBC convened its first BBC Social Media Summit, at which participants—industry leaders and scholars of journalism—discussed changes in journalistic innovations, values, norms, editorial standards, and practices as a result of integrating the use of social media into traditional journalistic procedures. The BBC made snippets of the proceedings available on Twitter, and published blog articles and videos on the College of Journalism's blog and YouTube channel. The first day's discussions were limited to guests and representatives of news organizations and took up such questions as how national and international news organizations incorporated social media in their reporting and their newsrooms. Discussions on the second day of the conference, open to about 150 journalists in each session, raised important questions about verification, ethics, cultural changes, editorial issues, audience expectations, and news coverage. On April 20, 2013, the *New York Times*, the Knight Foundation, and the BBC held a second summit in New York for media practitioners, academics, and social media gurus. On May 16, 2014, a similar, third summit was convened in London.[16]

Another example of the expansion of the temporal-spatial training envelope is the BBC's offering consulting and training since 2012 to other news organization. As one BBC journalist said,

We run a social media consultancy. If a radio station in Cambridge wants media training, we may have a couple of options. They'll run some formal training course in the classroom, but there's a lot of one-to-one. We have a training model; it's not just classroom training.[17]

More generally, with social media education now available online, the temporal and physical aspects of education have changed remarkably. Content is available online 24/7 worldwide, through blogs, Facebook, and YouTube, a realization of the BBC's charter mandate to educate.

Conclusion

Journalists adept in the use of social media have contributed to changes in the form, content, and practice of journalism education, particularly by expanding the space of education.[18] Journalism training at the BBC is now geared toward developing practices in which traditional and newer forms of news gathering, dissemination, and discussion merge, with open-ended possibilities. The integration of social media has in turn reopened age-old questions concerning ethical standards, the quality of content and reporting, the diversity of the audiences targeted, and the manner in which news is consumed as well as broadcast.[19] As the BBC has positioned itself as a leader in incorporating new technologies and platforms into news reporting and dissemination, news media organizations across the UK have benefited from the public broadcaster's commitment to journalism training.

The BBC has reassessed its journalism and public service ethos within the new media ecology. This revaluation in turn raises a set of new questions about the role of public broadcasting in British society. Far from imposing a new notion of what the BBC is or should be, the revaluation has reaffirmed the BBC's original identity as a broadcaster independent of external political and commercial influences and an impartial provider of quality journalism. The BBC's public broadcasting writ is defined not just by traditional metrics, such as quality of content, independence, and diversity of publics served. Rather, the key words *scope* and *access* take on a particularly important significance in defining the role of the public broadcaster in new social media contexts.

Notes

1. Helen Boaden, "The Role of Citizen Journalism in Modern Democracy," paper presented at a conference, "e-Democracy," London, November 11, 2008; Richard Sambrook, "Citizen Journalism and the BBC: Nieman Report," Nieman Foundation for Journalism at Harvard University, Winter 2005, http://niemanreports.org/

articles/citizen-journalism-and-the-bbc; Nic Newman, "The Rise of Social Media and Its Impact on Mainstream Journalism: A Study on How Newspapers and Broadcasters in the UK and US Are Responding to a Wave of Participatory Social Media and a Historic Shift in Control towards Individual Consumers," Working Paper, Reuters Institute for the Study of Journalism (Oxford, September 2009), http://www.sssup.it/UploadDocs/6635_8_S_The_rise_of_Social_Media_and_its_Impact_on_mainstream_journalism_Newman_07.pdf; Editor, interview, 2012.

2. For a detailed account of these events, see Valerie Belair-Gagnon, *Social Media at BBC News: The Re-Making of Crisis Reporting* (New York: Routledge, 2015).

3. A more detailed analysis of these events is available in Belair-Gagnon, *Social Media at BBC News*.

4. See David L. Altheide, *An Ecology of Communication: Cultural Formats of Control* (Hawthorne, NY: Aldine de Gruyter, 1995). Altheide conceptualizes how new information technologies transform the media logic.

5. BBC, Journalism College Launched, *BBC News* (online), June 28, 2005, http://news.bbc.co.uk/2/hi/uk_news/4630895.stm (accessed April 10, 2012).

6. Department for Culture, Media and Sport (UK) (DCMS), *Broadcasting: Copy of Royal Charter for the Continuance of the British Broadcasting Corporation (Royal Charter)* (Norwich: HMSO, 2006).

7. DCMS, "A Public Service for All: The BBC in the Digital Age," White Paper (Norwich: HMSO, 2006).

8. In 2005, Kevin Marsh was named the first executive editor of the BBC College of Journalism. He initiated e-learning courses delivered by well-known journalists such as John Simpson and face-to-face courses.

9. Social media trainer, interview, London, August 21, 2012.

10. Social media trainer, interview, London, August 21, 2012.

11. Social media trainer, interview, London, August 21, 2012.

12. BroadcastNow, "BBC Launches Editorial Standards Course on UGC," July 6, 2012, http://www.broadcastnow.co.uk/bbc-launches-editorial-standards-course-on-ugc/5044082.article (accessed October 27, 2015).

13. Ramaa Sharma, "Web Curation Tools for Journalists," BBC College of Journalism Blog, August 1, 2011, http://www.bbc.co.uk/blogs/blogcollegeofjournalism/posts/web_curation_tools_for_journal (accessed July 14, 2012).

14. Chris Walton, "Social Media Training Is Getting Results for the BBC," BBC College of Journalism blog, January 25, 2012, http://www.bbc.co.uk/blogs/collegeofjournalism/entries/7565de8f-9fe6-39ce-91b7-8efe49ec6a1a (accessed February 14, 2012).

15. Lise Doucet, "Big Stories: The Arab Spring," BBC College of Journalism blog, November 4, 2011,http://www.bbc.co.uk/journalism/blog/2011/11/big-stories-the-arab-spring.shtml (accessed April 10, 2012).

16. See the web page http://www.nytimes.com/packages/html/social-media-summit.

17. Chris Walton, project editor, College of Journalism, BBC Academy, interview, London, August 21, 2012.

18. For an in-depth account of social media at BBC News, see Belair-Gagnon, *Social Media at BBC News*.

19. Mark Settle, Smartphones for News: How the BBC Academy Is Helping Journalists Get More Mobile Than Ever, BBC College of Journalism blog, July 17, 2012, http://www.bbc.co.uk/academy/news/view/smartphones_news (accessed July 19, 2012); Nic Newman, ed., *Reuters Institute Digital News Report 2012: Tracking the Future of News* (Oxford: Reuters Institute for the Study of Journalism, 2012).

Bibliography

Altheide, David L. *An Ecology of Communication: Cultural Formats of Control*. Hawthorne, NY: Aldine de Gruyter, 1995.

BBC. "Journalism College Launched." *BBC News* (online), June 28, 2005. http://news.bbc.co.uk/2/hi/uk_news/4630895.stm.

Belair-Gagnon, Valerie. *Social Media at BBC News: The Re-Making of Crisis Reporting*. London: Routledge, 2015.

Boaden, Helen. "The Role of Citizen Journalism in Modern Democracy." Paper presented at a conference, "e-Democracy." London, November 11, 2008.

BroadcastNow. "BBC Launches Editorial Standards Course on UGC," July 6, 2012, http://www.broadcastnow.co.uk/bbc-launches-editorial-standards-course-on-ugc/5044082.article.

Department for Culture, Media and Sport (UK) (DCMS). *Broadcasting: Copy of Royal Charter for the Continuance of the British Broadcasting Corporation (Royal Charter)*. Norwich: HMSO, 2006.

DCMS. "A Public Service for All: The BBC in the Digital Age." White Paper. Norwich: HMSO, 2006.

Doucet, Lise. "Big Stories: The Arab Spring." BBC College of Journalism, November 4, 2011. http://www.bbc.co.uk/journalism/blog/2011/11/big-stories-the-arab-spring.shtml.

Newman, Nic. "The Rise of Social Media and Its Impact on Mainstream Journalism: A Study on How Newspapers and Broadcasters in the UK and US Are Responding to a Wave of Participatory Social Media and a Historic Shift in Control towards Individual Consumers." Working Paper. Oxford: Reuters Institute for the Study of Journalism, 2009. http://www.sssup.it/UploadDocs/6635_8_S_The_rise_of_Social_Media _and_its_Impact_on_mainstream_journalism_Newman_07.pdf.

Newman, Nic, ed. *Reuters Institute Digital News Report 2012: Tracking the Future of News*. Oxford: Reuters Institute for the Study of Journalism, 2012.

Sambrook, Richard. "Citizen Journalism and the BBC: Nieman Report." The Nieman Foundation for Journalism at Harvard University, Winter 2005. http://niemanreports.org/articles/citizen-journalism-and-the-bbc.

Settle, Mark. "Smartphones for News: How the BBC Academy Is Helping Journalists Get More Mobile Than Ever." BBC College of Journalism, July 17, 2012. http://www .bbc.co.uk/academy/news/view/smartphones_news.

Sharma, Ramaa. "Web Curation Tools for Journalists." BBC College of Journalism blog, August 1, 2011. http://www.bbc.co.uk/blogs/blogcollegeofjournalism/posts/ web_curation_tools_for_journal.

Walton, Chris. "Social Media Training Is Getting Results for the BBC." BBC College of Journalism blog, January 25, 2012. http://www.bbc.co.uk/blogs/collegeof journalism/entries/7565de8f-9fe6-39ce-91b7-8efe49ec6a1a.

II Challenges and Disruptions

The chapters in part I outlined a series of possibilities realizable through the use of social media in different educational contexts. These possibilities, while exciting, pose questions about the disruptive potential of social media for existing educational institutions, laws, and practices.

Part II explores the theme of disruption with four chapters that examine challenges to existing educational models. In chapter 6, Chris Dede (Timothy E. Wirth Professor of Learning Technologies, Harvard University Graduate School of Education) offers a broad and historically conscious discussion of changes now under way in traditional models of education. This chapter highlights aspects of the institutional and cultural shift now taking place with the extension of social media's reach into everyday learning. The remaining chapters in this part examine several aspects of this institutional and cultural shift. In chapter 7, John Palfrey (head of school, Philips Andover Academy) discusses how young people understand privacy in their social media practices and what this means as policymakers, educators, and parents develop workable policies for social media use in educational contexts. In chapter 8, Nicholas Bramble (former fellow of the Information Society Project, Yale Law School) and Yite John Lu (intellectual property litigation associate, Irell and Manella LLP) describe some challenges that online education poses for the accreditation and assessment of educational quality. And in chapter 9, Nicholas Bramble explores how educational sharing, mixing, and reworking sit in tension with existing copyright laws, and the ways in which copyright regulation reform could allow educators and students to make more extensive use of the educational possibilities of social media.

These four chapters show that while social media offer reasons to be optimistic about the future of education, the near term will involve a set of challenges and require hard choices to be made by policymakers, educators, and parents. As with any disruption of established models, the arrival of social media in education is provoking contentious debates about goals, values, priorities, and costs. There will also be intense debate among stakeholders about who—administrators? teachers? parents? students? hardware and software providers?—should take the lead in forming new policies. How these debates play out will have a significant effect on the extent to which and the ways in which social media are used in a variety of educational contexts.

Chapter 6: Social Media and Challenges to Traditional Models of Education

Chris Dede

An increasing proportion of people in all age groups are using social media as the dominant means of informal learning, developing strengths and preferences in how they create and share knowledge and the types of authority they accept as certifying its accuracy. As a growing number of students enter schools and colleges with beliefs and preferences about learning and knowledge derived from social media use, these institutions will experience pressure to acknowledge types of learning and knowing discrepant with classical models of instruction, authority, and epistemology. To prepare students for the twenty-first century and a global, knowledge-based civilization, Web 2.0 tools may empower a strategic vision of a redesigned K–20 formal educational system that leverages current technologies to implement sophisticated learning, teaching, and assessment anyplace and anytime, lifelong and lifewide.

Chapter 7: Reframing Privacy and Youth Media Practices

John Palfrey

This chapter examines how youth understand and exercise privacy on social media, and offers ways for concerned groups (parents, educators and legislators) to change their perceptions of the risks and rewards of social media use. It identifies the challenges of converged online lives and discusses these challenges in relation to new opportunities created by social media. The chapter concludes with a discussion of ways to empower youth to make decisions regarding their own privacy in a converged and mediated world.

Chapter 8: The Growth of Online Universities: How to Solve the Accreditation Dilemma, Protect Students, and Expand Access to Higher Education

Nicholas Bramble and Yite John Lu

This chapter explores the challenges of accreditation for new learning models based on the Internet and social media. It unfolds in three parts. The first describes the current U.S. environment for online universities, comparing examples of established for-profit and emerging low-cost universities. The second part gives an overview of accreditation in the United States and abroad, and explores accreditation barriers for online universities. Finally, the third part recommends the implementation of new formal and informal accreditation standards, along with the establishment of an agency that would track and evaluate the progress of new online learning models with respect to these accreditation standards.

Chapter 9: Copyright Reform and Educational Progress

Nicholas Bramble

This chapter explores challenges related to the use of copyrighted material in educational environments. It identifies several problems in current legislation and enforcement of copyright and shows the ways in which the current copyright regime is detrimental to educational goals. It proposes several changes in law and practice, with the goals of encouraging knowledge of great works and fostering collaboration and creativity among students.

6 Social Media and Challenges to Traditional Models of Education

Chris Dede

Introduction

The use of social media for learning purposes is based on fundamental beliefs about learning, knowledge, and expertise that are quite different from the foundational assumptions underlying the structure and practices of traditional educational institutions (schools, colleges). An increasing proportion of people in all age groups are using social media as the dominant means of informal learning, developing strengths and preferences in how they create and share knowledge and in what types of authority they accept as certifying its accuracy. As more students enter schools and colleges with beliefs and preferences about learning and knowledge they have developed through using social media, these institutions will face pressures to acknowledge types of learning and knowing discrepant with classic models of instruction, authority, and epistemology.

Web 2.0 Social Media and the Redefinition of Knowledge and Expertise

Web 2.0 interactive media are redefining ░░░░ ░░░ and with whom we learn, in ways that challenge and upend ░ For example, Wikipedia knowledge is c promises among various points of view. How do we in higher education help stu between facts, opinions, and values, and the interrelationships that create meani collective agreement, what does it meaı subject knowledge to teach a topic? Sinc can now be easily found online (along what core skills and competencies does twenty-first-century work and citizenshi growth of interactive media, how might we reconceptualize education? I do not provide answers to these questions here. But I do suggest ways to think about the issues raised by the new, pervasive Internet tools.

The term "Web 2.0" references a change in leading-edge applications on the Internet from the presentation of material by website providers to the active co-construction of resources by communities of contributors. Whereas a decade ago the Web centered on developer-created material (e.g., informational websites) generated primarily by a small fraction of Internet users, Web 2.0 tools (e.g., Wikipedia) now help large numbers of people build online communities for creativity, collaboration, and sharing. Interactive media that facilitate these Web 2.0 purposes include social bookmarking, wikis, podcasts, blogs, and software for personal expression and sharing (e.g., Facebook, YouTube, Twitter, Flickr). RSS feeds, sophisticated search engines, and similar harvesting tools to help individuals find the needles they care about in a huge haystack of resources. And with web application programming interfaces, community builders do not need specialized technical expertise to create new media.

At first glance, this evolution might seem simply to reflect simply a change in agency, from publication by a few to collective contribution by many. But the implications of Web 2.0 go much deeper. The tacit epistemologies that underlie its activities differ dramatically from what I will call here the classical perspective: the historical understanding of knowledge, expertise, and learning on which formal education is based. In the classical perspective, knowledge entails grasping accurate interrelationships among facts, based on unbiased research that produces compelling evidence about systemic causes and correlations. For example, students learn that changes in the color of the sky at various times of day owe to the differential scattering of various wavelengths of light by gas molecules in Earth's atmosphere. In the classical view of knowledge, there is only one correct, unambiguous interpretation of factual interrelationships. In a classical education, the content and skills that experts feel every person should know are presented as factual truth, compiled in curriculum standards and assessed with high-stakes testing.

In this classical perspective, experts with substantial credentials in academic fields and disciplines seek new knowledge through formal, evidence-argumentation, using elaborate methods to generate findings and tions. Premier reference sources, such as *Encyclopaedia Britannica*, lar materials, such as textbooks, embody "authenticated" mpiled by experts, peer reviewed, and transmitted to learn-lly, a single right answer is believed to underlie each phenomenon, even though experts may not yet have developed a full understanding of the systemic causes that provide an accurate interpretation of some situations.

In contrast, in a Web 2.0 world, knowledge is generated by collective agreement about a description that may combine facts with other dimensions of human experience, such as opinions, values, and spiritual beliefs. As an illustration, the Wikipedia entry "Social Effect of Evolutionary Theory" wrestles with constructing a point of view that most readers would consider reasonable, accurate, and unbiased, without derogating the religious precepts some might hold.[2] In contrast to articles in the *Encyclopaedia Britannica*, Wikipedia articles are either undisputed (tacitly considered accurate) or disputed (still resolving through collective argumentation), and Wikipedia articles cover topics that are not central to academic disciplines or to a wide audience (e.g., the cartoon dog Scooby-Doo).

The epistemology that leads to validity of knowledge in Web 2.0 media such as Wikipedia is peer review from people seen, by the community of contributors, as having unbiased perspectives. Expertise involves understanding disputes in detail and proposing syntheses that are widely accepted by the community. Possible warrants for expertise are wide-ranging and may draw on education, experience, rhetorical fluency, reputation, or perceived spiritual authority in articulating beliefs, values, and precepts.

Certainly, the contrasts between classical knowledge and Web 2.0 knowledge are continua rather than dichotomies, and one can find web communities with epistemologies located between the sharp distinctions noted above. Still, a gradual redirection to new types and ways of knowing is apparent and has important implications for learning and education. For example, formal schooling today remains based on the classical view of knowledge, expertise, and learning, transmitted through the following channels:

1. Curriculum standards that guide the development of instructional resources (e.g., textbooks) and assessments (e.g., high-stakes tests) stem from disciplinary experts' determinations of what students should learn.
2. Presentational or assimilative pedagogies convey "truth" from content experts to students, who learn by listening.
3. Students who have mastered large amounts of factual material and are fluent in academic skills are believed to be well prepared for a successful, prosperous, fulfilling life.

Advocates for a Web 2.0 view of knowledge, expertise, and learning would challenge each of these three precepts of formal education. Many have documented politically motivated inaccuracies in textbooks, including biases against minorities and women, interpretations that privilege the perspective of the dominant subculture, and omissions of material about the contributions and interpretations of diverse groups, such as people of color. Experts may sometimes speak truth to power, but too often those considered experts are anointed, funded, and rewarded to provide rationales for politically expedient actions. Curriculum standards frequently reflect a hodgepodge of what students might need to become experts in the various disciplines rather than what they might need to assume roles as effective workers, citizens, and self-fulfilled people in the twenty-first-century global civilization. Presentational pedagogies typically result in learning that is ephemeral, uninspiring, and unlikely to transfer to life situations.

In part because of the weaknesses in the classical model of education, many students who excel academically do not fare well later in life; the challenges of work, citizenship, and daily life do not resemble the multiple-choice items on high-stakes tests. Can a Web 2.0 view of knowledge, expertise, and learning overcome these problems? Based on the communal creation and sharing processes described above, an educational system oriented around Web 2.0 perspectives might posit the following:

1. The curriculum includes considerable variation from one community to another in what constitutes socialization, expertise, and essential knowledge, based on the types of content and skills valued within a particular geographic or online subculture.
2. Active learning pedagogies emphasize constructivist teaching approaches that encourage students' co-creation of knowledge.
3. Assessment is based on students' creations and collaborative efforts (e.g., contributions to a wiki) showing participation in peer review.

Many of those now involved in formal education might see Web 2.0 perspectives both as a desirable evolution in pedagogy and assessment and as a troubling "Dark Ages" reversion in terms of content. Many communities have made poor decisions about what constitutes factual knowledge, such as when the House of the 1897 Indiana State Legislature unanimously recommended to the Senate a bill that would have established "a new mathematical truth" and changed the value of pi.[3] Most decisions involve a complex mix of facts, beliefs, and values in which accuracy about the factual component is important. For example, individuals and governing bodies require accurate, factual information in order to make personal choices and formal laws and regulations, respectively. A detailed discussion of the potential impact of Web 2.0 epistemology on society is beyond the scope of this chapter; overall, like many other technology-driven repositionings, Web 2.0 aids with some problems but exacerbates others and creates novel challenges.

At present, the response of many educators is to stand on the conservative side of this epistemological clash. Many faculty force students to turn off electronic devices in classrooms; instead, students could be using search tools to bring in current information and events related to the class discussion. Some faculty ban the use of online sources and deride the validity of any perspective that does not come from a printed work by a disciplinary scholar. Many see social networking sites as useless or dangerous and do not recognize the diagnostic value of folksonomies for understanding the language and conceptual frameworks that students bring to the classroom. This refusal to acknowledge the weaknesses of the classical perspective and the strengths of Web 2.0 epistemologies is as ill-advised as completely abandoning classical epistemology for Web 2.0 meaning-making.

In considering this seismic shift in how students learn and what they know, I find helpful the following analogy of the contrast among three systems of governance:

1. In a hierarchical meritocracy, experts selected on the basis of intelligence run the country.
2. In a pure democracy, the entire population makes collective decisions about every aspect of governance.
3. In a representative democracy, a small group of people selected by the entire population makes decisions.

Any one of these three systems could work well if all participants were well informed, rational, and of good will, so the fundamental issue is which system works best given the human condition, which includes ignorance, irrationality, and the lust for power. The United States is a representative democracy, a synthesis that attempts to offset the weaknesses of the other two. A synthesis of classical and Web 2.0 views of knowledge, expertise, and learning would consider the weaknesses and strengths in both approaches, to make for a smooth transition during this seismic shift in epistemology.

Web 2.0 Social Media and Creating and Sharing Knowledge

Web 2.0 social media can be categorized into three groups, representing a progression of how many participants utilize these media.[4]

1. Sharing
   - Social bookmarking
   - Photo and video sharing

- Social networking
- Writers' workshops/fanfiction

2. Thinking
   - Blogs
   - Podcasts
   - Online discussion forums
   - Twitter

3. Cocreating
   - Wikis or collaborative file creation
   - Mashups or collective media creation
   - Collaborative social change communities

Like all category systems, the number of groups is somewhat arbitrary, and, depending on how they are used, particular media can blur from one category into another. For example, writers' workshop/fanfiction can approach cocreation rather than sharing if authors routinely and extensively revise based on iterative feedback from other community members.

As with many scholarly fields, the education research community describes its purpose as generating and sharing knowledge.[5] This is seen as a well-defined process invariant across disciplines: scientific research, whether in education, physics, anthropology, molecular biology, or economics, is a continual process of rigorous reasoning supported by a dynamic interplay among methods, theories, and findings. It builds understandings in the form of models or theories that can be tested. Advances in scientific knowledge are achieved by the self-regulating norms of the scientific community over time, and not, as sometimes believed, by the mechanistic application of a particular scientific method to a static set of questions.[6]

Adapting Web 2.0 tools to aid the education research community makes sense, insofar as these media can promote richly documented, rapid interchanges among groups of scholars sharing and discussing research representations, theories, methods, findings, and models.

Enhancing Knowledge Creation and Sharing

A geographically distributed community of scholars studying a particular topic in education might use a research infrastructure mingling many of these Web 2.0 social media to enhance both the pace and the quality of their work. At the level of sharing, through communal bookmarking (e.g., http://www.diigo.com), the group could continuously scan the educational context for resources of interest, including nonarchival material such as unpublished papers and YouTube videos. Photo- and video-sharing tools (e.g., http://voicethread.com) could enable sharing and annotating research data as multimedia artifacts, such as student products and video records of teaching. A ning (a user-created social network) could provide background information to foster informal professional exchanges among members of this community, empowering the "social scholarship" Christine Greenhow, Beth Robelia, and Joan E. Hughes describe.[7] A wiki (e.g., http://www.wikispaces.com) could serve as the basis for a negotiated exposition of theoretical principles; the theoretical wiki at the U.S. National Science Foundation (NSF)–funded Pittsburgh Science of Learning Center (http://www.learnlab.org/research/wiki/index.php/Main_Page) illustrates the value of this. Mashups (e.g., http://healthmap.org/en) could offer ways to contextualize individual data sets against a larger context of practice.

Such a research infrastructure could also serve other purposes beyond enhancing the scholarly productivity of its community. For example, federal agencies such as the NSF are now mandating external evaluations of their funded research projects to document that the processes of scholarship used are appropriate and effective. The participation of a particular research project in a larger scholarly community as described above could serve as such an evaluation. Also, case studies based on scholarly processes richly documented in such communities could enhance the teaching of research methods by offering richly grounded examples, including alternative perspectives on complex designs involving mixed methods.

A next step would incorporate Web 2.0 social media in education research beyond enhancing current scholarly practices for producing knowledge to initiating a new form of professional dialogue through communities that attempt to generate "wisdom." I am aware that this suggestion is provocative, controversial, and disruptive; nonetheless, I believe such an experiment is worth conducting.

Web 2.0 Social Media and Creating/Sharing Wisdom

For the last several millennia, scholars have wrestled with various definitions of wisdom.[8] Historical definitions of individual wisdom stress, in various proportions, an integrated perspective that includes expertise about the pragmatics of individual and social life, as well as the natural world; attitudes and behaviors based on considerations of virtue and morality; and an awareness and acceptance of one's own fallibility and limitations. Wise cultures are seen as collectively having these characteristics and as maximizing the development of wise persons through generating and sharing wisdom, in part through communal reflection and social dialogue.

According to James E. Birren and Cheryl M. Svensson, "Wisdom is perhaps the most complex characteristic that can be attributed to individuals or cultures."[9] The particular type of wisdom I am discussing has five dimensions:

1. a cognitive dimension involving rich understanding of a variety of intellectual disciplines and fields;
2. a practical-experiential dimension of sophisticated, pragmatic comprehension about how one should act, given the unresolvable questions, philosophical issues, and unavoidable problems (such as personal mortality) associated with everyday life;[10]
3. an interpersonal dimension of insightfully appreciating the interactions and contributions of diverse groups, cultures, and societies in shaping civilization;
4. an ethical dimension encompassing what the ancient Greeks meant by "knowing and doing the good"; and
5. a metacognitive dimension of reflective judgment, an awareness of the limitations of knowing and how these have an impact on resolving ill-defined problems.[11]

This definition draws on, but is more limited than, the concept of extraordinary wisdom delineated by William L. Randall and Gary M. Kenyon.[12]

The key contrast I wish to make is between this five-dimensional definition of wisdom and widely accepted definitions of knowledge. A person who is knowledgeable about academic content and skills would incorporate on part of the definition of wisdom above, the cognitive dimension. Someone who is knowledgeable about making optimal life choices would possess the practical-experiential dimension (teachers' professional subset of this dimension is often described in education as the "wisdom of practice"). These people could also metacognitively understand that these types of knowledge cannot in themselves provide complete answers to all questions. However, the interpersonal and ethical dimensions of wisdom transcend the epistemology-based expertise of knowledge to include moral, axiological, and subjective/interpersonal capacities of high value to oneself and others.

In other words, knowledge involves understanding the dynamic forces that shape one's life, including the natural and social contexts, but does not intrinsically include a capacity to make value-driven, moral choices that empower use of that understanding for personal and collective well-being across the full dimension of human needs. As an illustration, if one uses Abraham Maslow's hierarchy of needs as a referent, knowledge provides substantial leverage in relieving the physiological "deficiency" needs that encompass the bottom four levels of his hierarchy (survival needs, safety and security, love and esteem from others, feelings of self-worth and belonging). But knowledge alone falls short in attaining Maslow's fifth, self-actualized level of "growth" needs (e.g., spontaneity, creativity, closeness to others, appreciation for all aspects of life, making contributions that through ethical means resolve troubling problems with complex moral dimensions).[13] People who focus their personal learning solely on mastery of knowledge often lack many of these "growth" characteristics, and knowledgeable people who are self-actualized have attained their "wise" capacities through developing interpersonal and ethical understandings outside the realm of knowledge.

To ground this contrast between wisdom and knowledge in a specific example, I'll consider here the attempt to resolve a "wicked" problem in education. In his book, *Wicked Problems and Social Complexity,* Jeff Conklin indicates that these types of problems have four characteristics:

1. Stakeholders have different worldviews for framing the problem.
2. Constraints that define the problem and resources to resolve it change over time.
3. The problem cannot be fully comprehended without attempting solutions and studying the ways they fail.
4. The problem is never completely solved.[14]

Attaining educational equity is such a problem. Hypothetically, a team of researchers could with much effort generate the complicated systemic relationships that together create inequities in education and could develop dynamic models that contrast the likely effects of various ameliorative interventions. Such a team could also assess the psychosocial, economic, and cultural impacts of educational inequities—and interventions to reduce inequities—on various groups, in order to generate estimates of the potential benefits and costs of different actions decision makers could take to affect this issue. Such knowledge-based contributions would have great value but would fall short of resolving the difficult policy and practice questions that would then arise because these questions are in the province of wisdom rather than knowledge.

To articulate a few such questions as an illustration, I'll consider the complex influence of information and communication technologies (ICTs) in creating and reducing educational inequities. To lesson inequities, should stakeholders in education slow the adoption of new interactive media in schooling because the economic resources required could instead be used to address other issues related to inequities, such as hungry children, large class sizes, and underpaid teachers? If so, that decision would involve bypassing at present the potential benefits of ICTs to student and teacher motivation, learning, and assessment. Or should stakeholders in education instead push forward with these technologies, even though inequities may initially widen owing to issues of unequal access outside the school, because new media's potential to engage and individualize is strategically important for enabling learners diverse in their backgrounds the opportunity to reach their full potential—and because the online identities Greenhow and co-workers describe may help students with low academic self-efficacy reengage with classroom learning?[15] Knowledge can inform our thinking about these complex questions, but wisdom that draws on interpersonal and ethical dimensions is required to develop good answers.

How could the research infrastructure for knowledge production described above enable an experiment in generating wisdom? An interconnected suite of Web 2.0 tools customized for research would provide three capabilities:

1. a virtual setting in which various stakeholders could dialogue
2. about rich artifacts related to practice and policy
3. with a set of social supports to encourage community norms that respect not only theoretical rigor and empirical evidence but also interpersonal, experiential, and moral and ethical understandings.

For example, in terms of the complicated problem sketched above, teachers could bring detailed knowledge about students, curriculum, and instruction into such a community, and community representatives could articulate social and cultural norms reflective of their diverse values.[16] These three capabilities of a research infrastructure seem essential for a community attempting to generate wisdom about educational issues; only in the past few years have ICTs made these affordances widely available, practical, and inexpensive.

Why would the education research community want to sponsor such an experiment in complementing knowledge production with a process for articulating wisdom? The very idea may seem unwise: what about the "objectivity" of research? Beyond what theory and empirical evidence can offer, how can scholars in education judge the relative value of various moral, axiological, and subjective/interpersonal perspectives as they contribute to wisdom? Is this not the province of philosophers and preachers, community organizers, and proselytizers?

Perhaps in attempting to foster collective wisdom, I am demonstrating only my individual foolishness. However, the more I see the limited impact of "pure" knowledge (i.e., knowledge applied without wisdom) in solving wicked problems, the more I believe that we as professional scholars have a responsibility to go beyond generating just findings and theories—even though assuming such a responsibility means acknowledging the value of contributions from people whose epistemologies, standards, and values differ from our own. Quite possibly, an experiment in generating wisdom along the lines I suggest might fall far short, yet an "interesting" failure could provide the seeds of new insights into how to tackle the wicked problem of moving beyond the limitations of knowledge.

The National Research Council's 2002 report on education research says, "Advances in scientific knowledge are achieved by the self-regulating norms of the scientific community over time, not, as sometimes believed, by the mechanistic application of a particular scientific method to a static set of questions."[17] The advent of Web 2.0 social media does not change this observation; the power of research communities lies in the people who compose them rather than in the technological infrastructures that enhance the activities of those people. Emerging interactive media offer fascinating opportunities to enhance our scholarship; perhaps they offer even the opportunity to experiment with a superset of scholarly norms that provides leverage on wicked problems, such as the evolution of formal education beyond industrial-era schools.

Web 2.0 and Transforming Industrial-Era Schooling into Distributed Education

Along with many others, I believe that a new structure for formal education is necessary to enable our nation's graduates to compete in the twenty-first-century, knowledge-based global economy.[18] The one-room rural schoolhouse, emblematic of agricultural America, was replaced a century ago with the industrial-era schools we still have today. A comparable shift is necessary now; valiant attempts to keep the obsolete structure of today's schools and colleges but change people, policies, and practices fall well short of delivering high-quality educational outcomes for all students. Our schools and pedagogy do not even reflect recent developments in our knowledge about the human mind. If we redesigned education and teaching not just to make historical models of industrial-era schooling more efficient but to prepare students for the twenty-first century, what types of learning environments might sophisticated ICTs enable us to create?

The U.S. Department of Education's 2010 National Educational Technology Plan provides a pathway toward developing a twenty-first-century model of formal education to replace industrial-era schooling.[19] As a member of the technical working group that developed the plan, I can attest to the long hours of work that went into developing a comprehensive analysis. This is not a narrow, tactical plan for technology investments that aid industrial-era schooling but a strategic vision of a redesigned K–20 formal educational system that leverages current technologies to implement sophisticated learning, teaching, and assessment any place and anytime, lifelong and lifewide.

The plan appropriately begins its reconceptualization of formal education by describing powerful ways of learning accessible to all students through universal design. The next section delineates dramatically different types of assessments emerging to empower students' and teachers' learning through rich diagnostic feedback. Later sections on infrastructure and on productivity delineate the types of investments in technology needed to realize its vision and the ways a redesigned model of education could generate cost savings that would repay these investments.[20]

In terms of redesigning the formal educational system, the heart of the plan is the section on teaching. Here I would go beyond what the plan describes. As discussed by the "teaching" subset of the plan's working group, schools as custodial institutions are a starting point for considering the work of teaching. In contrast, a "distributed" model of human and technical infrastructure encompasses a wider context of formal learning outside classrooms that includes parents, museum and library staff, community members, and older peers as educators who collaborate with teachers in achieving equity and excellence.[21] The many provisions of modern technology now support both a broader suite of teaching roles and a range of educational delivery systems beyond the walls of a school.

An analogy to public health professionals illustrates the value of a model for teaching and learning distributed through time and space and across multiple demographics, rather than one localized to a small set of classroom teachers just during school hours. Largely because of the efforts of public health professionals, life expectancy has increased more than 60 percent in the last century.[22] Advances in medical interventions account for some of this improvement, but a greater factor is various types of public health roles distributed through society who help people learn to embrace wellness behaviors and to lead healthy lifestyles. For example, reductions in smoking and in obesity depend largely on the educational efforts not just of doctors and nurses but also of state and local boards of health, pharmacists, personnel in fitness-related organizations (e.g., personal trainers), coaches and athletes, teachers, reporters, and concerned citizens. In contrast to the objectives of formal education, the types of learning involved in public health are relatively simple, and the coordination among roles is minimal and informal. Nonetheless, this example illustrates a public sector responsibility crucial to society in which expanding education beyond a single narrow place and group of professionals (physicians' offices staffed by doctors and nurses) has reaped enormous benefits whose financial savings have more than offset the costs involved.

With modern technologies, a comparably distributed system of teaching and learning could complement education in schools with "educator" roles throughout children's lives. As an illustration of how complementary roles could function in a distributed model of formal education, collaborative media could be used to help coordinate between museum educators and both teachers and students. Teachers could use technology to make public the progression of curricular goals through the school year and the content on skills on which students need most help. In turn, museums could gear their exhibits and activities toward fostering these types of learning, making special outreach efforts to students for whom school-based learning was insufficient. Museums also could craft strong professional development experiences for teachers, with abstract concepts richly grounded in artifacts and with curators providing content expertise. Virtual outreach beyond the walls and schedule of the museum could include both web-based educational activities, such as immersive educational simulations, and "augmented realities" that help people learn about digitized artifacts virtually embedded in physical settings throughout the region and accessible by cell phone.[23] Faculty from local campuses could provide support in the design and evaluation of these museum-based educational resources.

Members of a student's family or community could choose to play a different type of complementary educational role in a distributed model. Teachers interact with dozens or hundreds of students each day and must balance a focus on the individual and on the group, but people outside the schools who are involved with a child's life know how to engage and support that particular individual. The local context—present and past—in which a student lives provides numerous ways in which to ground, exemplify, and practice the knowledge and skills teachers are attempting to communicate. However, fully realizing the academic value of students learning from people and resources in their lives outside school depends on a skilled teacher coordinating and orchestrating those informal experiences. Schools of education could shift their training and credentialing to encompass not only teachers but also parent tutors, informal educator coaches, and community mentors.

Distributed education is not a new concept, but at last—as the plan describes—we have the technologies needed to actualize this vision. Whether we have the political will remains to be seen. The time to act is now, when enormous investments are instead being used to shore up the obsolete model of industrial-era schooling. "Plan" is a verb, not a noun, and hopefully in the coming decade we will transform formal education as far beyond the industrial-era school as that institution moved beyond the one-room rural schoolhouse.

Conclusion: Web 2.0 and Personalized Learning

Personalized learning is emerging as a pathway for school success. As described in the U.S. National Educational Technology Plan, "personalization refers to instruction that is paced to learning needs [i.e., individualized], tailored to learning preferences [i.e., differentiated], and tailored to the specific interests of different learners. In an environment that is fully personalized, the learning objectives and content as well as the method and pace may all vary."[24] The Software and Information Industry Association report on personalized learning adds that

Educational equity is not simply about equal access and inputs, but ensuring that a student's educational path, curriculum, instruction, and schedule be personalized to meet her unique needs, inside and outside of school. Educational equity meets each child where she is and helps her achieve her potential through a wide range of resources and strategies appropriate for her learning style, abilities, and interests, as well as social, emotional, and physical situation.[25]

As discussed earlier, this is a very different pedagogical model than characteristic of industrial-era schooling, with one-size-fits-all processing of students.

An educational strategy that exemplifies personalization is connected learning. Online learning and e-learning are terms that convey a dated conception of what is possible with information technology. Both have roots in the early models of distance education, where the objective was to port classroom-style learning to off-campus students through an alternative delivery mechanism, whether via the postal service, cable television networks, or the Internet. In contrast, Ito and her colleagues note that connected learning

is socially embedded, interest-driven, and oriented toward educational, economic, or political opportunity. Connected learning is realized when a young person is able to pursue a personal interest or passion with the support of friends and caring adults, and is in turn able to link this learning and interest to academic achievement, career success or civic engagement.[26]

This model is based on evidence that resilient, adaptive, and effective learning involves individual interests coupled with social support to overcome adversity and provide recognition. To utilize connected learning, educators must link schooling to interdisciplinary problems and collaboration beyond classrooms and campuses. When learning is connected, it forms pathways; one activity feeds forward to another. Learners are not often engaged in unrelated activities—they form their identity and intentionality as they pursue their interests. With connected learning, the focus is on continuing pathways, not on gates or gatekeeping. The point is to connect the dots and to connect learning with life. Like personalized learning, this vision of life-wide learning is further articulated in the U.S. National Educational Technology Plan.[27] I cannot conceive of personalized learning or connected learning taking place without extensive use of Web 2.0 tools. These media provide both the personal focus and the social network requisite for these forms of lifewide learning. New forms of social media are appearing monthly, and it's exciting to imagine the opportunities that will arise in the years ahead. Because of their impact, future generation will have different definitions of learning, knowledge, and wisdom.

Notes

1. Christopher J. Dede, "A Seismic Shift in Epistemology," *EDUCAUSE Review* 43, no. 3 (2008): 80–81.

2. For the Wikipedia page on the social effect of evolutionary theory, see http://en.wikipedia.org/wiki/Social_effect_of_evolutionary_theory (accessed May 31, 2010).

3. Arthur E. Hallerberg, "Indiana's Squared Circle," *Mathematics Magazine* 50 (1977): 136–140.

4. Christopher Dede, "Technologies That Facilitate Generating Knowledge and Possibly Wisdom: A Response to 'Web 2.0 and Classroom Research,'" *Educational Researcher* 38, no. 4 (2009): 260–263.

5. National Research Council, Committee on Scientific Principles for Education Research, *Executive Summary of Scientific Research in Education,* ed. R. J. Shavelson and L. Towne (Washington, DC: National Academy Press, 2002), 1–10, 2.

6. Ibid., 2.

7. Christine Greenhow, Beth Robelia, and Joan E. Hughes, "Web 2.0 and Classroom Research: What Path Should We Take *Now?,*" *Educational Researcher* 38, no. 4 (2009): 246–259.

8. James E. Birren and Cheryl M. Svensson, "Wisdom in History: The Primacy of Affect-Cognition Relations," in *A Handbook of Wisdom: Psychological Perspectives*, ed. Robert J. Sternberg and Jennifer Jordan (Cambridge: Cambridge University Press, 2005), 3–31.

9. Ibid., 28.

10. Paul B. Baltes and Jacqui Smith, "Toward a Psychology of Wisdom and Its Ontogenesis," in *Wisdom: Its Nature, Origins, and Development*, ed. R. Sternberg (Cambridge: Cambridge University Press, 2005), 87–120.

11. James E. Birren and L. M. Fisher, "Conceptualizing Wisdom," in Sternberg and Jordan, *A Handbook of Wisdom*, 3–31.

12. William L. Randall and Gary M. Kenyon, *Ordinary Wisdom: Biographical Aging and the Journey of Life* (Westport, CT: Praeger, 2001).

13. Abraham H. Maslow, *Motivation and Personality* (New York: Harper and Brothers, 1954).

14. Jeff Conklin, *Wicked Problems and Social Complexity* (New York: Wiley, 2006).

15. Greenhow, Robelia, and Hughes, "Web 2.0 and Classroom Research."

16. Thomas Hatch et al., eds., *Going Public with Our Teaching: An Anthology of Practice* (New York: Teachers College Press, 2005).

17. National Research Council, *Executive Summary of Scientific Research in Education*, 2.

18. Christopher Dede, "Reflections on the Draft National Educational Technology Plan 2010: Foundations for Transformation," *Educational Technology* 50, no. 6 (2010): 18–22.

19. U.S. Department of Education. "2010 National Educational Technology Plan" (Washington, DC, 2010), http://www.ed.gov/technology/netp-2010.

20. Ibid.

21. Ibid.

22. National Institute on Aging, "Global Health and Aging" (Washington, DC: NIH, 2010), http://www.nia.nih.gov/research/publication/global-health-and-aging/living -longer.

23. Christopher Dede, "Reinventing the Role of Information and Communications Technologies in Education," in *Information and Communication Technologies: Considerations of Current Practice for Teachers and Teacher Educators*, ed. Louanne Smolin, Kimberly Lawless, and Nicholas Burbules (Malden, MA: Blackwell, 2007), 11–38.

24. U.S. Department of Education, "2010 National Educational Technology Plan," 12.

25. Software and Information Industry Association, "Innovate to Educate: System [Re]Design for Personalized Learning; A Report from the 2010 Symposium," prepared in collaboration with ASCD and the Council of Chief State School Officers, Mary Ann Wolf, author (Washington, DC: SIIA, November 2010), 6, http://siia.net/pli/presentations/PerLearnPaper.pdf.

26. Mizuko Ito et al., *Connected Learning: An Agenda for Research and Design* (Irvine, CA: Digital Media and Learning Research Hub, 2013), 6, http://dmlhub.net/publications/connected-learning-agenda-research-and-design.

27. U.S. Department of Education, "2010 National Educational Technology Plan."

Bibliography

Baltes, Paul B., and Jacqui Smith. "Toward a Psychology of Wisdom and Its Ontogenesis." In *Wisdom: Its Nature, Origins, and Development*, ed. R. Sternberg, 87–120. Cambridge: Cambridge University Press, 2005.

Birren, James E., and L. M. Fisher. "Conceptualizing Wisdom: The Primacy of Affect-Cognition Relations." In *A Handbook of Wisdom: Psychological Perspectives*, ed. Robert J. Sternberg and Jennifer Jordan, 317–332. Cambridge: Cambridge University Press, 2005.

Birren, James E., and Cheryl M. Svensson. "Wisdom in History: The Primacy of Affect-Cognition Relations." In *A Handbook of Wisdom: Psychological Perspectives*, ed. Robert J. Sternberg and Jennifer Jordan, 3–31. Cambridge: Cambridge University Press, 2005.

Conklin, Jeff. *Wicked Problems and Social Complexity*. New York: Wiley, 2006.

Dede, Christopher. "Immersive Interfaces for Engagement and Learning." *Science* 323, no. 5910 (2009): 66–69.

Dede, Christopher. "Reflections on the Draft National Educational Technology Plan 2010: Foundations for Transformation." *Educational Technology* 50, no. 6 (2010): 18–22.

Dede, Christopher. "A Seismic Shift in Epistemology." *EDUCAUSE Review* 43, no. 3 (2008): 80–81.

Dede, Christopher. "Technologies That Facilitate Generating Knowledge and Possibly Wisdom: A Response to "Web 2.0 and Classroom Research." *Educational Researcher* 38, no. 4 (2009): 260–263.

Dede, Christopher. "Reinventing the Role of Information and Communications Technologies in Education." In *Information and Communication Technologies: Considerations of Current Practice for Teachers and Teacher Educators*, ed. Louanne Smolin, Kimberly Lawless, and Nicholas Burbules, 11–38. Malden, MA: Blackwell, 2007.

Greenhow, Christine, Beth Robelia, and Joan E. Hughes. "Web 2.0 and Classroom Research: What Path Should We Take Now?" *Educational Researcher* 38, no.4 (2009): 246–259.

Hallerberg, Arthur E. 1977. "Indiana's Squared Circle." *Mathematics Magazine* 50:136–140.

Hatch, Thomas, Dilruba Ahmed, Ann Lieberman, Deborah Faigenbaum, Melissa Eiler White, and Désirée H. Pointer-Mace, eds. 2005. *Going Public with Our Teaching: An Anthology of Practice*. New York: Teachers College Press, 2005.

Ito, Mizuko, Kris Gutiérrez, Sonia Livingstone, Bill Penuel, Jean Rhodes, Katie Salen, Juliet Schor, Julian Sefton-Green, and S. Craig Watkins. *Connected Learning: An Agenda for Research and Design*. Irvine, CA: Digital Media and Learning Research Hub, 2013, http://dmlhub.net/publications/connected-learning-agenda-research-and-design.

Kitchener, Karen S., and Helene G. Brenner. "Wisdom and Reflective Judgment: Knowing in the Face of Uncertainty." In *A Handbook of Wisdom: Psychological Perspectives*, ed. Robert J. Sternberg and Jennifer Jordan, 212–229. Cambridge: Cambridge University Press, 1990.

Maslow, Abraham H. *Motivation and Personality*. New York: Harper and Brothers, 1954.

National Institute on Aging. "Global Health and Aging." Washington, DC: NIH, 2010. nia.nih.gov/research/publication/global-health-and-aging/living-longer.

National Research Council, Committee on Scientific Principles for Education Research. *Executive Summary of Scientific Research in Education*, ed. Richard J. Shavelson and Lisa Towne, 1–10. Washington, DC: National Academy Press, 2002.

Randall, William L., and Gary M. Kenyon. *Ordinary Wisdom: Biographical Aging and the Journey of Life*. Westport, CT: Praeger, 2001.

Software & Information Industry Association. "Innovate to Educate: System [Re] Design for Personalized Learning; A Report from the 2010 Symposium." Prepared in collaboration with ASCD and the Council of Chief State School Officers, Mary Ann Wolf, author. Washington, DC: SIIA, November 2010. http://www.ccsso.org/Documents/2010%20Symposium%20on%20Personalized%20Learning.pdf.

U.S. Department of Education. "2010 National Educational Technology Plan." Washington, DC, 2010. http://www.ed.gov/technology/netp-2010.

7 Reframing Privacy and Youth Media Practices

John Palfrey

Introduction

Young people use digital media, and social media in particular, in ways that are changing how they learn and grow up. These practices are changing how they relate to one another, to information, and to institutions. These changes can be good for teaching and learning, but they are not without complications. Privacy is chief among the concerns that we should bear in mind as we hurtle into a predominantly digital age, but not necessarily for the reasons that many adults and educators think. The main fear that parents and teachers express about privacy—that young people don't care about it—is neither true nor the main issue to address.

When it comes to youth and technology, issues of concern about the future—rather than issues related to opportunities—often dominate the public discourse. This perspective is understandable on several levels. First, parents and grandparents are often baffled by, and sometimes concerned about, the habits of their children and the generations that follow. The habitual use of social media by many youth is surely no exception to that rule. Second, the information technology environment is in the midst of radical transformations in patterns of technology usage, changes that bring with them much innovation, not to mention challenges to existing hierarchies. And third, adults perceive that their children are more likely to use these new information technologies in ways that are, at best, perplexing and, at worst, dangerous to themselves and to society. However, the data collected by social scientists about young people, how they use technologies, and the challenges and opportunities they face often are at odds with this public perception.

Chief among the worries that we researchers hear from parents is that young people share too much information about themselves online. Adults say they fear that kids don't care about their privacy. The fear is that young people are doing themselves harm by leaving tracks that others can follow online. Many parents fret over an erosion of the reasonable expectation of privacy in the online environment. Public outcry and class action lawsuits can prompt changes in the privacy policy and terms of service at large social networking sites, such as Facebook and Google.

These privacy issues appear cheek by jowl with issues of reputation, trust, and credibility in the lives of young people. Here, too, the perception about young people as invariably sharing too much information without a corresponding sense of obligation to one another is not matched by the data collected by social scientists in the field.[1]

Social science research suggests something quite different: many youth do care about privacy and their personal reputations. But research shows something else, a problem that is worrisome in a different way than we might expect. Many youth who have access to these technologies, and who lead lives heavily mediated by them, do not have sufficient skills and tools to keep private from others that which they wish to protect—even when they spend a great deal of time online and in gaming environments. Furthermore, what they wish to keep private is often different from what adults believe they should keep private.

There is a broad range of views among youth about privacy, just as there is among adults. The issues of privacy and information disclosure online do not break neatly along generational lines. Finally, there are plenty of youth—and adults—who recognize that much can be gained from being in public; such people are constantly assessing whether or not the opportunities of publicity outweigh the potential consequences. When thinking about privacy, educators and policymakers must also take into account the opportunities created by public participation.

Media Use by Young People

The use of digital media has led to transformations in learning, socializing, and communications practices among youth—many of which are overwhelmingly positive. Since technologies and youth practices change rapidly, data are, at best, a snapshot of a moving target.[2] As difficult as this research task is, researchers do know several important things about current youth media practices. First, young people as a group are using media, and digital media in particular, more than ever before. Many youth use multiple types of digital media at the same time, a practice called multitasking or switch-tasking.[3] For many young people, activities like content generation, remixing, collaboration, and sharing are important aspects of daily life.⁴ These digitally mediated practices are often very important to their overall methods of learning, especially in informal or connected types of learning.

The motivations for digital media use vary widely among youth, but most fall into two broad categories. Many of the media uses are friendship-driven: most youth interact online with people they already know from their offline lives, using the Internet to maintain existing relationships.⁵ Other media uses are interest-driven, with opportunities to develop expertise in specialized skill areas such as animation or blogging. In either context, the casual use of digital media is an important way to develop social and technological skills. Young people learn during their informal media use, just as they do in formal educational settings.

Though we often generalize about youth media practice in America, it is important to note that not all children are "born digital." In other words, not all youth have access to equal forms of digital media on the Internet. This digital divide, often also called the participation gap, limits opportunities for learning and development for many youth, especially those in lower socioeconomic brackets. Youth who do not have access to the Internet at home might miss out on opportunities to develop important social and technical skills. Youth who do not have the opportunity to develop familiarity and confidence with digital media may have trouble navigating social interactions in online communities or recognizing biased, unreliable information. These disadvantages place at increased risk the youth on the wrong side of this digital divide.

Access to digital technologies alone does not guarantee parity in experience. Youth who depend on computers in libraries and schools, which often block access to certain sites and services, are at a disadvantage compared to peers with better access. The notion of the participation gap, between those with sophisticated skills to use digital media and those without, has been developed in detail both theoretically and through empirical data by researchers, including Henry Jenkins and his colleagues.⁶

The full picture of how digital media are changing learning and socializing is still emerging. One challenge associated with research in this area is that we are only now observing children who have grown up with email, social networking sites, cell phones, and other technologies. We know enough today, though, to make a compelling case that engagement with digital media has great educational potential. A recent ethnographic study examined peer-based learning practices among youth, and found that digital media provide the opportunity for intense, self-directed, interest-driven study.⁷ So-called "geeking out"—defined as developing specialized expertise and sharing it with others—does not resemble traditional class-room-based education, yet it fosters important technological and social skills, including confidence, leadership, and communication. Youth benefit from socializing in digitally mediated environments, learning the social skills necessary to participate in creative and collaborative work environments.[8] As we seek to protect youth from the unforeseen risks of online engagement, including loss of privacy, it is essential that we do not foreclose on the benefits made possible by self-directed, informal learning and socializing through new technologies. Furthermore, the desire to reduce the risks posed to youth by online engagement should not preclude educators' experimentation with new technologies in the classroom.

Most of the studies about the educational possibilities afforded by networked technology usage to date focus on college students, a readily accessible population that presents fewer methodological challenges to researchers than do young children. According to many studies, most college students use Google, Wikipedia, and the advice of friends as starting points for everyday life research. For course research, the most popular resources are course materials, Google, and scholarly databases. While students welcome online access to library resources, their frustrations include focusing research topics, sorting through results to find relevant resources, and assessing the credibility of sources.

Educators at all levels are not, however, effectively realizing the potential of digital media in formal educational settings. Educational content in digital formats is often disorganized, decentralized, and difficult to find. Children and parents need assistance in locating reliable, age-appropriate educational content. It is unclear whether there is enough quality educational content accessible online for students at different age levels, for non-English speakers, or for children with disabilities or special needs. Technology can generally improve educational curricula by enabling instructors to address individual needs. Technologies can also help support new and enhanced pedagogies to provide multiple avenues for expression, engagement, and content presentation.[9] Some promising recent efforts have focused on harnessing video-gaming interfaces to supplement curricula.[10]

Technology can also play a crucial role in making information more accessible to youth with disabilities. For example, mobile devices such as cell phones and smartphones can facilitate communication between hearing-impaired students and their teachers and classmates.[11] Assistive technologies can and should go beyond basic accessibility, so that students have an educational experience that is not merely adequate but enhanced. Too often, concerns raised by market participants, including copyright interests, stand in the way of sound new teaching practices to help all young people learn. Likewise, fears around communication technologies often get in the way of educational opportunities. Research suggests that interventions involving computer-mediated communication can help those on the autism spectrum learn necessary social skills,[12] but only if educators are empowered to use such tools. The work of the Center for Applied Special Technology (CAST) is exemplary for leveraging digital media research to improve learning technologies for all students.

The Challenges of Convergent Lives and Privacy Online

Parents are often concerned that their children share too much personal information online. They worry that potential predators could use that information to harass or harm children, either online or offline. Since data disclosed online are often searchable, and hard to delete, youth who behave too openly may suffer consequences in the future, when their personal information is accessed in unforeseen ways by potential employers, educational institutions, or other parties.[13] These fears, though widespread, are not generally borne out in much of the research available today.

Young people use digital media and related technologies in ways that express their identity. Young people express themselves on social networking sites like Facebook and Instagram, environments in which they are shaping an identity. They choose how to express themselves by the photographs they upload to these social networking sites, but they also do so in a way that is not distinct from identity creation in the offline world. The notion that there is a separate digital world with a unique set of online identities makes little sense to someone who has grown up immersed in digital technologies.

What we might think of separately as online life and offline life are united, by and large. For young people, it is not online life and offline life—it's just life. These hybrid lives, which join the digitally mediated and the face-to-face, are where social life is playing out. Often, identity shaping by young people happens in a way that works just like the traditional role-playing we would expect of young people as they shape their identities. They are shaping multiple forms of their identity in these convergent lives.

The most important point about this convergence is that the digitally mediated experiences young people are having are related to and, much of the time, intertwined with their offline experiences. There is a lesson at the heart of this convergence for those of us who are parents and teachers: it does not make much sense to disaggregate the online and physical spaces in which learning and development are occurring. Educators need to plan, and act, in the knowledge that the experiences youth create for themselves in these multiple environments are tightly connected. Educational institutions and parents ignore these lessons at their peril.

Nothing about this new, converged series of environments is simple. At the heart of online identity formation lies a series of paradoxes. Although young people think they are creating multiple identities, there is also the ability for onlookers to see all of these identities at once. This is an interesting, and profound, change. Previously, onlookers trying to track down and then observe these identities seriatim could not see them all at once, could not see this multiplicity. Though young people may think there is more control and experimentation in terms of their identities today, it may be only that a more complete version of young people emerges through this medium.

Youth do, in fact, care about privacy. The willingness of today's youth to reveal information can be different from the patterns of their parents and grandparents, but not necessarily in the ways that many adults believe. Studies on this subject demonstrate that both youth and adults have a range of concerns about privacy. Some children and teens do show less concern than adults about their privacy online, although the data are inconclusive on this score. But studies also show that teens are often more vigilant than adults in terms of privacy-protecting behaviors, even though they are more likely to engage in what some consider less ethical approaches, such as flaming (disparaging individuals in public online fora) and providing false information.[14] When youth are concerned about risks to their privacy, they will engage in protective behaviors, such as adjusting their privacy settings, refusing to provide information, providing false information, or avoiding certain websites.[15] However, most youth (like most adults) do not read websites' privacy policies or practices, and may be unaware when their information is at risk of disclosure to third parties or unintended audiences.[16] These findings put pressure on the notion that the current model of "notice and consent"– or "notice and choice"–style privacy protections on commercial websites are the most effective ways to empower Internet users to manage their personal information. This variation in styles should lead to better notification of young people about their privacy choices on social media sites.

Young people tend to view the Internet as a social environment.[17] The relationships that youth maintain are not segmented between "online" and "offline" friendships. The social dynamics of friendship for many youth make the sharing of information online part of a coherent sense of identity. Most youth interact online with people they already know offline. On the other hand, some youth report chatting with strangers online, especially while playing online games.[18] Youth tend to focus more on the potential benefits of information disclosure than they do on potential harms.[19] Studies of twelve-year-old and older teens have found that youth take a risk–benefit approach to sharing information, becoming more willing to disclose if they anticipate benefits from sharing.[20] For many young people, being part of popular online social networking sites carries meaningful social benefits.[21]

The context in which information is solicited or shared is very important. Youth often don't see information as strictly public or strictly private. They distinguish between different levels of privacy; for example, on Facebook, youth may divide friends into different lists, to which they may grant graduated levels of access to different types of information. Youth might share passwords for their social media accounts with friends for perceived social benefits[22] while simultaneously keeping their online activities private from parents.[23] As the authors of a recent study observed, "Youth see benefits in sharing information online, but among peers rather than with adults in their lives."[24]

It is a dangerous mistake to conclude that differences in privacy attitudes are merely generational. Attitudes toward privacy and reputation also vary considerably among youth themselves. Age, gender, and Internet experience are important variables; research indicates that the most Internet-savvy, experienced users are the most concerned about privacy and the most likely to take privacy-protecting steps.[25] When youth are aware of and concerned about risk, they engage in protective behaviors, such as refusing to provide information, providing false information, or avoiding certain websites.[26] However, youth are not always concerned about risk when they should be. And many adults demonstrate the same information-sharing practices as youth.

Youth also vary in terms of their behavior related to certain types of personal information. Studies have found that teens share email addresses and passwords with one another,[27] possibly to demonstrate trust or to get technical help with accounts.[28] Public information often includes first names, photographs, and information about interests, but surnames, phone numbers, and addresses are shared less frequently.[29] Teenagers sometimes intentionally lie about their information, often because they believe that inaccurate information is necessary for online safety.[30] One study found that females are more likely to have private profiles than males.[31] Most relevant studies have looked at social networking practices among college students; supplementary research on younger children is needed to discover what information they typically share. In addition to profile information and passwords, youth commonly share user-created content, such as photographs, videos, or blog entries.[32]

Social networking sites require youth (and all users) to share at least some amount of personal information in order to participate in the environment. The choice of what information to disclose is part of the dynamic process of defining identity for young people. Research shows that youth do not always understand and use the most advanced privacy-protecting settings on social networking sites.[33] Some studies suggest that children may be more likely than adults to restrict access to their information on social networking sites.[34] However, if privacy settings are too complex, they threaten to confuse or turn off youth (and adults) and render themselves without utility.

For-profit firms are using a variety of means, including but not limited to social networking sites, to mediate the identity formation of young people. Adolescents are primary targets for digital marketing. An increasing number of market research firms, advertising agencies, and trend analysis companies are monitoring how youth incorporate digital media into their daily lives and are developing marketing strategies tailored to the specific psychological needs of young people. Market research is woven into the patterns of everyday socialization of youth. This process of integration creates a feedback system for marketers that enables them to refine their techniques in real time.[35]

Major food and beverage companies, including Coca-Cola, McDonald's, Burger King, and KFC, are exploiting the relationship that adolescents have with digital media by developing new online marketing campaigns. These efforts create intimacies between teenagers and the products and brands that surround them. Marketers use a wide range of digital marketing practices across a variety of platforms—social networking sites, video game sites, mobile services, online video-sharing sites, instant messaging apps, and virtual worlds. These campaigns take advantage of the key features that are emblematic of the ways in which young people interact with digital media—ubiquitous connectivity, personalization, peer-to-peer networking, engagement, immersion, and content creation. In contrast to traditional commercial advertising on television, in today's digital marketing system, advertising, editorial content, and content delivery are intertwined.[36]

Online advertising—banner ads, popups, search engine optimization, spam comments, and emails—constitutes for youth an inescapable part of using today's digital media. This raises an important question: can young people distinguish advertising from noncommercial content? While early research suggested that children could not reliably identify advertising content,[37] more recent work has suggested that youth may be savvy enough to spot the ads.[38] But even as children become increasingly familiar with the Internet, advertisers become better at blurring the boundaries between commercial and noncommercial content and at embedding persuasive messages on social networking sites, advergames, and in branded online environments intended for younger and younger children. So far, there is insufficient research to predict whether this blurring might yield different outcomes for youth than ads rendered through traditional media, such as television commercials.

There are real concerns facing youth and their privacy in a digital age. Youth are subject to a great deal of surveillance, online and offline; their activities are frequently monitored by parents and other adults in ways they perceive violate their privacy; and information about them is constantly being collected and is subject to exploitation by marketers seeking to sell them things. We need a series of related strategies to address these connected but distinct risks that our youth are facing.

Empowering Youth to Protect Themselves

Policy interventions should address the extent to which youth media occurs at the intersection of the public and the private and in a converged environment of the online and the offline. The growing body of research into youth media practices points to a broad range of policy levers that could be pulled to improve youth privacy in online social environments and other digital spaces. Regulatory interventions of the sort where the state disallows certain practices are among those choices but are certainly not the only way to proceed.

New policies should pursue five core approaches to improving youth online privacy protections. First, policymakers and educators must commit to grounding decision making in sound research as the privacy practices of young people change over time. Practices are changing rapidly in the digital era, and it is important to understand the manner in which youth are engaging in life, both online and offline, and how they think about the concepts of public and private. What is considered by youth to be public or private has not changed overnight as a result of the advent of digital media. But a great deal of social life for youth is occurring in networked public spaces, which means that a great deal of information is recorded about the everyday lives of youth, whether through their active disclosure or otherwise. Policymakers and educators need to commit to understanding these practices before, and as, they make hard choices.

Second, adults need to acknowledge and take responsibility for their roles in violating young people's privacy, especially in ways that can backfire. Parents should be aware that discussing media content with their children has been proven effective in reducing the amount of personal information disclosed—at least more so than simply prohibiting or limiting children's access.[39] Teens whose parents monitor or participate in their Internet use care more about their privacy than those who do not.[40] However, youth also may perceive monitoring by parents as a violation of their privacy.[41] One recent study of parent-child pairs found that children were more resistant to protective strategies involving parental monitoring and coviewing than they were to user empowerment strategies, or even some forms of government or industry protection.[42] Resources to help parents understand the ever-changing and complicated privacy settings used by websites like Facebook can be very constructive, but parents should be advised that filtering and monitoring strategies can backfire by undermining their children's trust, especially as they grow older.[43]

Third, governments and schools should emphasize teaching media literacy skills relating to privacy in a digital era in a manner that is not focused on scare tactics. These media literacy trainings can help close the participation gap that divides youth who have access to the technology from those who have both access and the good skills to use them effectively. A growing number of excellent media literacy curricula are available or under development, including offerings from New Media Literacies, the GoodPlay Project, and Common Sense Media. These media literacy efforts may take the form of specific courses or modules that can fit within the context of nearly any discipline-based course offering already offered by a school or district.

Fourth, companies (e.g., Facebook) that hold a great deal of information about young people need to be held accountable for their efforts to inform and empower their users about online privacy. Improvements in the ease with which youth can manage their privacy settings could help to address, in part, the participation gap between the most sophisticated Internet users and the most naïve. Youth who are less Internet-savvy, including younger children or teens without home Internet access, might have the most trouble navigating privacy settings, and thus may be at increased risk of unwitting public disclosure of personal information. While privacy settings should be subtle enough to permit granular control of personal information across one's various connections, social network hosts should also take responsibility for making these controls easier to find, understand, and use. Help should be provided, especially for younger users, and there should be a straightforward and transparent way to identify what profile information is publicly available. Social networking site providers should also allow users to access what information is kept about them, how it is used, and who can see it. Social networking site providers should set privacy defaults that favor increased security for personal information so that the least sophisticated users are protected from unwanted information disclosure.

Fifth, as a matter of public policy, we need to rethink, and improve on, the dominant "notice and choice" and self-regulatory framework for data held in digital forms about youth in particular. A new model for our regulatory regime must ensure a greater level of user control over and awareness of personally identifiable information over the long term. Companies that hold large amounts of data about youth or contributed by youth need to take on a larger role in safeguarding those data than they do today. We should consider restricting what is done with the data held by these companies, given that young people's convergent, hybrid, digital-era socializing involves so much sharing of information with private parties. And commercialization of the online learning spaces for children should be sharply curbed, without limiting the experimentation that is thriving today in the field of education.

Conclusion

In making our policy choices about protecting youth privacy online, policymakers and educators ought to emphasize initiatives that enable young people to manage the information they share about themselves online and offline. From the youth perspective, this information is not what we would traditionally deem to be public, to the extent that truly public information may be accessed without restriction by anyone else. Nor is the information intended to be purely private. The information is being shared with a purpose, in a semipublic fashion and within a context of trust and an expectation that access to the information will be limited. We also know that young people make mistakes about when they share information about themselves, as we all do, and that neither the law nor most companies are doing much to help them in this respect. Those of us who work with young people directly can help, but the solution must extend beyond the work of teachers and parents to include the state and the private owners of online spaces as central actors.

Notes

1. danah boyd, *It's Complicated: The Social Life of Networked Teens* (New Haven, CT: Yale University Press, 2014); Urs Gasser, "Perspectives on the Future of Digital Privacy," *Zeitschrift für Schweizerisches Recht* 134 (2015): II.

2. Andrew Schrock and danah boyd, "Online Threats to Youth: Solicitation, Harassment, and Problematic Content," in *Enhancing Child Safety and Online Technologies: Final Report of the Internet Safety Technical Task Force to the Multi-State Working Group on Social Networking of State Attorneys,* Internet Safety Technical Task Force (Durham, NC: Carolina Academic Press, 2008), 73–145.

3. Victoria J. Rideout, Ulla G. Foehr, and Donald F. Roberts, *Generation M2: Media in the Lives of 8- to 18-Year-Olds* (Menlo Park, CA: Kaiser Family Foundation, 2010); Urs Gasser and John G. Palfrey, "Mastering Multitasking," *Educational Leadership* 66, no. 6 (2009): 14–19.

4. Mizuko Ito et al., *Living and Learning with New Media: Summary of Findings from the Digital Youth Project,* The John D. and Catherine T. MacArthur Foundation Reports on Digital Media and Learning, November 2008, http://digitalyouth.ischool.berkeley .edu/files/report/digitalyouth-WhitePaper.pdf.

5. danah boyd, "Taken out of Context: American Teen Sociality in Networked Publics" (PhD diss., University of California, 2008); J. Palfrey and U. Gasser, *Born Digital: Understanding the First Generation of Digital Natives* (New York: Basic Books, 2008).

6. Henry Jenkins et al., *Confronting the Challenges of Participatory Culture: Media Education for the 21st Century* (Cambridge, MA: MIT Press, 2009), https://mitpress.mit .edu/sites/default/files/titles/free_download/9780262513623_Confronting_the _Challenges.pdf.

7. Mizuko Ito et al., *Hanging Out, Messing Around, and Geeking Out: Kids Living and Learning with New Media* (Cambridge, MA: MIT Press, 2009).

8. Ibid.

9. See http://www.cast.org.

10. James P. Gee, *What Video Games Have to Teach Us about Learning and Literacy* (New York: Palgrave, 2007).

11. Tracy Gray et al., *Unleashing the Power of Innovation for Assistive Technology* (Washington, DC: American Institutes for Research, 2010).

12. Moira Burke, Robert Kraut, and Diane Williams, "Social Use of Computer-Mediated Communication by Adults on the Autism Spectrum," paper presented at the Conference on Computer-Supported Cooperative Work, Savannah, GA, February 6–10, 2010, http://www.thoughtcrumbs.com/publications/Burke_CSCW2010 _CMC_and_Autism.pdf.

13. danah boyd, "Why Youth (Heart) Social Network Sites: The Role of Networked Publics in Teenage Social Life," in *Youth, Identity, and Digital Media*, ed. D. Buckingham, 1–26, The John D. and Catherine T. MacArthur Foundation Series on Digital Media and Learning (Cambridge, MA: MIT Press).

14. Alice E. Marwick, Diego Murgia-Diaz, and John Palfrey, "Youth, Privacy and Reputation," unpublished literature review (2010).

15. Seounmi Youn, "Determinants of Online Privacy Concern and Its Influence on Privacy Protection Behaviors among Young Adolescents," *Journal of Consumer Affairs* 43, no. 3 (2009): 389–418.

16. Ibid.

17. boyd, "Taken out of Context"; Ito et al., *Living and Learning with New Media*.

18. Schrock and boyd, "Online Threats to Youth."

19. Rafi Santo et al., *Meeting of Minds: Cross-Generational Dialogue on the Ethics of Digital Life*, a report in collaboration of Global Kids, Common Sense Media, and the GoodPlay Project at Harvard University's Project Zero, October 2009, http://www.macfound.org/atf/cf/%7Bb0386ce3-8b29-4162-8098-e466fb856794%7D/DML-FOCUS-DIALOGUE-REPORT-0910.PDF.

20. Youn, "Determinants of Online Privacy Concern"; Seounmi Youn, Teenagers' Perceptions of Online Privacy and Coping Behaviors: A Risk-Benefit Appraisal Approach," *Journal of Broadcasting & Electronic Media* 49, no. 1 (2005): 86–110.

21. boyd, "Why Youth (Heart) Social Network Sites."

22. Valerie Steeves and Cheryl Webster, "Closing the Barn Door: The Effect of Parental Supervision on Canadian Children's Online Privacy, *Bulletin of Science, Technology & Society* 28, no. 1 (2008): 4–19.

23. Anne West, Jane Lewis, and Peter Currie, "Students' Facebook 'Friends': Public and Private Spheres," *Journal of Youth Studies* 12, no. 6 (2009): 615–627.

24. Santo et al., *Meeting of Minds*.

25. Ian C. Grant, "Online Privacy: An Issue for Adolescents," in *Proceedings of the Child and Teen Consumption Conference* (Copenhagen: Copenhagen Business School, April 2006).

26. Marwick, Murgia-Diaz, and Palfrey, "Youth, Privacy and Reputation"; Youn, "Determinants of Online Privacy Concern."

27. Steeves and Webster, "Closing the Barn Door"; Amanda Lenhart, Oliver Lewis, and Lee Rainie, *Teenage Life Online: The Rise of the Instant-Message Generation and the Internet's Impact on Friendships and Family Relationships*, Pew Internet and American Life Project (Washington, DC: Pew Research Center, June 21, 2001), http://www

.pewinternet.org/files/old-media/Files/Reports/2001/PIP_Teens_Report.pdf (accessed December 29, 2009).

28. boyd, "Taken out of Context."

29. Amanda Lenhart and Mary Madden, *Teens, Privacy and Online Social Networks*, Pew Internet and American Life Project (Washington, DC: Pew Research Center, 2007), http://www.pewinternet.org/Reports/2007/Teens-Privacy-and-Online-Social -Networks.aspx (accessed December 29, 2009).

30. boyd, "Taken out of Context."

31. Amanda Burgess-Proctor, Justin Patchin, and Sameer Hinduja, "Cyberbullying and Online Harassment: Reconceptualizing the Victimization of Adolescent Girls," in *Female Crime Victims: Reality Reconsidered*, ed. V. Garcia and J. Clifford (Upper Saddle River, NJ: Prentice Hall, 2009), 162–176.

32. Amanda Lenhart, Mary Madden, Aaron Smith, and Alexandra Macgill, *Teens and Social Media*, Pew Internet and American Life Project (Washington, DC; Pew Research Center, 2007), http://www.pewinternet.org/~/media//Files/Reports/2007/PIP_Teens _Social_Media_Final.pdf (accessed September 22, 2015).

33. Bernhard Debatin, Jennette P. Lovejoy, Ann-Kathrin Horn, and Brittany Hughes, "Facebook and Online Privacy Attitudes, Behaviors, and Unintended Conse-quences," *Journal of Computer-Mediated Communication* 15, no. 1 (2009): 83–108.

34. Lenhart, Madden, and Smith, *Teens and Social Media*.

35. Kathryn Montgomery and Jeff Chester, "Interactive Food and Beverage Market-ing: Targeting Adolescents in the Digital Age," *Journal of Adolescent Health* 45, no. 3 (2009): S18–S29.

36. Ibid.

37. Lucy L. Henke, "Children, Advertising, and the Internet: An Exploratory Study," in *Advertising and the World Wide Web*, ed. D. Schumann and E. Thorson (Mahwah, NJ: Erlbaum, 1999), 73–80.

38. Lucy L. Henke, "After the Internet: A Third-Year Follow Up and Comparative Analysis of Children's Perceptions and Use of the Internet," in *Proceedings of the Academy of Marketing Studies* 7, no. 25 (2002).

39. May O. Lwin, Andrea J. S. Stanaland, and Anthony D. Miyazaki, "Protecting Children's Privacy Online: How Parental Mediation Strategies Affect Website Safe-guard Effectiveness," *Journal of Retailing* 84, no. 2 (2008): 205–217); Youn, "Parental Influence and Teens' Attitude"; Marwick, Murgia-Diaz, and Palfrey, "Youth, Privacy and Reputation."

40. Deborah M. Moscardelli and Richard Divine, "Adolescents' Concern for Privacy When Using the Internet: An Empirical Analysis of Predictors and Relationships

with Privacy-Protecting Behaviors," *Family and Consumer Sciences Research Journal* 35, no. 3 (2007): 232–252.

41. Ito et al., *Living and Learning with New Media*; West, Lewis, and Currie, "Students' Facebook 'Friends.'"

42. Sahara Byrne, "Parents versus Child Reports of Internet Behaviors and Support for Strategies to Prevent Negative Effects of Online Exposure," paper presented at the Berkman Center for Internet and Society, Harvard University, Cambridge, MA, December 15.

43. After Facebook revised its privacy controls in the fall of 2009, Common Sense Media the following year provided a guide for parents confused by the new settings: "How to Get a Handle on Facebook's Privacy Settings," http://www.common sensemedia.org/new-facebook-privacy-settings-what-parents-need-know.

Bibliography

boyd, danah. *It's Complicated: The Social Lives of Networked Teens*. New Haven, CT: Yale University Press, 2014.

boyd, danah. "Taken out of Context: American Teen Sociality in Networked Publics." PhD diss., University of California, 2008.

boyd, danah. "Why Youth (Heart) Social Network Sites: The Role of Networked Publics in Teenage Social Life." In *Youth, Identity, and Digital Media Volume*, ed. D. Buckingham, 1–26. The John D. and Catherine T. MacArthur Foundation Series on Digital Media and Learning. Cambridge, MA: MIT Press, 2007.

Burke, Moira, Robert Kraut, and Diane Williams. "Social Use of Computer-Mediated Communication by Adults on the Autism Spectrum." Paper presented at the Conference on Computer-Supported Cooperative Work, Savannah, GA, February 6–10, 2010. http://www.thoughtcrumbs.com/publications/Burke_CSCW2010_CMC_and _Autism.pdf.

Burgess-Proctor, Amanda, Justin Patchin, and Sameer Hinduja. "Cyberbullying and Online Harassment: Reconceptualizing the Victimization of Adolescent Girls." In *Female Crime Victims: Reality Reconsidered*, ed. V. Garcia and J. Clifford, 162–176. Upper Saddle River, NJ: Prentice Hall, 2009.

Byrne, Sahara, "Parents versus Child Reports of Internet Behaviors and Support for Strategies to Prevent Negative Effects of Online Exposure." Paper presented at the Berkman Center for Internet and Society, Harvard University, Cambridge, MA, December 15, 2009. http://cyber.law.harvard.edu/interactive/events/luncheons/ 2009/12/byrne.

Debatin, Bernard, Jennette P. Lovejoy, Ann-Kathrin Horn, and Brittany Hughes. "Facebook and Online Privacy: Attitudes, Behaviors, and Unintended Consequences." *Journal of Computer-Mediated Communication* 15, no. 1 (2009): 83–108.

Gasser, Urs. "Perspectives on the Future of Digital Privacy." *Zeitschrift für Schweizerisches Recht* 134 (2015): II.

Gasser, Urs, and John G. Palfrey. "Mastering Multitasking." *Educational Leadership* 66, no. 6 (2009): 14–19.

Gee, James P. *What Video Games Have to Teach Us About Learning and Literacy*. New York: Palgrave, 2007.

Grant, Ian C. "Online Privacy: An Issue for Adolescents." In *Proceedings of the Child and Teen Consumption Conference*. Copenhagen: Copenhagen Business School, April 2006.

Gray, Tracy, Heidi Silver-Pacuilla, Cynthia Overton, and Alise Brann. *Unleashing the Power of Innovation for Assistive Technology*. Washington, DC: American Institutes for Research, 2010.

Henke, Lucy L. "Children, Advertising, and the Internet: An Exploratory Study." In *Advertising and the World Wide Web*, ed. D. Schumann and E. Thorson, 73–80. Mahwah, NJ: Erlbaum, 1999.

Henke, Lucy L. "After the Internet: A Third-Year Follow Up and Comparative Analysis of Children's Perceptions and Use of the Internet." *Proceedings of the Academy of Marketing Studies* 7, no. 25 (2002).

Ito, Mizuko, Sonja Baumer, Matteo Bittanti. danah boyd, Rachel Cody, Becky Herr-Stephenson, Heather A. Horst, et al. *Hanging Out, Messing Around, and Geeking Out: Living and Learning with New Media*. Cambridge, MA: MIT Press, 2009.

Ito, Mizuko, Heather A. Horst, Matteo Bittanti. danah boyd, Becky Herr-Stephenson, Patricia G. Lange, C.J. Pascoe, et al. *Living and Learning with New Media: Summary of Findings from the Digital Youth Project*. The John D. and Catherine T. MacArthur Foundation Reports on Digital Media and Learning, November 2008. http:/digitalyouth.ischool.berkeley.edu/files/report/digitalyouth-WhitePaper.pdf.

Jenkins, Henry, with Ravi Purushotma, Margaret Weigel, Katie Clinton, and Alice J. Robison. *Confronting the Challenges of Participatory Culture: Media Education for the 21st Century* (Cambridge, MA: MIT Press, 2009). https://mitpress.mit.edu/sites/default/files/titles/free_download/9780262513623_Confronting_the_Challenges.pdf.

Lenhart, Amanda, and Mary Madden. *Teens, Privacy and Online Social Networks*. Pew Internet and American Life Project. Washington, DC: Pew Research Center, 2007. http://www.pewinternet.org/Reports/2007/Teens-Privacy-and-Online-Social-Networks.aspx (accessed December 29, 2009).

Lenhart, Amanda, Mary Madden, Aaron Smith, and Alexandra Macgill. *Teens and Social Media*. Pew Internet and American Life Project. Washington, DC: Pew Research Center, 2007. http://www.pewinternet.org/~/media//Files/Reports/2007/PIP_Teens _Social_Media_Final.pdf (accessed December 29, 2009).

Lenhart, Amanda, Lee Rainie, and Oliver Lewis. *Teenage Life Online: The Rise of the Instant-Message Generation and the Internet's Impact on Friendships and Family Relationships*. Pew Internet and American Life Project. Washington, DC: Pew Research Center, June 21, 2001. http://www.pewinternet.org/files/old-media/Files/Reports/ 2001/PIP_Teens_Report.pdf.pdf (accessed September 22, 2015).

Lwin, May O., Andrea J. S. Stanaland, and Anthony D. Miyazaki. "Protecting Children's Privacy Online: How Parental Mediation Strategies Affect Website Safeguard Effectiveness." *Journal of Retailing* 84, no. 2 (2008): 205–217.

Marwick, Alice E. *Status Update: Celebrity, Publicity, and Branding in the Social Media Age*. New Haven, CT: Yale University Press, 2013.

Montgomery, Kathryn, and Jeff Chester. "Interactive Food and Beverage Marketing: Targeting Adolescents in the Digital Age." *Journal of Adolescent Health* 45, no. 3 (2009): S18–S29.

Moscardelli, Deborah M., and Richard Divine. "Adolescents' Concern for Privacy When Using the Internet: An Empirical Analysis of Predictors and Relationships with Privacy-Protecting Behaviors." *Family and Consumer Sciences Research Journal* 35, no. 3 (2007): 232–252.

Palfrey, John, and Urs Gasser. *Born Digital: Understanding the First Generation of Digital Natives*. New York: Basic Books, 2008.

Rideout, Victoria, Ulla G. Foehr, and Donald F. Roberts. *Generation M2: Media in the Lives of 8- to 18-Year-Olds*. Menlo Park, CA: Kaiser Family Foundation, 2010.

Santo, Rafi, Carrie James, Katie Davis, Shire Lee Katz, Linda Burch, and Barry Joseph. *Meeting of Minds: Cross-Generational Dialogue on the Ethics of Digital Life*. A report in collaboration of Global Kids, Common Sense Media, and the GoodPlay Project at Harvard University's Project Zero, October 2009. http://dmlcentral.net/wp-content/ uploads/files/meetingofminds.pdf.

Schrock, Andrew, and danah boyd. "Online Threats to Youth: Solicitation, Harassment, and Problematic Content." In *Enhancing Child Safety and Online Technologies: Final Report of the Internet Safety Technical Task Force to the Multi-State Working Group on Social Networking of State Attorneys*. Internet Safety Technical Task Force, 73–145. Durham, NC: Carolina Academic Press, 2008.

Steeves, Valerie, and Cheryl Webster. "Closing the Barn Door: The Effect of Parental Supervision on Canadian Children's Online Privacy." *Bulletin of Science, Technology & Society* 28 (1) (2008): 4–19.

Watkins, S. Craig. *The Young and the Digital: What the Migration to Social-Network Sites, Games, and Anytime, Anywhere Media Means for Our Future.* Boston: Beacon Press, 2009.

West, Anne, Jane Lewis, and Peter Currie. "Students' Facebook 'Friends': Public and Private Spheres." *Journal of Youth Studies* 12 (6) (2009): 615–627.

Youn, Seounmi. "Determinants of Online Privacy Concern and Its Influence on Privacy Protection Behaviors among Young Adolescents." *Journal of Consumer Affairs* 43, no. 3 (2009): 389–418.

Youn, Seounmi. "Parental Influence and Teens' Attitude toward Online Privacy Protection." *Journal of Consumer Affairs* 42, no 3 (2008): 362–388.

Youn, Seounmi. "Teenagers' Perceptions of Online Privacy and Coping Behaviors: A Risk-Benefit Appraisal Approach." *Journal of Broadcasting & Electronic Media* 49, no. 1 (2005): 86–110.

8 The Growth of Online Universities: How to Solve the Accreditation Dilemma, Protect Students, and Expand Access to Higher Education

Nicholas Bramble and Yite John Lu

Introduction

Advances in telecommunications, Internet access, social networking software, and open educational resources facilitate the education of individuals and communities in numbers that were previously unimaginable. The ease of sharing digital content can alleviate the scarcity of educational resources and access, particularly in underserved areas of the United States and in developing countries. Barriers to educational access have already begun to fall in the face of low-cost distance learning and new forms of information distribution. At this still early stage in the looming transformation of higher education, few have examined how existing laws, educational policies, and institutional stakeholders will determine the course of this restructuring process. In particular, the process of accreditation poses an underrecognized threat—and a possible solution—to the development of newer online educational models. In this chapter, we advocate for the modernization of accreditation. We seek to identify how information regulations and policies governing access to digital educational technologies could better address the specialized needs of both educators and students. And, in the words of President Barack Obama, we also seek to discuss "establishing a new, alternative system of accreditation that would provide pathways for higher education models and colleges to receive federal student aid based on performance and results."[1]

Most fundamentally, students of new online universities and learning communities will suffer if accreditation agencies continue to refrain from providing ongoing, in-depth evaluations of the quality of these initiatives. When novel online learning methods and institutions are left to languish, it can be argued, the goals of accreditation are no longer being met. As of 2014, not one peer-driven online learning institution had gained the most significant form of regional accreditation, whereas a wide and confusing

variety of programmatic and hybrid agencies had evolved to assess the
increasing number of online colleges.[2] However, as more students learn and
take courses through formal and informal online mechanisms, some
measure of more consistent evaluation will be necessary to (1) protect students against for-profit online learning institutions that seek to make
money primarily as diploma mills, (2) save employers the cost of performing their own internal assessments of online educational initiatives, (3)
ensure that new online learning institutions gain access to government
funding for student loans and operational expenses where appropriate, and
(4) enable online institutions to meet measurable quality standards pegged
to the world of low-cost online education rather than to the traditional
comprehensive four-year campus model. A modified, more comprehensive
accreditation system could improve access to knowledge for tens of
millions of currently underserved American students and facilitate the
development of a more competitive and more data-driven educational
marketplace.

Accordingly, this chapter considers how policymakers might design an
accreditation system more attuned to the specific infrastructure and operational features of free or low-cost online educational initiatives. The externalities of failing to recalibrate the accreditation system are significant: a
lack of action here will either force operators of online education programs
to engage in high-cost attempts to comply with an accreditation system
still premised on traditional campus-based education or consign these
innovative learning models to the margins of the conversation about higher
education. The world of digital learning is changing, but we have not yet
seen a corresponding adaptation and reimplementation of the values served
by accreditation. This chapter explores the failure (so far) of current accreditation systems to account for new learning models that make education
available to a radically expanded group of people, and seeks to ensure that
these programs are not stymied in their infancy by outdated accreditation
requirements.

The first section of this chapter describes the current U.S. environment
for online universities, comparing examples of established for-profit and
emerging low-cost universities. The second section gives an overview of
accreditation in the United States and abroad, and explores accreditation
barriers for online universities. Finally, the third section recommends the
implementation of new formal and informal accreditation standards, along
with the establishment of an agency that would track and evaluate the
progress of new online learning models with respect to these accreditation
standards.

1. The Role of Accreditation in Forming the Digital Education Landscape

The rise of online learning institutions can be seen as a reaction to a postsecondary educational market increasingly characterized by three features. First, a large number of flexible part-time students, in the United States and abroad, need to learn certain subjects without necessarily committing to a degree program. Second, traditional campus-based institutions seeking to attract such students are charging higher tuition prices for a broad curriculum, some of which may be irrelevant to the outcomes and certifications these students seek. Third, more fly-by-night institutions are simply trading a degree or license—and perhaps some very basic training—for the student's money. These diploma mills[3] are a logical outgrowth of a world in which existing institutions have failed to meet students' needs, demands, and financial capabilities. Diploma mills motivate the need to validate online learning institutions.

An expanded accreditation program can help solve some of the problems associated with these market features. Through the process of accreditation, a governmental organization or private membership agency seeks to "ensure that education provided by institutions of higher education meets acceptable levels of quality."[4] In most countries, a ministry of education or other governmental agency makes the necessary judgment as to whether institutions of higher education meet certain quality standards. In the United States, however, this process is administered not directly by the government but by private agencies that the government has deemed reliable assessors of quality in education and training. Accreditation is most often accomplished through a lengthy process of ascertaining whether an institution has met certain minimum quality standards, typically concerning the provision of a suitable curriculum, faculty, administration, admissions process, library, and physical infrastructure.

To set the stage for proposals to modernize and streamline the accreditation process, this section begins by exploring how online learning initiatives have grown in number, established partnerships with campus-based universities, and in many cases gained accreditation. It then describes a new set of low-cost online postsecondary learning institutions and outlines their struggles for accreditation. Finally, it discusses the differences in student demographics, faculty ratios, educational content, and teaching methods among campus-based online courses, for-profit online universities, and low-cost or free online learning initiatives. Although these differences may be significant, they help illustrate the different paths that online learning institutions (and initiatives) are taking to achieve financial viability and cultural visibility. The overarching question raised in this section, and answered later in the chapter, is how current examples of emerging low-cost online learning institutions can gain some measure of accreditation and evaluation, as their campus-based and for-profit university peers do, while maintaining their low operating costs.

Existing Online Universities That Have Gained Accreditation and Peer Recognition

Much of the growth in online education can be traced to existing campus-based universities that have built online distance learning programs.[5] In contrast to independent initiatives, many of these programs are already accredited by virtue of their connections to the traditional campus-based university: common faculty, shared library resources, and so on. Such extensions of traditional postsecondary learning institutions typically need not clear the same accreditation hurdles faced by newer and independent education providers.

Stand-alone online universities have also grown in number. The University of Phoenix is the largest online university in North America, as well as the largest private university, with an enrollment of more than 250,000 full-time-equivalent students.[6] The cost of attendance is approximately $395 per course unit (more for upper division credits), or about $48,000 for a bachelor of arts or a bachelor of science degree.[7] In part because the University of Phoenix has features in common with campus-based community colleges and universities, accreditation of the university's degree programs has proceeded in a largely traditional manner. The University of Phoenix system has obtained regional accreditation (the gold standard of accreditation) for more than thirty years.[8] Thus, the University of Phoenix is positioned to function as a full-fledged substitute for traditional campus-based universities rather than as a complementary institution.

StraighterLine, a lower-cost alternative, provides a less typical example of a for-profit online university: it focuses on individual courses instead of degrees, and gains recognition for these courses in an informal manner through partnerships with accredited campus-based universities.[9] StraighterLine, which itself is not accredited, offers a range of freshman-equivalent courses, such as introductory math, economics, and English,[10] and encourages its students to finish their degrees at other, more established universities. This model is intended to facilitate a mutually beneficial relationship with partnership colleges—StraighterLine does not compete with campus-based colleges for the entirety of a student's higher education, and partnership colleges acquire new students without needing to fund their own distance learning or recruitment programs. Once a StraighterLine student goes through this pipeline and enrolls at an accredited partner college, that accredited college will award course credit for completion of StraighterLine courses.

Yet students at one college associated with StraighterLine organized a protest, claiming that the accreditation partnerships "cheapen the quality and value of a degree" by allowing anyone to gain Fort Hays State University credit after taking StraighterLine online courses.[11] In the wake of the protest, and after a regional accreditor questioned the appropriateness of the partnerships, two partner colleges ended their involvement with StraighterLine. This example of student-based resistance underscores the difficulty that upstart education models will face. They must convince not just employers and educators but also students that increased course portability and low-cost supplements represent an opportunity rather than a threat.

Yet together, and along with a bevy of both for-profit models such as Minerva[12] and nonprofit or government-funded models such as Western Governors University and the Open University, these institutions are putting pressure on traditional education infrastructure, and on the accreditation system upholding that infrastructure.

The Uphill Struggle Faced by Low-Tuition or Tuition-Free Providers of Online Higher Education

Compared to the more traditional online universities listed above, the innovations of peer-to-peer learning in higher education are largely in the areas of scalability and modularity. Peer-driven learning models are highly scalable in the sense that, theoretically, they place no limit on the number of students who can be involved in higher education. Like Wikipedia,[13] these schools can leverage mass contributions and utilize peer production models (in terms of both content and student evaluations), eliminate expensive overhead, and radically expand student-to-faculty ratios. Peer-driven models can exploit the principle of modularity—the idea that components within a given architecture can be designed independently of one another but still work together.[14] They can do this by unbundling courseware and individual learning modules from larger degree programs, and from university accreditation and oversight structures. A modular educational system would enable students to export and import educational records, course credit, and other markers of learning progress to and from learning institutions. The challenge, of course, is to figure out how to reassemble these modules into a meaningful expression of a given student's experience and skills.[15]

Peer-driven structures expose students to a large variety of points of view and allow them to build on each other's knowledge on a scale that faculty-led classroom discussions are unlikely to achieve. The peer-to-peer learning model is typically implemented as a community-based structure in which networks of students teach and learn from each other through discussion forums and other collaborative online spaces. In the same vein as other peer networks, this learning model can enable improvements in capacity, low costs of ownership, and self-organization and decentralized coordination of limited resources. Network contributors can create and manage new elements of a knowledge system without needing to run each modification through a centralized bureaucratic structure.

For example, if it turns out that students have a strong need to learn a new programming language, students and other contributors can put together a quick plan of attack to learn that language without obtaining university-level approval. Of course, the development of new courses need not be peer-driven; it can also be motivated by an individual's desire to share and sell particular expertise. As Kevin Carey points out, "Right now, only organizations that provide whole degree programs can receive aid. But what if you want to specialize and provide nothing other than the world's greatest Linear Algebra class at a super-affordable price?"[16]

Open educational resources and other digital learning assets can also be distributed and adjusted to provide local benefits without restricting the ability of others to enjoy these benefits.[17] And the assessment method at these learning institutions can be peer-driven as well; as with the correspondence model of education, instructors do not assist students unless specifically requested. Instead, students are encouraged to use existing online sources (including, in some cases, their own peers) as resources. However, the differences that make these learning networks more flexible and more scalable can also pose a significant problem for purposes of accreditation.

For example, University of the People is a tuition-free online university that offers associate's and bachelor's degrees in business administration and computer science. After several years of seeking to obtain accreditation, the university obtained accreditation for these programs from a national group called the Distance Education and Training Council.[18] The university uses active and retired professors—some paid, mostly volunteers—along with librarians, graduate students, and professionals to develop the course programs, facilitate learning, evaluate curricula, and oversee assessments.[19] Students within a given course are divided into classes of about twenty people, with whom they work to learn course material. Students are expected to comply with instructions in the course syllabus and are required to engage in self-guided discussion forums by posting responses to questions and comments issued in advance by the course instructor—and to pass a final exam.[20] Students pay a one-time application fee (ranging from $10 to $50) and an exam administration fee of $100 per exam, with scholarships available.[21]

Another example of a peer-driven provider of higher education is Peer 2 Peer University (P2PU), which describes itself as an "open education project that organizes learning outside of institutional walls and gives learners recognition for their achievements."[22] P2PU offers courses in a variety of subjects, including finance, computer programming, and design of educational materials.[23] The course material is organized, designed, and taught by volunteers, who may or may not be experts in the field. Perhaps the most notable aspect of P2PU is its educational assessment process, which is entirely peer-driven. P2PU's founders compare its assessment process to the feedback mechanisms used in open-source software communities, where "the participants in a learning group provide feedback to each other, reviewing and improving each other's work."[24] Students taking P2PU courses "will assess each other's work" and receive an online certificate from the university upon completion of each course.[25]

This brief overview of online universities and newer peer-driven postsecondary learning initiatives helps illustrate operational differences between the two models, and demonstrates how the two models might serve different student populations, in terms of both size and demographics. This comparison sets the stage for a more detailed discussion of accreditation of these new learning models.

2. Continuing Relevance of Accreditation to the Development of Pathways for Online Learning Models

This section develops the argument that a comprehensive and empirical accreditation system must take stock of differences in faculty, learning methods, assessment methods, and types of educational content between traditional online universities and peer-driven universities. Such a system should be inclusive of new educational models while clearly labeling the potential challenges and shortcoming of those models.

It is important to make clear why accreditation is still relevant to an inquiry into the future of online universities and higher learning. After all, one might ask, if the goal of higher education is self-development and skill acquisition, and these new online initiatives do an adequate job of meeting this goal, then why is it necessary to gain the approval of an accreditation agency? Might it even be helpful to these innovative new models to wall them off from credit-rating agencies, standard-setting intermediaries, and other barriers to entry that might hinder ambitious new initiatives?

The first part of this section addresses these questions at a high level, by describing the purposes of accreditation and the relevance of these purposes as education extends beyond the synchronous campus-based model. We then examine several different domestic and international accreditation systems and the extent to which these systems' requirements are amenable to low-cost and tuition-free online education models.

Is Accreditation Necessary for the Low-Cost Online University?

For a number of reasons, accreditation is likely a necessary step if low-cost online universities are to have a substantial impact on student welfare and the existing structures of higher education. The U.S. Department of Education warns that "unaccredited institutions are not reviewed against a set of standards to determine the quality of their education and training."[26] Accreditation, in whatever form it is granted, provides both a stamp of approval and a standardized set of metrics that satisfies both employers and students by limiting the costs of weighing the comparative merit of schools.

First, employers undoubtedly will be interested in a job applicant's educational history to see whether the applicant is qualified for the position. Accreditation provides quick and simple information as to whether the applicant's educational institution meets basic minimum standards of quality. Accreditation thus partially solves a collective action problem wherein employers are separately unwilling and unable to certify the qualifications of prospective employees; it allows employers to outsource the task of certification to universities and to the accreditation agencies that police quality standards. As a standard-setting process, accreditation sets forth a level metric on which a large group of entities can be categorized, rated, and compared.

This collective-action problem also holds true for universities determining whether or not to accept prior degrees or transfer credits from other institutions. A graduate program or a university accepting transfer students would, like an employer, tend to treat the question of accreditation as a simple heuristic for determining which students and which transfer credits to accept. The accreditation heuristic relieves employers and universities of the burden of performing their own subjective background research into the comparative merits and quality standards of established versus unestablished institutions.

Of course, accreditation is not a perfect predictor of credit-transferability. Even at the regionally accredited University of Phoenix, many students still clamor for the ability to transfer credit to degree programs at more traditional universities.[27] Such tensions indicate that accreditation does not automatically result in a university's full recognition by the surrounding academic community, particularly when the university in question is operating on a new business and academic model. At the same time, accreditation clearly enables a university to link up with existing academic and employment infrastructure, and then enter into negotiations over credit transferability. Absent the denominator of accreditation, such negotiations become far more difficult for new educational initiatives.

Second, beyond its importance to employers, accreditation is an important signal of educational quality to students. Prospective students may lack the resources or understanding necessary to perform a detailed inquiry into the quality of a university or program. This is particularly true of online universities without a central physical campus, where the primary information available to prospective students is what institutions decide to promote on their (often fairly undifferentiated) websites. Secondary information on these institutions tends to emerge from discussion boards, user review communities, and occasional journalistic surveys and directories of online universities.[28] Students need independent guidance on the quality of an institution before they invest significant time and effort pursuing their studies there; a well-functioning accreditation agency that reviews online universities would help meet this need.

It is worthwhile to pause here on the problem of false credentials—a problem that has become increasingly common in postsecondary education and is exemplified by the rise of unaccredited and fraudulent educational institutions that grant a degree to all applicants in exchange for payment, but offer little (if any) actual education. The rise of these diploma mills both justifies and challenges the accreditation system. On the one hand, it becomes even more important for an impartial agency to police the boundary between authentic and fraudulent postsecondary institutions. On the other hand, the rise of diploma mills is symptomatic of the radical expansion of educational availability, and the fact that it has become increasingly difficult for regional accreditation agencies to monitor every last corner of the online educational world for falsity and fraud and to provide effective disclosures at the right times to students and employers.

Finally, accreditation is important for financial and organizational sustainability. Most importantly in this regard, accreditation identifies institutions as worthy of public and private investment.[29] For example, an

institution must be accredited to receive federal funding in the United
States, and accreditation is often a prerequisite for receiving state funding
as well.[30] Furthermore, students cannot receive government financial aid in
the United States unless the institution they attend is accredited; the same
is true for many other countries.[31] Recognizing this fact, President Obama
recently called on Congress to

consider value, affordability, and student outcomes in making determinations about
which colleges and universities receive access to federal student aid, either by incorporating measures of value and affordability into the existing accreditation system;
or by establishing a new, alternative system of accreditation that would provide
pathways for higher education models and colleges to receive federal student aid
based on performance and results.[32]

Finally, accreditation can help populate and organize an educational institution. Peer-driven learning models, in particular, require a critical mass of
participants to be self-sustaining.[33] Accreditation can drive students and
volunteers to sign up for a peer-to-peer education model, thereby rendering
it more sustainable, and promoting the institution in the eyes of other
accreditors and education policymakers.

Why Seek U.S. Accreditation?

In the United States, accreditation is a complex and not entirely coherent
process controlled by a variety of national and regional stakeholders who
impose different quality standards in the course of assessing postsecondary
institutions.[34] Nonetheless, gaining accreditation in the United States
signals the reputational quality of an institution of higher education.[35] For
a postsecondary online institution aiming to draw in a global learning community, obtaining this mark of approval from a regional or national accreditor is particularly significant.

The U.S. Department of Education does not accredit educational institutions. Instead, the Secretary of Education publishes a list of private recognized accreditation agencies, regional or national in scope, that conduct
"non-governmental, peer evaluation of educational institutions and programs" to determine if an institution meets basic operational quality standards.[36] Despite the lack of direct government oversight, once an institution
is accredited, the federal government provides that institution with all the
growth-oriented benefits of accreditation, including financial aid for its students.[37] Thus accreditation can be crucial to the long-term growth and sustainability of an institution.

Accreditation agencies in the United States are either regional or national
in scope. Six accreditation agencies have the authority to accredit universities in separate regions of the country;[38] these regional agencies are

recognized to confer the highest level of accreditation.[39] Their funding comes primarily from the dues and accreditation fees paid by institutions and programs that either have been accredited or are seeking accreditation.[40] In contrast, national accreditation agencies are a much newer phenomenon and typically specialize in discrete segments of the higher education industry, such as healthcare or midwifery degree programs. The Department of Education recognizes five general (i.e., nonspecialized) national accreditation agencies, including the Distance Education and Training Council (DETC).[41] The DETC is particularly important for accrediting peer-driven online learning institutions due to its specialty in accreditation of distance learning, its long history in evaluating correspondence learning programs, and its perceived openness to innovative learning models.[42]

Regional accreditors recognize that "new providers, often lacking traditional institutional hallmarks ... [are] raising fresh questions as to the essential nature and content of an educational experience and the resources required to support it."[43] However, many accreditation values, policies, and practices were designed with traditional instructor-led campus-based education in mind.[44] As a result, the quality review process typically involves peer review and a number of site-based tasks including "visiting campuses, examining classrooms, touring facilities, and, in general, scrutinizing the resources and capacity of an academic community, especially the teaching and learning environment."[45]

Established regional accreditation agencies have resolved to sustain certain values—many of which are based in the experiences of those traditional universities. Several of these requirements relevant or troublesome to peer-driven online models:

1. education is best experienced within a community of learning where competent professionals are actively and cooperatively involved with creating, providing, and improving the instructional program;
2. learning is dynamic and interactive, regardless of the setting in which it occurs;
3. instructional programs leading to degrees having integrity are organized around substantive and coherent curricula which define expected learning outcomes;
4. institutions accept the obligation to address student needs related to, and to provide the resources necessary for, their academic success;
5. institutions are responsible for the education provided in their name;
6. institutions undertake the assessment and improvement of their quality, giving particular emphasis to student learning;
7. institutions voluntarily subject themselves to peer review.[46]

From this list of requirements, it becomes clear that several characteristics of online peer-driven learning institutions will be problematic as these institutions pursue accreditation. Their students have little face-to-face contact with instructors, and the institutions lack a local presence in most cases. The increased use of open education resources under the peer-driven model creates a degree of separation between curriculum design and delivery: instructors rely on resources and modules produced by other people not responsible to the instructors, and sometimes must tailor their curricula to those resources, rather than tailoring resources to their curricula. Open resources may be localizable to a given student's language and educational needs, but higher student-to-faculty ratios with peer-driven models eliminate the most common mechanism for individualized learning—an attentive and accessible faculty member. Peer models also bring about a large separation in time between when a student asks a question and a faculty member is able to answer that question (and vice versa). Some current peer-driven models have starkly lower levels of traditional student services such as advising, mentoring, and library services, although the availability of these services varies from institution to institution. And finally, the prevalence of volunteer faculty at some online learning institutions raises question of faculty commitment and the sustainability of teaching quality.

In the third section below, we will discuss how online learning institutions and accrediting agencies alike can move away from some of these more inflexible rules, and instead develop mission-driven values and standards to assess the quality of these new forms of institutions.

Why Seek Accreditation Internationally?

If the goal of peer-driven online postsecondary learning institutions is to provide opportunities for higher education for those who otherwise do not have access, then many students of these institutions will come from countries other than the United States. Thus, peer-driven institutions and education policymakers interested in promoting such universities should not restrict their accreditation focus solely to the United States.

Different countries are at different stages of development in relation to their quality review processes.[47] In some countries, such as the United Kingdom and Australia, changes to the higher education system (including a shift from an elite to a mass system and the ending of a binary distinction between universities and polytechnics) are introducing or altering external review processes that necessarily encompass distance education programs.[48] And China will likely increasingly look to online higher education models as a means to alleviate growing socioeconomic inequalities between wealthy and poorer citizens.[49]

Peer-driven learning institutions seeking to educate students in another country must navigate the different accreditation procedures for distance education within each country. They must also ensure that qualifications earned in one country are recognized for academic and professional uses in other countries. International recognition of accreditation is especially relevant for online universities because of public concerns about the validity of distance learning providers, false claims of accreditation, fraudulent degree certificates, and plagiarism by students. In some countries, national centers provide advice or have the power to decide on the comparability of qualifications.[50] Thus it is likely that peer-driven universities will need to develop layered accreditation strategies depending on the scope of the credential they seek to award, and tailor their educational strategies to different geographical, cultural, historical, and technological contexts.

3. Proposal: Adaptation of Accreditation Methodologies and Development of a Framework for Measuring Learning Progress

Beyond implementing strategies to bring new higher education models within the current ambit of regional accreditation standards, there are changes that policymakers and accreditors themselves can make to bring new online institutions into the fold, rather than leaving them to look for recognition from alternative sources or potentially fraudulent agencies. Most fundamentally, instead of tailoring the accreditation process toward an all-or-nothing version of high-prestige accreditation, an agency with the reputation of one of the regional accreditors could utilize a more scalar model—giving an accreditation score on a scale of 1 to 10 based on granular metrics rather than a binary up-or-down vote, for instance. An agency could also offer a lower-prestige certification for new education models that necessarily have different characteristics and appeal to a different student population than campus-based universities. Policymakers, in turn, might seek to adjust governmental aid policies so that online educational institutions receive a portion of state funding proportional to their score on a battery of accreditation tests and measures of student skills.

The sustainability of any new educational model, after all, depends on at least a modicum of cultural and governmental recognition. Without clear rules and criteria or attentive analysis and comparison of different universities, the marketplace for new online education models will remain confusing to customers, and potentially detrimental to access to education. Policymakers would be well-advised to consider the importance of providing students (and educators alike) with the kind of clear and detailed information that is needed to decide how and where to devote one's educational

hopes and efforts. In a world of increasingly detailed consumer information, accreditation agencies can best serve the public interest by recognizing the variety of motivations and economic capabilities of students seeking
an education, rather than by biasing review methodologies and evaluation
standards toward a single institutional ideal. In practice, accreditors can act
on this intuition by making available detailed information and ratings
about institutions and initiatives which, while not fitting the traditional
educational mold, offer hope for the radical expansion of educational availability. Even as the function of policing fraudulent diploma mills rises in
importance, accreditation agencies should recognize a concomitant need to
review and compare new models, and offer these initiatives a path toward
legitimization instead of leaving them to fend for themselves in an unregu-
lated market.

In the end, it is likely that accreditation of new online educational institutions will be accomplished not solely on a country-by-country basis, but
instead through some combination of international and distance-learning
accrediting organizations, company and industry certifications and skill
tests, institutional affiliations (including resource partnerships with existing universities), and other informal ex post recognitions of merit. It would
be helpful to prospective students of these institutions to have an objective
and data-driven means of tracking a new university's progress through
these various hurdles. Accordingly, a regional, national, or international
accreditation agency targeted toward online learning models might be
better off acting as a meta-evaluator of how well such institutions are doing
on the metrics described above.

Furthermore, the structure of the educational world is changing rapidly
as students begin to take courses at a variety of institutions rather than at
just one stable and centralized campus. The future of education will likely
be a conversation between formal and informal accreditation models,
between traditional campus-based universities and open/closed online
learning models, and between institutionally bundled and a la carte educational content. As students combine credit for courses into a master study
plan or educational record, roughly analogous to an electronic health
record, a variety of questions arise concerning credit portability, curricular
coherence, and course modularity, as well as data ownership and data
privacy. A new accreditation agency would be well-positioned to begin to
answer the question of how to design an accreditation system that allows
people to combine courses from many sources into a useful and verifiable
cross-platform degree. Such an agency might be more interested in accrediting a student's learning progress than in accrediting the particular institutions, websites, or apps at which this learning has taken place.

As governmental bodies recognize and accredit new models of formal and informal education, they, too, face challenging questions as to how to allocate financial aid to these institutions and how to distribute necessary educational resources to the students of such institutions. Accreditation status will likely remain a useful mechanism in determining how governmental funds should be distributed. But governments should not consign themselves to allocating funding on a purely institutional basis; they can also put that funding toward measurable student outcomes and to specific courses and certification programs, particularly in areas that currently lack a strong supply of qualified graduates.

Businesses, too, will be challenged by the rise of piecemeal and idiosyncratic online learning initiatives. Rather than filtering based on university degree, a company with specific hiring needs might offer a skill-based test to applicants, thus displacing the value of the diploma or credential itself and focusing on the skills actually learned during the educational process. As alternative education tools become more prominent, companies might eventually band together and develop an industry-wide test of post-college skills.

In the coming years, a variety of stakeholders in the educational system will likely demand a more flexible approach to the metrics by which we have traditionally measured postsecondary learning progress. The proposal above seeks to develop a standardized framework within which that demand can be satisfied.

Conclusion

While it is still unclear what the future of higher education will look like, this chapter has argued that the current formalistic, all-or-nothing accreditation model is ill-suited to address new and technologically innovative online learning models. It is likely that the stress points of the current education system—the lack of access to education for hundreds of millions of otherwise qualified students, evolving business demands, proliferation of diploma mills, low access to postsecondary education in developing countries, and students' and parents' desire to lower university costs without decreasing quality—will lead to changes in formal accreditation policies, and increased reliance on informal mechanisms of quality assurance. The emergence of new online learning models is a promising development in the direction of addressing these stress points. Rather than letting this new educational ecosystem be weakened by inflexible accreditation traditions, or haphazardly applying outdated metrics to these new learning models, we must recognize "the obligations which these possibilities impose"[51] and begin to develop new methodologies for tracking educational progress.

Notes

1. Barack Obama, "The President's Plan for a Strong Middle Class and a Strong America," White House, February 12, 2013, http://www.whitehouse.gov/sites/default/files/uploads/sotu_2013_blueprint_embargo.pdf.

2. See http://www.guidetoonlineschools.com/online-schools (listing more than five hundred schools that offered online degrees with some form of accreditation).

3. Congress has defined a diploma mill as an entity that offers "degrees, diplomas, or certificates, that may be used to represent to the general public that the individual … has completed a program of postsecondary education or training," "requires … little or no education or coursework to obtain such degree, diploma, or certificate" and "lacks accreditation by an accrediting agency." U.S. Congress, Higher Education Opportunity Act, Pub. L. No. 110–315 (2008), codified at 20 U.S.C. § 1003(5).

4. See U.S. Department of Education, "Accreditation in the United States—Overview," http://www.ed.gov/admins/finaid/accred/accreditation.html#Overview.

5. See I. Elaine Allen and Jeff Seaman, "Class Differences: Online Education in the United States, 2010," Babson Survey Research Group and the Sloan Consortium, 2010.

6. See   http://www.marketwatch.com/story/apollo-group-fourth-quarter-profit-tumbles-71-2013-10-22.

7. This estimate is based on a student obtaining the required 120 credits for a four-year degree at an average of $400 per credit.

8. In 1978, the University of Phoenix joined the North Central Association of Colleges and Schools, one of six regional accreditation groups in the United States. See http://www.ncahlc.org.

9. These partner colleges include Charter Oak State College, Fort Hays State University, Lake City Community College, and Potomac College (http://www.straighterline.com/how-it-works/credit-transfer). Taking courses at StraighterLine costs $99 per month (for a general membership) and an additional $49 for each course. StraighterLine, "Membership Pricing of Our Online Courses," n.d., http://www.straighterline.com/how-it-works/how-much-does-it-cost.

10. See Kevin Carey, "College for $99 a Month," *Washington Monthly*, September 2009. http://www.washingtonmonthly.com/college_guide/feature/college_for_99_a_month.php.

11. Ibid.

12. See Graham Wood, "The Future of College?," *Atlantic*, August 2014, http://www .theatlantic.com/features/archive/2014/08/the-future-of-college/375071.

13. Wikipedia quickly amassed a high number of encyclopedia entries—roughly equal in quality to those of *Encyclopaedia Britannica*—in part as a result of having an exponentially larger number of contributors who could coordinate the creation and management of new entries without needing to run each step through a centralized bureaucratic structure. See Jim Giles, "Internet Encyclopaedias Go Head to Head," *Nature* 438 (December 15, 2005): 900.

14. See Barbara van Schewick, *Internet Architecture and Innovation* (Cambridge, MA: MIT Press, 2012), 38.

15. For a more detailed discussion of how accreditation can be helpful in assembling a meaningful description of a student's skills, see part 2 below.

16. Kevin Carey, "President Obama's Bold Plan to Reshape American Higher Education," The Chronicle for Higher Education, February 13, 2013, http://chronicle.com/ blogs/conversation/2013/02/13/obamas-bold-plan-to-reshape-american-higher -education.

17. See Organisation for Economic Co-operation and Development, *Giving Knowledge for Free: The Emergence of Open Educational Resources,* OECD, Centre for Educational Research and Innovation, 2007, 11, http://www.oecd.org/edu/ceri/giving knowledgeforfreetheemergenceofopeneducationalresources.htm. Examples of open educational resources include courses, content modules, software tools (such as search tools and learning management systems), and resources for implementation of open learning (such as free and open intellectual property licenses and design principles for the spread of open content).

18. Shai Reshef, founder, University of the People, interviews, September 22, 2009, and July 13, 2010. See Tamar Lewin, "Free Online University Receives Accreditation, in Time for Graduating Class of 7," *New York Times,* February, 13, 2014, ttp://www .nytimes.com/2014/02/14/education/free-online-university-receives-accreditation -in-time-for-graduating-class-of-7.html.

19. Lewin, "Free Online University Receives Accreditation."

20. Ibid. See also Marc Parry, "New Tuition-Free 'University of the People' Tries to Democratize Higher Ed," *Chronicle of Higher Education,* August 26, 2009, http:// chronicle.com/blogPost/New-Tuition-Free-University/7831.

21. See Lewin, "Free Online University Receives Accreditation."

22. See the website for Peer 2 Peer University at http://p2pu.org.

23. See Peer 2 Peer University, "Courses," 2015, http://p2pu.org/course/list.

24. Peer 2 Peer University, "About P2PU," 2015, http://p2pu.org/About-P2PU.

25. Ibid.

26. U.S. Department of Education, "Diploma Mills and Accreditation—Accreditation," October 15, 2009, http://www2.ed.gov/students/prep/college/diplomamills/accreditation.html.

27. A radio report noted that "one of the biggest complaints students had was that [University of Phoenix] counselors misled them about credits." NPR, "Allegations against U. of Phoenix Persist," *Marketplace*, November 3, 2009, http://www.marketplace.org/topics/life/allegations-against-u-phoenix-persist. A University of Phoenix counselor who participated in this report was quoted as saying that "one of the things that we were told to do was, you say, 'we are regionally accredited, which means they're transferable anywhere,' which isn't true. They're eligible for transferability." The University of Phoenix responded by calling the report an "imbalanced, subjective, salacious story" (http://www.phoenix.edu/about_us/media-center/fact-checker/2009/11/university-of-phoenix-responds-to-npr-syndicated-marketplace-report.html).

28. See, for example, "Schools with Undergraduate Distance Learning Programs," *U.S. News and World Report*, Education Rankings and Advice, 2015, http://www.usnews.com/directories/online-education/main/index_html/level+u.

29. See U.S. Department of Education, "Guide to the Accrediting Agency Recognition Process," February 2010, http://www.chea.org/pdf/GUIDE%20to%20Accred%20%20Agency%20Recog%20DRAFT%20FEBRUARY%2016%202010.pdf.

30. See William A. Kaplin and Barbara Lee, *The Law of Higher Education,* 5th ed. (San Francisco: Jossey-Bass, 2014), 1531–1532.

31. The extent of government involvement in education reflects the notion that education is not merely about self-development, and that the state has taken an interest in promoting informed and enlightened citizens.

32. Obama, "The President's Plan for a Strong Middle Class and a Strong America."

33. The University of the People requires a critical mass of 15,000 students to be self-sustaining. Reshef, interview by phone, September 22, 2009, and July 13, 2010.

34. See California Postsecondary Education Commission, "Public Policy Accreditation & State Approval in California," 1984, 62.

35. See U.S. Court of Appeals, District of Columbia Circuit, Marjorie Webster Jr. College, Inc. v. Middle States Ass'n of Colleges, 302 F. Supp. 459, 471 (D.D.C. 1969) ("Accreditation has become the symbol of academic acceptability, and many states measure the educational excellence of their public institutions by the standards of the regional associations").

36. See U.S. Department of Education, "Accreditation in the U.S.," August 25, 2003, http://www2.ed.gov/admins/finaid/accred/accredus.html.

37. See U.S. Congress, Title IV of the Higher Education Act of 1965, Pub. L. No. 89–329, 79 Stat. 1219, Section 1232. Title IV assists students by supporting undergraduate scholarships, loans with reduced interest rates, and work-study programs.

38. See U.S. Court of Appeals, Ninth Circuit, Daghlian v. DeVry University, Inc., 582 F. Supp. 2d 1231, 1237–37 (C.D. Cal. 2007) (describing the "six nongovernmental regional accrediting agencies that operate independently in six different geographic regions"). These regional accreditation agencies include the Middle States Association of Colleges and Schools, New England Association of Schools and Colleges, North Central Association of Colleges and Schools, Northwest Association of Accredited Schools, Western Association of Schools and Colleges, and Southern Association of Colleges and Schools.

39. For instance, regionally accredited institutions may accept transfer credits from other regionally accredited institutions but typically refuse to accept transfer credit from institutions accredited only by national agencies.

40. Judith S. Eaton, "An Overview of U.S. Accreditation," Council for Higher Education Accreditation, 2011, 6, http://chea.org/pdf/Overview%20of%20US%20Accreditation%2003.2011.pdf.

41. U.S. Department of Education, "Regional and National Institutional Accrediting Agencies," http://www2.ed.gov/admins/finaid/accred/accreditation_pg6.html.

42. Mike Lambert, Executive Director, Distance Education and Training Council, interview by phone, November 5, 2009.

43. See Middle States Commission on Higher Education, "Distance Learning Programs: Interregional Guidelines for Electronically Offered Degree and Certificate Programs," 2002, https://www.msche.org/publications/Guidelines-for-the-Evaluation-of-Distance-Education-Programs.pdf.

44. Judith S. Eaton, *Maintaining the Delicate Balance: Distance Learning, Higher Education Accreditation, and the Politics of Self-Regulation* (Washington, DC: American Council on Education, 2002).

45. See Robin Middlehurst and Steve Woodfield, "International Quality Review and Distance Learning: Lessons from Five Countries," Council for Higher Education Accreditation, December 2004, 19, http://www.chea.org/pdf/CHEA_OP_Jan05.pdf.

46. See North Central Association Higher Learning Commission, "Statement of Commitment by the Regional Accrediting Commissions (CRAC) for the Evaluation of Electronically Offered Degree and Certificate Programs," n.d., http://www.niu.edu/assessment/manual/_docs/Best%20Practices.pdf; idem, "Best Practices for Electronically Offered Degree and Certificate Programs" (listing and discussing a series of best practices developed by regional accreditors "in response to the emergence of technologically mediated instruction offered at a distance as an important component of higher education"), n.d., http://www.ncahlc.org/download/Best_Pract_DEd.pdf.

47. Robin Middlehurst and Carolyn Campbell, *Quality Assurance and Borderless Higher Education: Finding Pathways through the Maze* (London: Observatory on Borderless Higher Education, 2003).

48. Middlehurst and Woodfield, 16–17.

49. Fengshou Sun and Armando Barrientos, "The Equity Challenge in China's Higher Education Finance Policy," *Higher Education Policy* 22 (2009): 191.

50. Within the European Union, all countries have National Academic Recognition Centers (NARICs), although some exercise only advisory capacity. Middlehurst and Woodfield.

51. John Dewey, "My Pedagogic Creed," 1897, http://dewey.pragmatism.org/creed.

Bibliography

Allen, I. Elaine, and Jeff Seaman. "Class Differences: Online Education in the United States, 2010." Babson Survey Research Group and the Sloan Consortium, 2010. http://files.eric.ed.gov/fulltext/ED529952.pdf.

California Postsecondary Education Commission. "Public Policy Accreditation and State Approval in California." 1984.

Carey, Kevin. "College for $99 a Month." *Washington Monthly*, September 2009. http://www.washingtonmonthly.com/college_guide/feature/college_for_99_a_month.php.

Carey, Kevin. "President Obama's Bold Plan to Reshape American Higher Education," *The Chronicle of Higher Education*, February 13, 2013, http://chronicle.com/blogs/conversation/2013/02/13/obamas-bold-plan-to-reshape-american-higher-education.

Dewey, John. "My Pedagogic Creed." 1897. http://dewey.pragmatism.org/creed.

Eaton, Judith S. *Maintaining the Delicate Balance: Distance Learning, Higher Education Accreditation, and the Politics of Self-Regulation*. Washington, DC: American Council on Education, 2002.

Eaton, Judith S. "An Overview of U.S. Accreditation." Council for Higher Education Accreditation, 2011. http://chea.org/pdf/Overview%20of%20US%20Accreditation%2003.2011.pdf.

Elman, Sandra E. "Academic Freedom and Regional Accreditation: Guarantors of Quality in the Academy." *New Directions for Higher Education* 88 (1994):89.

Giles, Jim. "Internet Encyclopaedias Go Head to Head." *Nature* 438 (December 15, 2005): 900–901.

Kaplin, William A., and Barbara Lee. *The Law of Higher Education*, 5th ed. San Francisco: Jossey-Bass, 2014.

Lewin, Tamar. "Free Online University Receives Accreditation, in Time for Graduating Class of 7." *New York Times,* February, 13, 2014. http://www.nytimes.com/2014/02/14/education/free-online-university-receives-accreditation-in-time-for-graduating-class-of-7.html.

Middle States Commission on Higher Education. "Distance Learning Programs: Interregional Guidelines for Electronically Offered Degree and Certificate Programs," 2002. https://www.msche.org/publications/Guidelines-for-the-Evaluation-of-Distance-Education-Programs.pdf.

Middlehurst, Robin, and Carolyn Campbell. *Quality Assurance and Borderless Higher Education: Finding Pathways through the Maze.* London: Observatory on Borderless Higher Education, 2003.

Middlehurst, Robin, and Steve Woodfield. "International Quality Review and Distance Learning: Lessons from Five Countries." Council for Higher Education Accreditation, December 2004. http://www.chea.org/pdf/CHEA_OP_Jan05.pdf.

NPR. "Allegations against U. of Phoenix Persist." *Marketplace,* November 3, 2009. http://www.marketplace.org/topics/life/allegations-against-u-phoenix-persist.

North Central Association Higher Learning Commission. "Statement of Commitment by the Regional Accrediting Commissions (CRAC) for the Evaluation of Electronically Offered Degree and Certificate Programs." n.d. http://www.niu.edu/assessment/manual/_docs/Statement%20of%20Commitment.pdf.

North Central Association Higher Learning Commission. "Best Practices for Electronically Offered Degree and Certificate Programs." n.d. http://www.aaup.org/NR/rdonlyres/BBA85B72-20E9-4F62-B8B5-CDFF03CD8A53/0/WICHEDOC.PDF.

Obama, Barack. "The President's Plan for a Strong Middle Class and a Strong America." White House, February 12, 2013. http://www.whitehouse.gov/sites/default/files/uploads/sotu_2013_blueprint_embargo.pdf.

Organisation for Economic Co-operation and Development. *Giving Knowledge for Free: The Emergence of Open Educational Resources.* OECD, Centre for Educational Research and Innovation, 2007. http://www.oecd.org/edu/ceri/givingknowledgefor freetheemergenceofopeneducationalresources.htm.

Parry, Marc. "New Tuition-Free 'University of the People' Tries to Democratize Higher Ed." *Chronicle of Higher Education,* August 26, 2009. http://chronicle.com/blogPost/New-Tuition-Free-University/7831.

Peer 2 Peer University. "Courses." http://p2pu.org/course/list.

Peer 2 Peer University. "About P2PU." http://p2pu.org/About-P2PU.

"Schools with Undergraduate Distance Learning Programs." *U.S. News and World Report,* Education Rankings and Advice, 2012. http://www.usnews.com/directories/online-education/main/index_html/level+u .

StraighterLine. "FAQs," n.d., http://www.straighterline.com/faq.

StraighterLine. "Membership Pricing of Our Online Courses," n.d. http://www
.straighterline.com/how-it-works/how-much-does-it-cost.

Sun, Fengshou, and Armando Barrientos. "The Equity Challenge in China's Higher
Education Finance Policy." *Higher Education Policy* 22 (2009): 191–207.

U.S Congress. Title IV of the Higher Education Act of 1965, Pub. L. No. 89–329
(1965).

U.S. Congress. Higher Education Opportunity Act, Pub. L. No. 110–315 (2008).

U.S. Court of Appeals, District of Columbia Circuit. *Marjorie Webster Jr. College, Inc. v.
Middle States Ass'n of Colleges*, 302 F. Supp. 459, 471 (D.D.C. 1969).

U.S. Court of Appeals, Ninth Circuit. *Daghlian v. DeVry University, Inc.*, 582 F. Supp.
2d 1231, 1237–37 (C.D. Cal. 2007).

U.S. Department of Education. "Accreditation in the United States: Overview
of Accreditation." June 12, 2015. http://www.ed.gov/admins/finaid/accred/
accreditation.html#Overview.

U.S. Department of Education. "Accreditation in the U.S." August 25, 2003. http://
www2.ed.gov/admins/finaid/accred/accredus.html.

U.S. Department of Education. "Diploma Mills and Accreditation—Accreditation."
October 15, 2009. http://www2.ed.gov/students/prep/college/diplomamills/
accreditation.html.

U.S. Department of Education. "Guide to the Accrediting Agency Recognition Process." 2011. http://www.chea.org/pdf/GUIDE%20to%20Accred%20%20Agency%20
Recog%20DRAFT%20FEBRUARY%2016%202010.pdf.

U.S. Department of Education, Office of Postsecondary Education. "Database of
Accredited Postsecondary Institutions and Programs." n.d. http://ope.ed.gov/
accreditation.

U.S. Department of Education. "Regional and National Institutional Accrediting
Agencies." 2012. http://www2.ed.gov/admins/finaid/accred/accreditation_pg6.html.

van Schewick, Barbara. *Internet Architecture and Innovation*. Cambridge, MA: MIT
Press, 2012.

Wood, Graham. "The Future of College?" *Atlantic*, August 2014. http://www
.theatlantic.com/features/archive/2014/08/the-future-of-college/375071.

9 Copyright Reform and Educational Progress

Nicholas Bramble

Introduction

Students craft, share, transform, and distribute complex creative works, such as films, literary adaptations, musical reinterpretations, websites, computer software, and mobile applications, in an increasing variety of educational contexts, often beyond typical school hours and school boundaries. Widespread access to broadband-based tools extends the learning day beyond typical school hours and school boundaries. By engaging in and sponsoring these activities, students, teachers, and school administrators contribute to and draw from the world of creative artifacts that surrounds them. And by sending these class projects around the world in the form of open educational resources, students and educators make it possible for others to learn from their work and modify it as well. Today, as a result of these actions, we are witnessing early growth in distributed educational networks that make these works, tools, and other raw materials of educational progress available to a radically expanded population of students.

In several senses, copyright law is not ready for this new world. Students and teachers frequently make at least some use of copyrighted content when they author these complex creative works, and they make additional uses of such resources when they share and distribute their creations with one another, with other classrooms and other schools, and on the public Internet. Yet at nearly every inflection point in this educational ecosystem, unjustifiably strong interpretations of the potential scope of copyright law threaten to deter these actions, even when students and educators are interacting with knowledge, tools, and artifacts for the purpose of learning and sharing information rather than for commercial exploitation.

Those who design public laws and private guidelines around copyright must carve out additional space to facilitate the growth of these innovative new learning environments. The pages that follow describe the online tools and media-sharing practices that will challenge copyright law, as well as the rules and practices that schools and governments will need to adopt to encourage the sharing of ideas and artifacts for educational purposes. This chapter suggests a number of ways that schools, copyright holders, courts, and legislators can treat educational uses of copyrighted works less as ill-formed "exceptions" to copyright law and more as systematically integrated practices essential to educational progress.

The recommendations in this chapter address three needs. First, they recognize that the way students experience learning has changed, and that the educational system is no longer a strictly hierarchical setting but is instead populated with increasingly interactive, multiparty, asynchronous flows of information. Second, these recommendations seek to protect the autonomy of teachers and promote their ability to make innovative uses of educational materials. Courts are beginning to offer more clarity regarding what constitutes fair use, but school districts and other institutions often adopt confusing and overly conservative guidelines on what teachers and students can and cannot do with educational tools. The changes proposed here would permit teachers and students to engage in creative activities more in line with the dynamic goals of copyright and fair use law. Finally, these recommendations promote the importance of computer labs, software and application design, and Internet interactivity in education, and seek to ensure that copyright law encourages rather than hampers student and teacher innovation.

1.   Incompatibility between Copyright Law and New Educational Resources and Environments

Faced with a changing educational environment, governments, schools, and students alike should understand the importance of a robust educational fair use exception for the future of learning and teaching. The best way to understand fair use is by recognizing that fair use is integral to the function of copyright law. Copyright law is focused on the dissemination of existing knowledge and the creation of new knowledge. However, as courts have noted, there exist cases where copyright liability "would stifle the very creativity which that law is designed to foster," and in these circumstances fair use was intended—by the courts and by Congress—to provide a solution.[1] The law states that "the fair use of a copyrighted work, ... for purposes such as criticism, comment, news reporting, teaching (including multiple copies for classroom use), scholarship, or research, is not an infringement of copyright" (17 U.S.C. § 107). The law also sets forth four factors in assessing whether a given use is fair:

1. the purpose and character of the use, including whether such use is of a commercial nature or is for nonprofit educational purposes;
2. the nature of the copyrighted work;
3. the amount and substantiality of the portion used in relation to the copyrighted work as a whole; and
4. the effect of the use on the potential market for or value of the copyrighted work.

It is therefore important to understand these fair use factors as contributing to the kind of dynamic creation and distribution of new knowledge on which the American educational system depends.

However, the current copyright regime allows every work of authorship with a modicum of creativity to be granted copyright protection without any requirement of registration or notice, and makes fair use difficult to ascertain and expensive to litigate. This has led to a variety of dangerous externalities in the educational context. For instance, a film containing archival and documentary footage of Martin Luther King, Jr., and the battle against segregation was forced out of print by the expense and legal complications of license renewals. Students were thus unable to use excerpts in class projects on the civil rights era.[2] Teachers seeking to use Beatles and Kanye West lyrics to promote literacy in the classroom were unable to afford the $3,000 licensing fees charged by the relevant rights holders.[3]

Descendants representing the estates of authors have asserted broader copyright protection than is available under the law of fair use, but because fair use is notoriously unclear and because copyright litigation is very expensive, users have been hesitant to engage fully with the writings of James Joyce, William Faulkner, J.R.R. Tolkien, and other authors and artists at the core of the Western canon.[4] To the detriment of visually impaired students, text-to-speech features on electronic book-readers such as the Amazon Kindle were turned off in response to a copyright complaint from the Authors Guild of America; as a result, several universities opted not to distribute the device to students, thus stalling the planned conversion of textbooks to cheaper e-versions.[5] An archiving organization rejected a student's attempt to deposit a documentary film into its archive until all the rights to images within the film had been cleared—a difficult task for someone working within a typical student budget.[6] Rather than encourage educators to incorporate video content into the curriculum simply by copying short scenes directly from a DVD, the Motion Picture Association of America has suggested that teachers should instead go through the cumbersome process of using a camcorder to record video from a television, and then show the resulting low-quality videotape of this footage to students.[7] A teacher and documentary filmmaker happened to record, in the corner of an otherwise unrelated shot, a television program that played 4.5 seconds of a Simpsons episode; the owner of the copyright in this episode sought to charge the filmmaker $10,000 for use of the snippet.[8] Stories like these are rampant, and demonstrate how the traditional educational autonomy exercised by teachers, students, and archivists is being challenged by overly broad assertions of copyright protection over educational materials and over uses of content for educational purposes.

The use of copyrighted works by educators can provide quick, convenient, and effective ways of demonstrating to students the relevance of course content. Educators face the persistent challenge of convincing students of the importance and relevance of the material being taught. Teachers may lack the time and means to take their students out of the classroom to show them firsthand the role course content plays in "the real world." But teachers can easily bring cultural artifacts and scientific experiments into the learning environment, and demonstrate the importance and relevance of the material. Educational fair use can expand the pool of open educational resources and thereby promote the embedding of teaching tools in everyday cultural experiences, rather than solely in the detached space of a lecture or textbook. Unfortunately, the copyright protection of many, if not most, cultural and educational artifacts that teachers might find useful, coupled with teachers' uncertainties about the scope of copyright law, can intimidate teachers and prevent them from making educational fair use of cultural materials.

Beyond barriers to the integration of outside cultural artifacts into the classroom, unclear and limited articulations of fair use stand in the way of the development of new online learning tools. These include multiplayer games, adaptive learning plans, platforms that let educators share their expertise and innovations, collaborative video-editing software, vocational simulations, and software that enables students to look for patterns among texts, videos, and other artifacts. Many of these new tools will require the use and integration of many layers of copyrighted content, since student collaboration and evaluation require back-and-forth distribution of the projects and software containing this content. Without a broad educational fair use exception, the developers of these tools—which may include students themselves—will not have sufficient legal certainty to move forward with such complex projects. For them, the risk of a potential copyright violation along the way is too high.

Uncertainty over fair use also impedes the growth of distance learning. Students whose educational institutions are isolated in one way or another— whether by geography or by limited funding—are poised to benefit from the cheap digitization and easy distribution of rich educational resources, as are students who are isolated from their educational institutions.

Adults with changing work and family schedules can now access online learning tools at their convenience. The spread of broadband access makes it possible to share high-bandwidth media content, lectures, and complex course modules with students who would otherwise be unable to access such materials through their local institution. For instance, a student without access to an Advanced Placement calculus course might want to watch video lectures, participate in group projects, browse lecture notes and past student projects, use software platforms such as Mathematica, and engage with homework assignments offered by distant institutions. (In science, distance participation also necessitates access to the labs, data, analytical software, and research papers housed at the host institution.) Students with broadband access can become active participants when using these resources: they learn to localize, customize, modify, and improve the materials in question, then upload them back to the server and allow other students to do the same. MIT's OpenCourseWare project and Khan Academy are prime examples of producers and distributors of open educational resources, and the massive open online courses offered by Coursera, edX, and Udacity are examples of how students engage with such resources.

These collaborative learning tools require greater legal protection. Because copyright law governs almost every point along the chain of technological and individual actions described here (e.g., the decision by an instructor to include outside content within these learning tools, or the decision by a student to create and share content within these tools), efforts to develop these tools require confidence and a willingness to incur legal risks. Since not all institutions are in the financial position of MIT or Google to insure against these risks, governments must act to ensure that educators and students alike have broad permission and similar power to engage in educational fair use of copyrighted content.

2. Actions That Governments and Institutions Can Take to Clarify the Scope of Fair Educational Use

Educators, creators, authors, and students are inhibited by unclear guidelines governing the scope of copyright liability, and would benefit from rational governmental and institutional articulations of the rules governing the use of copyrighted materials in educational environments. However, there is considerable variation between different institutions and even between different courts when it comes to defining the balance between fair use and infringement.

In part, this variability arises because fair use remains a largely judge-made doctrine, often involving a multifactor inquiry into the purpose, character, and market effect of a particular use, along with the relationship of that use to the copyrighted work (e.g., what "amount" of the work is being used?) and the "nature" of that copyrighted work. This doctrinal flexibility and subjectivity, whereby judges can weigh various factors depending on the circumstances of the context of use, has led to a great deal of creativity around the margins of copyright law. Perhaps not surprisingly, this flexibility has also led to crippling uncertainty among educators who must assess whether a given use will eventually be adjudged as fair.

Given the complexity of fair use analysis and the potential for crippling damage awards (ranging from hundreds of dollars to $150,000 for instances of "willful" infringement)[9], schools and other institutions have adopted guidelines asking students and teachers to exercise such extreme caution with regard to copyrighted materials that many uses once traditionally deemed to be fair are no longer exercised. For instance, one guideline from the MIT Press—the publisher of this text—states that "all quoted poetry or song lyrics require permission, regardless of length," and provides no exception for fair use.[10] The U.S. Congress initially tasked a group of users and copyright owners to negotiate general guidelines, but these parties had difficulty coming to any firm agreement.[11] Congress eventually imported into its recommendations a number of subjective criteria, such as "brevity," "spontaneity," and "cumulative effect," that are nowhere to be found in the fair use statute itself.

This failure to reach consensus over acceptable fair use guidelines has been repeated over the years in a wide number of contexts. In the absence of a clear national consensus, many other entities have developed their own guidelines. Unfortunately, these are inconsistent from organization to organization and from school to school, thus increasing the uncertainty faced by an educator or a student who seeks to make use of copyrighted materials. The Center for Social Media at American University and others have compiled a list of the variable levels of educational fair use at play in different institutions:

1. A professor described a policy at his college, in which the provost issued an ultimatum: only DVDs owned by the college can be used in the

classroom, and under no circumstances can faculty use VHS tapes, off-air broadcasts, or DVDs from other sources.

2. At one high school, the technology specialist refuses to let teachers use school equipment to screen videos unless they sign statements that they (and not the school administration) are legally liable for copyright violation.

3. A university professor who created a compilation reel of clips for her course was not allowed to post it on the course-management software so students could view the clips to do their homework assignments.

4. An administrator whose interpretation of copyright was dramatically different than a teacher's placed severe limits on what could be photocopied for classroom use, limiting the teacher's ability to use newspaper articles and other printed materials.

5. The "45-day rule," derived from the 1981 guidelines, ... states that video taped off-air should be erased or destroyed after 45 days.

6. One teacher was told that, to avoid legal issues when using copyrighted material in a student video, it was better to use three short 10-second clips than one long 30-second clip.

7. Many teachers believed that, as one teacher put it, "You can only use 10 percent of a film, TV show, or song." Others told us it was OK to use four sentences of print, and 60 seconds of video.[12]

Even those institutions that do have clear copyright and fair use policies rarely take the time to explain those policies to the individuals they affect; as the American University report noted, "no interviewee reported receiving any education or training about fair use."[13]

Inconsistent guidelines also make it harder to share and develop educational materials across multiple institutions. As more institutions engage in collaborative creation, the notion of institution-specific guidelines concerning fair use has become increasingly impractical, and is standing in the way of educational progress and creativity. A clear and broad fair use rule for the classroom context would dispel this institutional fear and uncertainty and would permit educators to coalesce around useful, positive standards of fair use.

One way to build and clarify fair use would be take a page from the current U.S. copyright statute, which specifies, prior to listing the four fair use factors, six characteristic sectors in which fair use should not constitute infringement: criticism, comment, news reporting, teaching, scholarship, and research. Although these six sectors are each related to the practices and goals of education, there have been few court cases setting forth the principle that educators and students should be given special rights to make fair use of copyrighted content. This is despite the widespread intuition, reflected in classroom practices, that such uses are part of the learning process.

To bring the law into harmony with existing learning practices, courts and legislatures should build on this categorical definition of fair use to promote embedding and durability in the educational context. Teachers and students are increasingly using online educational tools—including proprietary management systems such as Blackboard, open platforms such as Sakai, and open content sources such as MIT's OpenCourseWare—to design anthologies and timelines detailing students' interactions with (often copyrighted) works. In these projects, students mark up artistic, literary, and technological works with commentary, write reaction papers, and publish videos, and teachers attach their lecture notes to the works so that students can review the work at a later time. Such projects involve more than the mere duplication or quotation of a work; they involve transforming the work by embedding teacher and student interactions within the work.

Digital media are being used more and more frequently in the course of education. Teachers often scan images into digital slide presentations or play instructional podcasts that contain clips of relevant audio from other sources, and students copy charts and graphs from websites into their own research works. In distance and at-home learning environments, students need to view an image, video, or audio file for longer than just a discrete "class session," because of the asynchronous manner in which such students access course materials. Nontraditional and home-schooled students require a similar degree of access to the educational content that is used by traditional students within the physical classroom environment. However, under prevailing copyright laws such as the TEACH Act, a distance learning student is constrained from making the same uses of copyrighted content that students are able to make within the physical classroom environment.

There is thus a strong need to classify the "durable use" of copyrighted works in the educational context as noninfringing, so that students can incorporate external works into material such as digital student portfolios, online writing projects, and other interactive projects in which fair use of the work requires use for an extended period of time. Students are no longer using copyrighted works in a purely synchronous manner; rather, their interactions with works are sustained over longer periods of time. There is good reason for schools and colleges to retain the ability to evaluate later student works in the context of prior works. Such ongoing evaluation and dynamic use of student projects necessitates access to a digital student portfolio and any copyrighted materials contained and modified therein.

This concept of a digital student portfolio, dependent on durable rights of use and reuse of external content as well as rights to use the student's own work, promotes the usefulness of student projects beyond the immediate educational setting in which they were created. For instance, a student who incorporates song lyrics or video snippets into a research essay may want to archive her work for later performance at an achievement fair, talent show, or video-sharing site. Schools may wish to encapsulate projects within a broader digital portfolio that can be put to later educational use within exportable course modules, or distributed between multiple schools as part of a creative exchange project.

It is important to note that the use of these student projects precludes the application of technological and rights-management measures that may prevent even the temporary retention and reuse of the work on which the project is based. To engage in the transformative uses of content necessary for a truly interactive educational process, students must have some ability to shape, remodel, and reincorporate external educational content into a new form. This requires at least a temporary copy of the work to be made on the student's computing device. For instance, if students design a wiki around a copyrighted novel, they may want to edit that wiki by adding new passages from the novel, images from film adaptations of the novel, and excerpts from critical works that cite the novel. And if an educator or other authority identifies a student-created project of significant merit, that educator may wish to share the project with future students studying the work in question, and with students in other locations. The right to durable educational use of a work is particularly relevant in distance learning environments, where the duration and number of class sessions—not to mention the list of students taking part in the sessions—are difficult to estimate in advance.

To minimize teacher and student uncertainty regarding the status of copyrighted works, and to promote greater educational use of noncommercial works, educational institutions (or governments) could also institute a simple repository of creative works that teachers and students are explicitly free to use in the course of education, without fear of potential liability for copyright infringement. One way to populate this repository would be to introduce (or reintroduce) into copyright law a registration and renewal requirement that, if not satisfied, would result in a work's entrance into the educational public domain after a certain period of years. Such a requirement would partially solve the problem of orphan works by placing the burden on the author to maintain the copyright status of a work. If designed properly, this model would give the author the freedom (on copyright registration) to permit certain noncommercial and educational uses of her work.

A less mechanical—and perhaps more flexible—means of encouraging educational use of copyrighted works would be to fine-tune copyright and fair use statutes to promote innovative and transformative uses of content by students and teachers, and to ensure that existing educational uses are clearly accounted for by the law. In the United States, for instance, Congress could state that if the "purpose and character of the use" are primarily educational, then special and compelling weight should be assigned to the first fair use factor. The fact that a particular use of copyrighted materials is educational in character should serve as a prima facie indication that the use of the copyrighted material was fair, rebuttable only by a finding that the remaining three factors of the fair use inquiry all augur strongly against the fairness of the use in question. Additionally, it will be appropriate in some countries to institute a presumption that recipients of copies of copyrighted works in educational contexts are not potential consumers of those works in their intended market. In the United States and elsewhere, positioning the question of educational use as a threshold question in the fair use inquiry, rather than as merely one single factor within a broader inquiry, would further codify the already strong indication in many statutory texts that educational uses should be accorded generous treatment.

Such clear classifications of educational use of copyrighted content would help reduce the uncertainty faced by educators and students in deciding whether or not to use copyrighted material for educational purposes. Educators would no longer need to constantly look over their shoulders when engaging in innovative uses of content. The threat of a statutory penalty of up to $150,000 for each act of copyright infringement[14] would no longer discourage acts with even a slight probability of infringement.

Furthermore, these rules would pave the way for the development of novel educational resources, as teachers and students would be able to spend more time exploring, understanding, and recontextualizing the materials within a newly opened educational public domain. The reforms and enhancements to educational fair use set forth in this chapter provide several means of countering the inertia of the current copyright system, and of ensuring that educational systems are ready for the development of new, interconnected digital learning platforms. They would ensure, as Judge Pierre Leval has written, that fair use is perceived "not as a disorderly basket of exceptions to the rules of copyright, nor as a departure from the principles governing that body of law, but rather as a rational, integral part of copyright, whose observance is necessary to achieve the objectives of that law."[15]

Notes

1. U.S. Supreme Court, Campbell v. Acuff-Rose Music, Inc., 510 U.S. 569, 577 (1994), quoting Stewart v. Abend, 495 U.S. 207, 236 (1990).

2. See Katie Dean, "Bleary Days for Eyes on the Prize," *Wired,* December 22, 2004, http://www.wired.com/culture/lifestyle/news/2004/12/66106. Dean notes that the producers "cleared rights to broadcast on PBS, for educational distribution and for broadcast overseas," but that once these rights began to expire in the mid-1990s, it was difficult to coordinate the numerous stakeholders necessary to clarify renewal rights in these areas.

3. Center for Social Media, School of Communication, American University, "Documentary Filmmakers' Statement of Best Practices in Fair Use," November 18, 2015, 16–17, http://www.centerforsocialmedia.org/files/pdf/Final_CSM_copyright_report .pdf.

4. See D. T. Max, "The Injustice Collector: Is James Joyce's Grandson Suppressing Scholarship?," *The New Yorker,* June 19, 2006, http://www.newyorker.com/ archive/2006/06/19/060619fa_fact. See also Karen Sloan, "James Joyce Estate Agrees to Pay Plaintiff's Fees in Fair Use Dispute," *National Law Journal,* September 2009, http://www.law.com/jsp/article.jsp?id=1202434181383.

5. See: Geoffrey Fowler and Jeffrey A. Trachtenberg,, "New Kindle Audio Feature Causes a Stir," *Wall Street Journal Online,* February 10, 2009, http://online.wsj.com/ article/SB123419309890963869.html; see also Don Reisinger, "Universities Reject Kindle over Inaccessibility for Blind," CNet, November 16, 2009, http://news.cnet .com/8301-13506_3-10396177-17.html.

6. See Rick Morris, "Use of Copyrighted Images in Academic Scholarship and Creative Work," *IDEA* 33 (1993): 129.

7. Jacqui Cheng, "MPAA: Teachers Should Videotape Monitors, Not Rip DVDs," *Ars Technica,* May 7, 2009, http://arstechnica.com/tech-policy/news/2009/05/mpaa -teachers-should-video-record-tv-screens-not-rip-dvds.ars.

8. Lawrence Lessig, *Free Culture* (New York: Penguin Press, 2004), 95–97.

9. U.S. Congress, 7 U.S.C. § 504(c), http://www.law.cornell.edu/uscode/text/17/504.

10. MIT Press, "Author Guidelines," 2014, http://mitpress.mit.edu/content/author -guidelines.

11. See Historical and Revision Notes to H.R. 94–1476 (notes accompanying fair use statute) ("Representatives of the American Association of University Professors and of the Association of American Law Schools have written to the Committee strongly criticizing the guidelines, particularly with respect to multiple copying, as being too restrictive with respect to classroom situations at the university and graduate level").

12. This list consists of quotations from Renee Hobbs, Peter Jaszi, and Pat Aufderheide, "The Cost of Copyright Confusion for Media Literacy," https://www.macfound.org/media/article_pdfs/MEDIALITERACYREPORT.PDF. See also Center for Social Media, "Documentary Filmmakers' Statement of Best Practices in Fair Use," 10–12.

13. Ibid., 12.

14. See U.S. Congress, 17 U.S.C. § 504.

15. Pierre Leval, "Toward a Fair Use Standard," *Harvard Law Review* 103 (1990): 1107.

Bibliography

Center for Social Media, School of Communication, American University. "Documentary Filmmakers' Statement of Best Practices in Fair Use." Center for Social Media, November 18, 2005.http://www.centerforsocialmedia.org/files/pdf/Final_CSM_copyright_report.pdf.

Cheng, Jacqui. "MPAA: Teachers Should Videotape Monitors, Not Rip DVDs." *Ars Technica,* May 7, 2009. http://arstechnica.com/tech-policy/news/2009/05/mpaa-teachers-should-video-record-tv-screens-not-rip-dvds.ars.

Dean, Katie. "Bleary Days for Eyes on the Prize," *Wired,* December 22, 2004. http://www.wired.com/culture/lifestyle/news/2004/12/66106.

Fowler, Geoffrey, and Jeffrey A. Trachtenberg. "New Kindle Audio Feature Causes a Stir." *Wall Street Journal Online*, February 10, 2009. http://online.wsj.com/article/SB123419309890963869.html.

Lessig, Lawrence. *Free Culture.* New York: Penguin Press, 2004.

Leval, Pierre. 1990. "Toward a Fair Use Standard." *Harvard Law Review* 103.

Max, D. T. "The Injustice Collector: Is James Joyce's Grandson Suppressing Scholarship?" *The New Yorker,* June 19, 2006. http://www.newyorker.com/archive/2006/06/19/060619fa_fact.

MIT Press. "Author Guidelines." MIT Press, 2014. http://mitpress.mit.edu/content/author-guidelines.

Morris, Rick. 1993. Use of Copyrighted Images in Academic Scholarship and Creative Work. *IDEA* 33:129.

Reisinger, Don. "Universities Reject Kindle over Inaccessibility for Blind." CNet, 2009. http://news.cnet.com/8301-13506_3-10396177-17.html.

Sloan, Karen. "James Joyce Estate Agrees to Pay Plaintiff's Fees in Fair Use Dispute." *National Law Journal,* 2009. http://www.law.com/jsp/article.jsp?id=1202434181383.

U.S. Congress. 7 U.S.C. § 504(c). Remedies for infringement: Damages and profits. http://www.law.cornell.edu/uscode/text/17/504.

U.S. Copyright Office. "Fair Use." Washington, DC: Library of Congress, June 2015. http://www.copyright.gov/fls/fl102.html.

U.S. Supreme Court. Campbell v. Acuff-Rose Music, Inc., 510 U.S. 569, 577 (1994).

III Social Media and Education in the Coming Decade

Part I explored the new educational possibilities social media offer, with chapters on social media use in U.S. school districts, online youth-initiated communities, distance learning initiatives in developing countries, and social media–based education in news organizations.

These possibilities in turn raise questions about the disruptive potential of social media for existing educational institutions, laws, and industry practices. Part II therefore explored the ways in which social media are challenging and disrupting existing educational models. It examined challenges to norms of knowledge and authority that have emerged on social media, changing notions of privacy and identity, challenges that online educational institutions pose for accreditation and educational assessment, and tensions between the new ease of sharing and mixing and copyright protection laws.

Part III offers a series of examples that demonstrate in practice both the possibilities and the challenges social media offer as educational tools. In chapter 10, David Buckingham (professor of education and director of the Centre for the Study of Children, Youth and Media, University of London) explores ways to teach about media and what to teach. He cautions that educators who do not participate in the new media culture risk living in a society that is disconnected from that of their students. Chapters 11 and 12, by Shai Reshef (CEO, University of the People) and Daniel J. H. Greenwood (professor of law, Hofstra University, and CFO, University of the People), respectively, discuss a model for and the economics of an international, open-educational, online university: University of the People (UoPeople), powered by social media. Chapter 11 takes the reader through the vision, history, and implementation of UoPeople, especially the benefits and challenges of implementing such a model. Chapter 12 surveys business models for social media and education, especially that underlying UoPeople, and envisions new financial models for "our core institutions" of education. In chapter 13, Minhtuyen Mai (researcher at the HOPE Lab, University of Wisconsin–Madison), Adam Poppe (PhD candidate, Michigan State University), and Christine Greenhow (assistant professor of counseling, educational psychology, and special education, Michigan State University) consider social media–enabled education on a massive scale. The chapter presents the history of and current trends in massive open online courses (MOOCs), suggesting the benefits and challenges to implementing MOOCs in various contexts. Finally, chapters 14 and 15 consider teachers' and students' experiences in social media–enabled formal and informal educational spaces. In chapter 14, Jiahang Li (assistant professor of counseling, educational psychology, and special education, Michigan State University) presents a case study of a formal teacher education program that integrated social media for its professional development model. In chapter 15, Benjamin Gleason (PhD candidate, Michigan State University) examines two informal learning programs for high school–age teens that foster informal learning about technology, literacy, and science and civic engagement through participatory play.

The examples in these six chapters demonstrate in practice the possibilities and pitfalls when social media are introduced either to complement or to enrich existing formal educational programs (e.g., the teacher education program) or as the catalyst for disruption and reform (e.g., UoPeople, MOOCs, and informal learning programs founded on notions of participatory play). All chapters seek to resist technodeterminism or utopian idealism to present a more balanced and critical approach of how social media are shaping and in turn shaped by learning, teaching, and social practices in various contexts among different types of learners. Each chapter concludes with implications or recommendations for the educational community.

Chapter 10: Do We Really Need Media Education 2.0? Teaching Media in the Age of Participatory Culture

David Buckingham

This chapter makes the case for what and how we should teach *about* media, in K–12 schools and universities. Buckingham takes a measured approach, advocating the teaching of both traditional media criticism as well as digital media skills related to content creation and participation. Further, Buckingham urges educators to resist what he calls "technofetishism," or celebrating technology in education for its own sake. Nevertheless, he acknowledges that educators who do not participate in new media culture risk losing the so-called "right to teach" by living in a different society from that of their students.

Chapter 11: University of the People: A Model for International, Tuition-Free, Open Education Powered by Social Media

Shai Reshef

In this chapter, the founder of an experimental, Internet-based university (University of the People) describes its history and discusses how lessons shared via social media might enable the growth of a free, international system of higher education accessible to all. The author asserts that such a system could harness the collective intelligence of millions who now are blocked by financial and other obstacles from obtaining higher education. UoPeople is a nonprofit, tuition-free, accredited online university that draws on open-source technology, open educational resources, peer-to-peer learning, and the assistance of academic volunteers. Founded in 2009, the university has served more than two thousand students from more than 170 countries. The chapter also describes the challenges involved in implementing such a model. Insights for people and organizations considering launching similar enterprises are offered.

Chapter 12: Technology and the Economics of Education

Daniel J. H. Greenwood

This chapter surveys business models for social media education. Noting that the marginal cost for educating one more student online is zero, while the average cost of creating new research products and training a new scholar is quite high, Greenwood suggests that the traditional economic model underpinning universities is unsustainable in a digital world. While holding out UoPeople as an example of how wealthy countries can generously distribute knowledge to the rest of the world, Greenwood argues that such endeavors can bankrupt the more complex, face-to-face educational institutions that are needed to drive innovation and develop new faculty. The author discusses several new financial models for the core U.S. educational institutions. His recommendations include more substantial government subsidy and a revamp of the current patent and copyright systems.

Chapter 13: Social Media and Education on a Massive Scale: The Case of MOOCs

Minhtuyen Mai, Adam Poppe, and Christine Greenhow

This chapter presents the definition and emergence of massive open online courses (MOOCs), a relatively new phenomenon in education, borne out of new technological and social media affordances. A central theme of the chapter is that the hype surrounding this instructional approach has outpaced scholarship. The chapter presents the benefits of and challenges to implementing MOOCs in higher education and concludes with both the educational opportunities they suggest and the challenges they pose for teachers, administrators, and others in the educational community.

Chapter 14: Social Media and Teacher Education: the Case of STARTALK

Jiahang Li

This chapter discusses the relationship between social media and teacher education. Drawing on the results of case study research, the chapter identifies several affordances that social media offer teacher education, including promoting collaborative learning, building a community of practice, and generating content. It introduces an exemplary case of foreign language teacher education programs, STARTALK, to illustrate the affordances and challenges of social media adoption in teachers' professional development. Li concludes with suggestions for teacher educators and directions for future research.

Chapter 15: Teens' Participatory Play: Digital Media Learning through Civic Engagement

Benjamin Gleason

While teenagers have widespread access to the Internet at home and school, they lack opportunities to use digital media to support their social, cultural, and political participation. This chapter discusses an emerging model of civic engagement. Using the affordances of the Internet to engage teens in projects that are personally meaningful may allow young people to learn valuable technological, communicative, and artistic skills and develop professional expertise. The discussion explores two projects, Mouse and World's Fair 2064, as examples of how digital media can support teenagers' individual competences while also developing the capacity of the community to respond to pressing needs.

10 Do We Really Need Media Education 2.0? Teaching Media in the Age of Participatory Culture

David Buckingham

Introduction

In the UK, media education has a long history, going back more than seventy years. Media education is a dimension of mother-tongue language teaching ("subject English") throughout the secondary school, as well as an established specialist subject (media studies) for students aged fourteen to eighteen years. There is now a growing recognition among policymakers that all children should be taught about media as a core element of literacy education in particular.[1] As such, media education in the UK is guided by a fairly coherent conceptual framework, and there is a good sense of what works in the classroom. Media education in UK schools has always been about creativity as well as critique; it is about making media as well as analyzing media.

Of course, this is not to say there are no debates to be had, or no areas in need of development. Indeed, a growing body of research is addressing some of the contradictions and limitations of established practice in media education.[2] Much of the debate hinges on fundamental questions about knowledge and learning: what do we imagine young people *already* know about media, what do they need to know, and how might they learn it? The advent of digital media has some interesting implications in respect of these questions. As we shall see, some have claimed that contemporary changes in the wider media environment require us to rethink the fundamental aims and methods of media education—not just the content of the curriculum but also our pedagogy and our teaching methods. But are such changes really as fundamental as their advocates suggest? And is it necessarily the case that the age of Media 2.0 also requires Media Education 2.0?

Media Education 2.0 and the Complete Reinvention of Everything

Many contemporary teenagers are now growing up with the ensemble of participatory media collectively known as Web 2.0: social networking sites, photo- and video-sharing sites, blogs, podcasts, remixes and mashups, wikis, machinima, user-generated content, online games, social worlds, and so on. These new media have not replaced older media. On average, young people still spend much more time watching television than they spend online;[3] many of them even obstinately continue to read books. Nevertheless, if we base our teaching on forms of media that are, at least, only part of the environment that young people are now experiencing, there is clearly a danger that it may become irrelevant to their lives. This is not, I would argue, simply a question of curriculum *content*—of teaching students how to analyze websites as well as television ads, for example. Rather, enthusiasts for new media typically claim that such media entail a distinctively different orientation toward information, a different phenomenology of use, a different politics of knowledge, and a different mode of learning. If this is the case, it has potentially far-reaching implications for pedagogy—not just for *what* we teach but also for *how* we teach.

For William Merrin, a senior lecturer in media studies at Swansea University and likely originator of the term "Media Studies 2.0," these new media represent a fundamental challenge to our "right to teach":

Our fear of technology often extends to our own personal use of it. Whereas in the broadcast-era we broadly understood the basic technical principles of the dominant media and we understood their use—sharing that use with our students—today lecturers are being left behind in their knowledge of what technologies are out there, of their technical possibilities, of how they even work, of how to use them and of what they are being used for. Again, we no longer share a common culture with our students. Unless we can keep up with these changing technologies and uses and unless they become as integral a part of our lives as they are to our students' then we will lose both the ability and even the right to teach them. In an era in which we watched and studied TV we had a right to teach it: in the future, unless we're downloading, sharing, ripping, burning, messaging, networking, playing, building and producing then we'll lose that right.[4]

Questions could certainly be raised about the historical narrative that is offered here, in particular the notion that at some unspecified time in the past there used to be a "common culture," an experience of media shared among teachers (or lecturers) and students, that has now been lost. However, the more challenging question is about the "right to teach"—in effect, about the *legitimacy* of teaching about media in the age of Media 2.0.

Table 10.1

Media 1.0	Media 2.0
Old (analog) media	New (digital) media
Consumption	Production, participation
Hierarchy	Popular democracy
Media Studies 1.0	**Media Studies 2.0**
The media canon	Diversification of tastes
Western media	Global media
Textual analysis and political economy	Audience research
Conventional research methods	Creative research methods
Expert readers	Ordinary audience members
People need to be taught to be critical	People are already critical

The arguments developed by Merrin and by David Gauntlett across their various contributions to this debate hinge on a binary opposition between 1.0 and 2.0. A summary, drawing principally on Gauntlett, is shown in table 10.1.[5]

Like many such binary models, this one suffers from the tendency to deal in absolute oppositions, and to conflate quite different issues. For example, the distinction between Western media and global media does not simply map onto a distinction between old and new media—particularly in a situation where the majority of the population of the global south do not even have access to electricity, let alone broadband Internet.

Even so, there are interesting pedagogical issues here, which go back to the point about the right to teach. For example, according to Gauntlett, Media Studies 1.0 was characterized by "a belief that students should be taught how to 'read' the media in an appropriate 'critical' style."[6] In Media Studies 2.0, this is no longer necessary: "The patronising belief that students should be taught how to 'read' the media is replaced by the recognition that media audiences in general are already extremely capable interpreters of media content, with a critical eye and an understanding of contemporary media techniques, thanks in large part to the large amount of coverage of this in popular media itself."[7] There is an element of deliberate provocation here, but there are also interesting questions about learning. If students already participate in and produce their own media—supposedly in the extremely capable and critical way Gauntlett is suggesting—then what do they need to learn, and what do we have to teach them?

The Limits of Media 2.0

The advocates of Media Studies 2.0 are clearly subscribers to what Richard Barbrook and Andy Cameron many years ago called the "Californian ideology"—a kind of populist cyber-libertarianism that holds that ordinary people will somehow be empowered by technology and that digital media are inherently liberating and countercultural.[8] This approach is certainly apparent in the celebration of creativity and participation for their own sake, and in the valorizing of ordinary people.

The broader problems with this approach have been widely rehearsed.[9] It rests on a form of technological determinism—a view of technology as somehow autonomously producing social change. In this context, and in discussions of education more broadly, it is also implicated in the notion of the "digital generation": the idea that technology has brought about fundamental and absolute generational change, and that young people today are somehow automatically technologically savvy or media literate. As several critics have argued, this approach embodies a kind of generalization, an exoticism of youth, that ignores the diversity and the inequalities in young people's experiences and the continuities across generations.[10]

Claims about the potential of new media in terms of democratization and empowerment are by no means new. One need only look back to the arguments being made about cable TV in the 1970s[11] or about portable video in the 1980s[12]—in fact, most new media technologies have arrived amid claims about their inherently radical potential.[13] All of these media were apparently going to bring power to the people, undermine the control of knowledge by elites, enable ordinary people to express themselves and have their voices heard, and create new forms of collaboration—in precisely the revolutionary ways that are now purported to accompany the spread of digital media. And in each case, the ultimate effects were much more complex and equivocal than their advocates proclaimed.

In the case of Web 2.0, claims about its democratizing force point to widely accessible platforms for user-created and user-uploaded content, but it would seem that relatively few users of such services are active creators of content. For example, figures from the market research agency Hitwise suggest that among users of YouTube, the most accessible online video-sharing site, only 0.16 percent actually upload material, and much of what they upload is pirated clips from commercial media.[14] Research also suggests that there are some striking social differences in levels of participation here. For example, studies by Amanda Lenhart and co-workers[15] or Eszter Hargittai and Gina Walejko[16] point to significant "digital divides" in people's uses of these participatory media. These inequalities are clearly related to wider forms of social inequality; and they largely coincide with other differences, for example in how families from different social classes use the educational dimensions of the Internet or participate in creative or arts-related activities offline. To a large extent, the most active participants in the creative world of Web 2.0 are the usual suspects. Indeed, if online participation is as socially, culturally, and politically important as the enthusiasts suggest, it seems likely that, far from liquidating social inequality, it might actually accentuate it.

Finally, there is the question of the commercial interests that are at stake in these developments. One of the paradoxical characteristics of the Californian ideology is its appeal both to libertarian political radicals and to contemporary business gurus—not least Rupert Murdoch, whose proclamations about ordinary people "taking control" of the media have been widely circulated.[17] The political economy of Web 2.0 is still evolving, yet it is clear that the Internet is an exceptionally efficient medium for niche marketing, not least because of its potential for the targeting and surveillance of individual consumers. Indeed, much of this marketing is itself "user-generated" and "interactive" (as in the case of viral advertising).

Clearly, there are debates to be had about the wider social and political ramifications of Media 2.0. Such debates are beyond the scope of this article, but it could be argued that, far from precipitating a democratic revolution in communications, these new media are merely part of much broader moves toward individualization, self-surveillance, and self-promotion that are characteristic of how identities are formed and lived out in neoliberal consumer societies. While there is certainly a democratic promise here, the realization of that promise will require more than technology alone.

The Limits of Celebration

The Californian ideology has its own manifestations in education, where technology is widely believed to be transforming learning, changing the power relationships of classrooms, and creating autonomous, liberated learners. This form of educational cyber-utopianism is typically aligned with a range of fashionable but ill-defined concepts, of which creativity, informal learning, and (most recently) personalization are among the most prominent.[18] This rhetoric is strongly promoted by commercial technology companies, but it is also espoused by governments attracted to a technological fix for the problems of public education. In such rhetoric, it is often difficult to tell the difference between the overexcited claims of policymakers (and some academics) and the sales pitches of the computer companies.[19]

For some apparently progressive educational thinkers, the technology-driven classroom is somehow a vindication of the child-centered learning theories of the 1960s and 1970s, although others argue that digital technology has rendered the institution of the school redundant and that the real learning is now taking place in children's informal engagements with games or online social worlds. This celebratory argument typically entails a wholly positive, uncritical stance toward popular uses of technology. For example, those who extol the benefits of computer games for learning tend to ignore the commercial dimensions of games, and avoid awkward questions about their values and ideologies.[20] They also engage in a rather ill-defined valorization of informal learning, in which formal learning is seen as something inherently bad.

Addressing Digital Divides

Rather than diminishing the right to teach, I would argue that the advent of digital technology points to a need to extend the traditional mission of the school as a public institution. For instance, in the context of continuing digital divides, schools should play a key role in attempting to ameliorate inequalities in participation. As Henry Jenkins and others have argued,[21] schools have to address the "participation gap"—"the unequal access to the opportunities, experiences, skills and knowledge that will prepare youth for full participation in the world of tomorrow."[22] Like Jenkins, I see this gap as much more than unequal access to equipment; it is about cultural competencies, social skills, and knowledge. Jenkins offers an extensive list, which includes skills to do with play, experimentation, and problem solving; skills in handling different media sources and modes of communication, and in navigating across and between them; skills in networking and collaborating, locating information, and interacting with others; and skills having to do with judgment and critical evaluation.[23]

While some of the skills that Jenkins and others identify are certainly new, others are decidedly traditional. This has been confirmed by research I am currently conducting with colleagues on the role of the Internet in promoting civic participation (see www.civicweb.eu). While some have looked to the Internet as a means of reengaging young people who are currently disaffected from civic and political organizations, we have found that such opportunities are again largely taken up by the usual suspects, that is, those who already have an established interest in social or political issues and the skills and motivation to engage in political debate. To this extent, it is possible that the Internet may accentuate existing inequalities rather than help to overcome them. If disaffected and disadvantaged young people are to be enabled to participate, they need to develop relatively traditional skills in locating and evaluating information, constructing arguments, and thinking critically; these skills depend in turn on advanced forms of traditional literacy.

This is not to imply that nothing is changing. The Internet may, for example, be fostering new forms and styles of civic engagement that are at least potentially more inclusive. But participation, in civic engagement as in many other areas, still requires relatively traditional forms of cultural and educational capital. Addressing the "participation gap" therefore depends on addressing broader inequalities; the gap will not disappear simply as a result of widening access to technology.

The Place of Critique

The kinds of learning that are typically celebrated in discussions of digital technology in education tend to allow little space for critical reflection or the explicit development of critical skills. There seems to be an assumption that participation or creative production is a good thing in itself, and that it either stands in for or automatically generates critical understanding in its own right. Indeed, as we have seen, Gauntlett expresses a strong suspicion of critique, as though it necessarily represented a "patronizing" imposition of pedagogical authority. Media audiences, he argues, are "already extremely capable interpreters of media content."[24] In other words, they do not need to be taught to be critical.

As I have argued elsewhere, there is some justification in this suspicion of critique.[25] "Critical" itself is very much an "us versus them" term: people who are critical are often simply people who happen to agree with us, whereas those whom we disagree with are by definition uncritical. There is also a danger that "being critical" becomes one of the standardized routines or language games of the media classroom—a game in which students simply give back to the teacher the forms of critical discourse they have been fed. The emphasis on critical analysis can sanction a rather superficial, rationalistic approach to media—even a form of superficial cynicism—that belies the complex (and not least emotional) ways in which we actually relate to media.

However, none of this should imply that audiences are always and already "extremely" capable and critical—that they already know everything they need to know. Nor does it mean that we can throw out the critical tools and perspectives that we use to analyze media. We can accept that audiences can be active, discriminating, and, indeed, critical, while also recognizing there are things young people generally do *not* know about media—and, indeed, that they need to learn. There is a body of knowledge here—about how the media work, about the media industries, about the history of media, about the uses and effects of media within society. It is a changing and contested body of knowledge, to be sure, but it is neverthe-less a body of knowledge, and one with shared criteria for determining what counts as truth. The danger here is in assuming that somehow criti-cism is about an illegitimate imposition of authority or that it implies that ordinary people are stupid or deluded. This points to a rather old-fashioned, narrow sense of criticism as necessarily negative, or at least a notion of criti-cism as merely a form of defense or inoculation against influence.

Again, Jenkins and his colleagues are correct to identify another gap here, one that has to do with critique.[26] As they suggest, we need to enable young people to become active participants in media culture, but participa-tion or creativity for its own sake is not enough. We also need them to be critical participants, and to develop a broader understanding of the economic, social, and cultural dimensions of media. Such critical under-standing does not follow automatically from the experience of creative pro-duction. As Carmen Luke argues in relation to literacy, learners do not develop critical literacy just through the experience of reading and writing; they have to step back from immediate experience, in order to reflect and to analyze.[27]

Media 2.0 and Media Education 1.0: A Blended Approach

The foregoing leads to the complex and time-honored question of how we integrate theory (critical analysis) and practice (creative production) in media education. How does learning transfer from the domain of reading media to the domain of writing, and vice versa? How do we promote mean-ingful rather than superficial critical reflection on what students do as par-ticipants or creators of media? How do we help them understand those experiences in the broader social and cultural context?

In fact, I believe that digital technology offers new ways of addressing this issue, and of bringing theory closer to practice. For example, in the case of digital editing and image manipulation, the technology can help make explicit the processes of choice, selection, construction, and manipulation that often seem to be locked away with analog forms. As students drag and drop shots onto the timeline in a digital editing program, the experience of drafting and redrafting a sequence, and debating as they go along, makes a significant difference to the nature of the learning: the experience of editing is not just easier but also more explicit than was the case with older analog technology.[28]

My colleague Andrew Burn has analyzed how teachers can use the remixing potential of digital media to bring theory closer to practice.[29] Quite well-established activities in media teaching, such as making a trailer to market an existing movie to a new audience (*Psycho* and *Romeo + Juliet* are two of Burn's examples), have become much more feasible and controllable than used to be the case with analog technology. This process also provides new opportunities for analysis and reflection, although (as Burn suggests) this needs to be an explicit expectation that is built into the process. Indeed, Burn's case studies show extensive evidence of students applying the "faux-expert non-procedures" of semiotics and political economy analysis to inform such reflection.

Ole Erstad and his colleagues and Kirsten Drotner have also recently written about this remixing, looking at how students search out material on the Internet for their digital design work, and then process and recombine it in various ways, using what they call copy-and-paste literacy.[30] However, they also suggest that there is a danger in being seduced by the superficial professional gloss of this kind of work, and by young people's apparent facility with the technology. Actually, there is a lot young people do not know and cannot do. The activity of media-making needs to be accompanied by forms of analysis and theoretical conceptualization, and a set of clear curricular aims on the part of teachers. Further teacher training and teacher professional development will be needed to assist teachers in clarifying their objectives and supporting students in critically evaluating their digital design work.

Finally, our own recent research on digital game-making provides further instances of this connection between theory and practice.[31] In this project, we worked with an educational software company and a group of schools to develop a game-authoring tool. The resulting package, MissionMaker, enables users to make three-dimensional games without the necessity of programming. One thing we learned quite quickly was that, even if students are very adept game players, they do not automatically possess the requisite skills or knowledge to make the games. Making games is very difficult; it involves computational thinking, logic, and an ability to imagine a user who is not just an audience (or a reader) but a player, interacting with the text. In order to move from being a player to being a maker of games, you need to take a step back from your immediate experience and engage in some hard, systematic analysis.

Conclusion

Do we really need Media Education 2.0? Perhaps we do, but we certainly still need Media Education 1.0 as well. The advocates of Media Education 2.0 do identify some key imperatives here. I do not accept Merrin's claim that we lose the right to teach if we are not ourselves actively participating in the whole range of contemporary media. That said, I agree that it is necessary to keep pace with our students' media experiences and their changing orientations toward media—although we need to beware of assuming that those experiences are all the same. However, keeping up with our students does not mean we should automatically import the latest technological gimmicks into the classroom, let alone start pimping up our Facebook profiles in some hopeless desire to be "down with the kids."

New media can offer new opportunities for participation, for creative communication, and for the generation of content, at least for some people in some contexts. However, the competencies that people need in order to take up those opportunities are not equally distributed, and they do not arise simply because people have access to technology. Furthermore, it would be wrong to assume that participation is always a good thing, or that it is necessarily democratic, countercultural, or liberating. Creative production can be a powerful means of learning, whether it involves remixing of various kinds, appropriating and adapting existing texts, or creating wholly new ones, or simply exploiting the potential for networked communication. However, all of these activities should also include critical reflection and analysis.

In sum, media education itself needs to adopt a more critical stance toward the celebration of technology in education, and the kind of market-driven technofetishism that is mistakenly seen by some as the cutting edge of educational change. There is a risk here that media education might be seen as just another way of importing computer technology into schools—or indeed as a sexy alternative to the wasteland of spreadsheets, file management, and instrumental training that constitutes most information technology courses. There is an opportunity in Media Education 2.0, but it should not involve abandoning the traditional critical imperatives of Media Education 1.0 for a sentimental appeal to creativity and participation.

Notes

A slightly different version of this article was previously published in Kirsten Drotner and Kim Christian Schrøder, eds., *Digital Content Creation: Perceptions, Practices and Perspectives,* New Literacies and Digital Epistemologies 46 (New York: Peter Lang, 2010), 287–304.

1. See David Buckingham, *Media Education: Literacy, Learning and Contemporary Culture* (Cambridge: Polity, 2003); Andrew Burn and James Durran, *Media Literacy in Schools: Practice, Production and Progression* (London: Paul Chapman, 2007).

2. Reviews of some of this work may be found in David Buckingham, *Media Education,* and David Buckingham, with Shakuntala Banaji et al., *The Media Literacy of Children and Young People: A Review of the Academic Research* (London: Ofcom, 2005). More recent examples are contained in David Buckingham and Sara Bragg, eds., "Media Education Goes Digital," special issue, *Learning, Media and Technology* 27, no. 2 (2007); and Sara Bragg, David Buckingham, and Sue Turnbull, eds., "Media Education," special issue, *Media International Australia* 120 (August 2006).

3. Ofcom, *Media Literacy: Report on UK Children's Media Literacy* (London: Ofcom, 2008).

4. William Merrin, "Media Studies 2.0: My Thoughts," *Media Studies 2.0 Forum* (blog), posted January 4, 2008.

5. The summary draws primarily from David Gauntlett, "Wide Angle: Is It Time for Media Studies 2.0?," *Media Education Association Newsletter* 5 (2007): 3–5.

6. Ibid., 3.

7. Ibid., 3.

8. Richard Barbrook and Andy Cameron, "The Californian Ideology," Hypermedia Research Centre, University of Westminster, 1996, http://www.hrc.wmin.ac.uk/theory-californianideology-main.html (accessed November 8, 2008).

9. See, for example, Kevin Robins and Frank Webster, *Times of the Technoculture* (London: Routledge, 1999).

10. David Buckingham, "Is There a Digital Generation?," in *Digital Generations: Children, Young People and New Media,* ed. David Buckingham and Rebekah Willett, 1–17 (Mahwah, NJ: Erlbaum, 2006); S. Herring, "Questioning the Generational Divide: Technological Exoticism and Adult Constructions of Online Youth Identity," in *Youth, Identity and Digital Media,* ed. David Buckingham (Cambridge, MA: MIT Press, 2008), 71–92.

11. Thomas Streeter, "The Cable Fable Revisited: Discourse, Policy and the Making of Cable Television," *Critical Studies in Mass Communication* 4, no. 2 (1987): 174–200.

12. David Buckingham, Maria Pini, and Rebekah Willett, "'Take Back the Tube!' The Discursive Construction of Amateur Film and Video Making," *Journal of Media Practice* 8, no. 2 (2007): 183–201.

13. Carolyn Marvin, *When Old Technologies Were New* (New York: Oxford University Press, 1988); Brian Winston, *Media, Technology and Society: A History* (London: Routledge, 1998).

14. Eric Auchard, "Participation on Web 2.0 Sites Remains Weak," Reuters, April 17, 2007, http://www.reuters.com/article/InternetNews/idUSN1743638820070418 (accessed December 3, 2007).

15. Amanda Lenhart et al., *Teens and Social Media,* Pew Internet & American Life Project (Washington, DC: Pew Research Center, 2007).

16. Eszter Hargittai and Gina Walejko, "The Participation Divide: Content Creation and Sharing and the Digital Age," *Information Communication and Society* 11, no. 2 (2008): 239–256.

17. Spencer Reiss, "His Space," *Wired* 14.07 (July 2006), http://www.wired.com/wired/archive/14.07/murdoch.html (accessed April 12, 2007).

18. See David Buckingham, *Beyond Technology: Children's Learning in the Age of Digital* Culture (Cambridge: Polity, 2007), for further discussion.

19. Ibid.

20. For example, James Paul Gee, *What Video Games Have to Teach Us about Learning and Literacy* (Basingstoke: Palgrave, 2003).

21. Henry Jenkins, with K. Clinton et al, *Confronting the Challenges of Participatory Culture: Media Education for the 21st Century* (Chicago: MacArthur Foundation, 2006), 1–68, http://www.nwp.org/cs/public/print/resource/2713 (accessed November 27, 2007).

22. Ibid., 3.

23. Ibid., xiv.

24. Gauntlett, "Wide Angle," 4.

25. See, for example, Buckingham, *Media Education.*

26. Jenkins et al., "Confronting the Challenges of Participatory Culture."

27. Carmen Luke, "Cyber-schooling and Technological Change: Multiliteracies for New Times," in *Multiliteracies: Literacy Learning and the Design of Social Futures,* ed. Bill Cope and Mary Kalantzis (London: Routledge, 2000), 69–91.

28. David Buckingham, Issy Harvey, and Julian Sefton-Green, "The Difference Is Digital? Digital Technology and Student Media Production," *Convergence* 5, no. 4 (1999): 10–20.

29. Andrew Burn, "Repackaging the Slasher Movie: Digital Unwriting of Film in the Classroom," *English in Australia* 1, nos. 127–128 (2000): 24–34; Andrew Burn and

James Durran, "Digital Anatomies: Analysis as Production in Media Education," in *Digital Generations: Children, Young People and New Media,* ed. David Buckingham and Rebekah Willett (Mahwah, NJ: Erlbaum, 2006), 273–294.

30. Ole Erstad, Øystein Gilje, and Thomas de Lang, "Re-mixing Multimodal Resources: Multiliteracies and Digital Production in Norwegian Media Education," in Buckingham and Bragg, "Media Education Goes Digital"; Kirsten Drotner, "Learning Is Hard Work: Digital Practices and Future Competencies," in *Youth, Identity and Digital Media,* ed. David Buckingham (Cambridge, MA: MIT Press, 2008), 167–184.

31. David Buckingham and Andrew Burn, "Game Literacy in Theory and Practice," *Journal of Educational Media and Hypermedia* 16, no. 3 (2007): 323–349; Caroline Pelletier, "Games and Learning: What's the Connection?," *International Journal of Learning and Media* 1, no. 1 (2009), http://ijlm.net/ (accessed March 18, 2009).

Bibliography

Auchard, Eric. "Participation on Web 2.0 Sites Remains Weak." Reuters, April 17, 2007. http://www.reuters.com/article/InternetNews/idUSN1743638820070418 (accessed December 3, 2007).

Barbrook, Richard, and Andy Cameron. "The Californian Ideology." Hypermedia Research Centre, University of Westminster, 1996. http://www.hrc.wmin.ac.uk/theory-californianideology-main.html (accessed November 8, 2008).

Bragg, Sara, David Buckingham, and Sue Turnbull, eds. "Media Education." Special issue, *Media International Australia* 120 (August 2006).

Buckingham, David. *Beyond Technology: Children's Learning in the Age of Digital Culture.* Cambridge: Polity, 2007.

Buckingham, David. "'Creative' Visual Methods in Media Research: Possibilities, Problems and Proposals." *Media Culture & Society* 31, no. 4 (2009): 633–652.

Buckingham, David. "Is There a Digital Generation?" In *Digital Generations: Children, Young People and New Media,* ed. David Buckingham and Rebekah Willett, 1–17. Mahwah, NJ: Erlbaum, 2006.

Buckingham, David. *Media Education: Literacy, Learning and Contemporary Culture.* Cambridge: Polity, 2003.

Buckingham, David, with Shaku Banaji, Andrew Burn, Diane Carr, Sue Cranmer, and Rebekah Willett. "The Media Literacy of Children and Young People: A Review of the Academic Research." London: Ofcom, 2005.

Buckingham, David, and Sara Bragg, eds. "Media Education Goes Digital." Special issue, *Learning, Media and Technology* 27, no. 2 (2007).

Buckingham, David, and Andrew Burn. "Game Literacy in Theory and Practice." *Journal of Educational Media and Hypermedia* 16, no. 3 (2007): 323–349.

Buckingham, David, Issy Harvey, and Julian Sefton-Green. "The Difference Is Digital? Digital Technology and Student Media Production." *Convergence* 5, no. 4 (1999): 10–20.

Buckingham, David, and Rebekah Willett, eds. *Video Cultures: Media Technology and Amateur Creativity*. Basingstoke: Palgrave, 2009.

Buckingham, David, Maria Pini, and Rebekah Willett. "'Take Back the Tube!' The Discursive Construction of Amateur Film and Video Making." *Journal of Media Practice* 8, no. 2 (2007): 183–201.

Buckingham, David, Rebekah Willett, and Maria Pini. *Home Truths? Video Production and Domestic Life*. Ann Arbor: University of Michigan Press, 2011.

Burgess, Jean. "Hearing Ordinary Voices: Cultural Studies, Vernacular Creativity and Digital Storytelling." *Continuum* 20, no. 2 (2006): 201–214.

Burn, Andrew. "Repackaging the Slasher Movie: Digital Unwriting of Film in the Classroom." *English in Australia* 1, nos. 127–128 (2000): 24–34.

Burn, Andrew, and James Durran. "Digital Anatomies: Analysis as Production in Media Education." In *Digital Generations: Children, Young People and New Media*, ed. D. Buckingham and R. Willett, 273–294. Mahwah, NJ: Erlbaum, 2006.

Burn, Andrew, and James Durran. *Media Literacy in Schools: Practice, Production and Progression*. London: Paul Chapman, 2007.

Chalfen, Richard. *Snapshot Versions of Life*. Bowling Green, OH: Bowling Green State University Press, 1987.

Cohen, Philip. *Really Useful Knowledge*. Stoke-on-Trent: Trentham, 1990.

Drotner, Kirsten. "Learning Is Hard Work: Digital Practices and Future Competencies." In *Youth, Identity and Digital Media*, ed. David Buckingham, 167–184. Cambridge, MA: MIT Press, 2008.

Erstad, Ole, Øystein Gilje, and Thomas de Lange. "Re-mixing Multimodal Resources: Multiliteracies and Digital Production in Norwegian Media Education." In "Media Education Goes Digital," ed. D. Buckingham and S. Bragg. Special issue, *Learning, Media and Technology* 27, no. 2 (2007): 183–98.

Gauntlett, David. "Wide Angle: Is It Time for Media Studies 2.0?" *Media Education Association Newsletter* 5 (2007): 3–5.

Gee, James Paul. *What Video Games Have to Teach Us about Learning and Literacy*. Basingstoke: Palgrave, 2003.

Grossberg, Lawrence. "Cultural Studies vs. Political Economy: Is Anybody Else Bored with This Debate?" *Critical Studies in Mass Communication* 12, no. 1 (1995): 72–81.

Hargittai, Eszter, and Gina Walejko. "The Participation Divide: Content Creation and Sharing and the Digital Age." *Information Communication and Society* 11, no. 2 (2008): 239–256.

Herring, Susan C. "Questioning the Generational Divide: Technological Exoticism and Adult Constructions of Online Youth Identity." In *Youth, Identity and Digital Media*, ed. David Buckingham, 71–92. Cambridge, MA: MIT Press, 2008.

Jenkins, Henry, with Katie Clinton, Ravi Purushotma, Alice J. Robison, and Margaret Weigel. *Confronting the Challenges of Participatory Culture: Media Education for the 21st Century*. Chicago: MacArthur Foundation, 2006. http://www.nwp.org/cs/public/ print/resource/2713 (accessed November 27, 2007).

Lenhart, Amanda, Mary Madden, Alexandra Rankin Macgill, and Aaron Smith. *Teens and Social Media*. Pew Internet & American Life Project. Washington, DC: Pew Research Center, 2007.

Luke, Carmen. "Cyber-schooling and Technological Change: Multiliteracies for New Times." In *Multiliteracies: Literacy Learning and the Design of Social Futures*, ed. Bill Cope and Mary Kalantzis, 69–91. London: Routledge, 2000.

Marvin, Carolyn. *When Old Technologies Were New*. New York: Oxford University Press, 1988.

Merrin, William. *Media Studies 2.0 Forum* (blog). http://twopointzeroforum.blogspot .com (accessed March 16, 2009).

Ofcom. *Media Literacy: Report on UK children's Media Literacy*. London: Ofcom, 2008.

Pelletier, Caroline. "Games and Learning: What's the Connection?" *International Journal of Learning and Media* 1, no. 1 (2009). http://ijlm.net/ (accessed March 18, 2009).

Reiss, Spencer. "His Space." *Wired* 14.07 (July 2006). http://www.wired.com/wired/ archive/14.07/murdoch.html (accessed April 12, 2007).

Robins, Kevin, and Frank Webster. *Times of the Technoculture*. London: Routledge, 1999.

Ross, A. *No-Collar: The Humane Workplace and Its Hidden Costs*. Philadelphia: Temple University Press, 2003.

Streeter, Thomas. "The Cable Fable Revisited: Discourse, Policy and the Making of Cable Television." *Critical Studies in Mass Communication* 4, no. 2 (1987): 174–200.

Winston, Brian. *Media, Technology and Society: A History*. London: Routledge, 1998.

11 University of the People: A Model for International, Tuition-Free, Open Education Powered by Social Media

Shai Reshef

Introduction

In the age of the Internet, many of the barriers that have constrained us and separated us are disappearing. Distances are dwindling, and time is shrinking as our capacity for global communication expands exponentially. We are no longer simply different people from different countries and ethnic groups, too often fighting each other. Rather, we are evolving toward a global humanity that has an unprecedented opportunity to join together to improve our future and our world. To realize our brightest vision for the future, we must strive for an educated global population.

As a basic right, higher education can transform the lives not only of individuals but eventually of the entire world's population. However, UNESCO estimates that by the year 2025, there will be 98 million qualified students worldwide who will be excluded from higher education because of a shortage of university seats.[1] This chapter describes a global, wholly online university powered by social media that was founded to address the needs of these would-be students. In the past, developing such a university, spread across the world and serving a heterogeneous mix of students at a cost low enough to make it accessible to all qualified applicants, would have been impossible. Fortunately, such an endeavor is now feasible. The following pages describe the University of the People (UoPeople), its vision and purpose, and the basic unmet human right this model of international, tuition-free education seeks to address..

Education: An Unfulfilled Human Right

More than anything else, education is the road to world peace. Educated people have more hope for a successful and productive future. Education enables people to lift themselves out of poverty and chronic hunger and gives them a greater stake in the world. The basic right to education is one that, if met, leads to bettering one's potential earnings. Education allows for a fuller life and individual self-realization, which bring more personal peace. Education helps eradicate prejudices: generally, educated people tend to be more open to the viewpoints and belief systems of others, and more willing to embrace foreign customs and people. The challenge, then, is to make education globally accessible. Access to knowledge and information must become an essential human right, on par with access to health care.

Millions around the world desire postsecondary education and its ensuing credentials but lack the opportunity to acquire them, for a variety of reasons. For many today, a postsecondary education is simply too expensive, while others confront insufficient facilities in their region to accommodate all the willing and able students. Some are unable to leave their families to relocate to a university, and some cultures exclude certain social castes, ethnic or religious groups, or women from attending universities. These differences are often geographically or economically based. For example, according to the UNESCO Institute for Statistics, 70 percent of potential students in the United States attend a higher education institution, in comparison to only 6 percent in sub-Saharan Africa.

Vision for an Open and Global University

University of the People is a nonprofit, tuition-free, accredited online university. Dedicated to opening access to higher education globally, UoPeople is designed to help qualified high school graduates overcome financial, geographic, social, and personal constraints keeping them from college-level studies. The university currently offers two-year associate and four-year bachelor degree programs in business administration and computer science, with additional programs in health sciences and an online master of business administration in the planning stages.

The vision behind UoPeople was formulated at the convergence of three recent technological, cultural and societal transformations. These transformations are (1) the development and widespread adoption of the Internet and social media and their exponentially growing capacity and penetration, (2) the rapidly increasing quantity and quality of free information and software available online, and (3) the positive social dynamics of online social networking. These transformations are all highly significant, but particularly germane to the theme of this book is that open access to information, knowledge, and social interactions through digital media accessed over the Internet enabled the establishment of a university of the people. Moreover, the UoPeople model was founded on the belief that access to higher education could promote world peace and global economic development. I next present the history of this model, then explain its instructional strategy and look at the results of recent evaluation efforts.

History

From my previous work in for-profit education, and having chaired KIT eLearning, the online learning partner of the University of Liverpool and the first online university outside the United States, I have witnessed how powerful online learning can be. Students from all over the world were attracted to the idea of learning online while continuing their jobs. On their own time and at their convenience, students were able to obtain a high-quality European education through KIT eLearning. However, after some time I realized that earning an online degree was nothing more than wishful thinking for most people around the world, simply because of its lack of affordability. This realization was the spark that led to the founding of UoPeople.

UoPeople opened its gates in January 2009. Admissions began in April 2009, and classes began in September 2009. The university was accredited in February 2014. Since its founding, the university has admitted more than two thousand students from one hundred seventy countries on six continents.

After the initial launch in 2009 and promotion in the media, hundreds of volunteers offered their help for this new kind of university. The majority of them were university professors from the United States, among them emeriti faculty, but librarians, professionals, graduate students, and other academic specialists from around the world also offered their expertise.

It is noteworthy that most countries without the infrastructure or the capacity to create affordable and meaningful higher education opportunities still have sufficient Internet access to provide a gateway to programs offered by UoPeople. Thus, the Internet has in some ways served as an equalizer, enabling educational opportunity for the world's people even as other factors divide them.

A major goal of UoPeople is to better students' standards of living; therefore, it initially granted degrees offering the greatest promise for attractive employment. For instance, the degrees most sought both by prospective students and by their employers (excluding degrees in fields that require on-site learning or that are characterized by regional differences in content) are in business administration and computer science.

Within five years, UoPeople has formed partnerships with, among others, the Information and Society Project at Yale Law School, for research; New York University, to accept students; Microsoft, for scholarships and access to its certificate programs, mentoring, internships, and employment opportunities; and Hewlett-Packard, for general support, scholarships for women, and internships.

Admissions

Since the language of instruction at UoPeople is English, sufficient proficiency in English is a prerequisite to admission. Another prerequisite is successful completion of high school, clearly documented with a valid high school diploma. Regrettably, this means that when the gates of the university opened, though thousands of students applied, only hundreds met the requirements for admission.

Those who attend UoPeople compose a diverse student body. They range in age from eighteen to seventy-two years. With 45 percent female and 55 percent male, our students hail from all over the world (United States, 35 percent; East Asia, 10 percent; and the rest from Europe, Oceania, and Central and South America) and work in a broad spectrum of occupations. The United States, Nigeria, Indonesia, China, Brazil, Vietnam, and Saudi Arabia are among the most heavily represented countries. Some of these countries have high rates of illiteracy and low rates of higher education.

Instruction Powered by Social Media

Instruction at UoPeople is facilitated by two converging trends. First, open access to knowledge is becoming more commonplace. The extent to which information and knowledge are being offered without cost online is impressive, especially if we consider how much information could be protected under intellectual property laws and then monetized. Some manifestations of this open-access movement are open-source technology, open educational resources (OER) and the Creative Commons movement, as well as the proliferation of MOOCs (massive open online courses). With such information freely available, anyone with access to the Internet can study whatever he or she chooses, often at no charge. However, most people need more structure and guidance to gain a sound—not to mention a formally recognized—education; open access is necessary but not sufficient.

Second, online social networking by means of social media is transforming how people interact in various ways, including how they exchange information. Particularly compelling in social networking behavior, especially in online communities, is people's willingness to compose thoughtful answers to questions posed on forums, wikis, and in other venues by complete strangers. The new culture emerging in online social networks, study communities, and other forms of online interaction has direct relevance for the future of academia.

Such transformations notwithstanding, an educated world still needs processes for organizing the transmission of knowledge, for instilling analytic and communication skills, and, most important, for certifying educational achievement. This need to institutionalize learning, including the requisite diploma, is one of the drivers behind UoPeople.

Thus, students who have been accepted to UoPeople are required to take twenty courses to complete an associate's degree and forty courses to complete a bachelor's degree. For any given course, students are grouped into classes of twenty to thirty. In this virtual classroom, students study in week-long cycles. Each week, students log into the classroom and find the lecture, reading assignment, homework assignment, and discussion question for that week. The weekly discussion question is at the core of UoPeople's courses. Students must address the weekly question through online discussion with their classmates. At least four times each week, students raise issues and present ideas on the subject, as well as reply to the contributions of their classmates. This method helps foster active engagement, deepening involvement and self-discipline.

If a student has a question that cannot be answered by a classmate or wants to research more deeply a topic not included in the class discussion, he or she can approach the course instructor, who is there to read all the material, supervise the discussion, and get involved if needed. By the end of each week, after the discussion is exhausted, students turn in their homework assignment, take a self-assessment quiz, and continue on to the next week of their studies. At the end of each course, students take an exam and get a final grade based on the exam grade as well as on their peers' assessment of their contribution to the class discussion and of their homework assignments.

As indicated by the logistics and requirements just outlined, the university expects its students to take the initiative, studying diligently on their own and discussing their thoughts online. In turn, the university has an obligation to provide a learning environment that stimulates and motivates its students. Though meeting this obligation is important for every university, it is particularly important for an online institution, for students are likely to drop out if they are dissatisfied. Recognizing this reality, we have tried to structure the pedagogical model to achieve an interesting and motivating learning environment, and we measure student satisfaction on an ongoing basis. According to anonymous responses on individual end-of-course surveys, more than 95 percent of UoPeople students recommend the program to their peers and cite UoPeople as a great place to study.

Model for Tuition-Free and Open Education

The UoPeople is striving to become financially accessible, charging only small administrative fees and no tuition. Students pay an application processing fee of $50. For each course they take, the university expects students to pay a $100 per examination fee; thus a full BA degree will cost $4,000. For those who cannot afford even this amount, the university offers a variety of scholarships to make sure that no student is excluded solely for financial reasons. Over time, through grants and philanthropy, the university hopes to continue to be able to offer financial aid for students in need. With economies of scale, these administrative fees are projected to sustain the operating budget of the university when the student enrollment reaches approximately four thousand, which is expected to happen in 2016. Also necessary for this model to succeed are rigorous cost-containment measures, the use of open-source technology and open-access material, and the volunteer staffing of both academic and administrative areas of the university.

Indeed, perhaps the most significant source of support for UoPeople comes from the enormous number of volunteers (more than three thousand) who generously donate their time and expertise to the university. For instance, most of the university's leadership participates on a volunteer basis, with individuals from leading institutions such as Columbia University, New York University, and others providing UoPeople with a world-class academic backbone. Some volunteers provide external services pro bono, some help with administration, and some are involved with course development, creating libraries and running departments. The university courses are written by volunteers. These are experts in the relevant subjects who write the courses, review other volunteers' work, and supervise and improve the courses once they are being taught. Furthermore, UoPeople uses open educational resources. That is, all of its course material is free for anyone to use, and any content created by the course developers and then used by instructors is made freely available online.

The university also has an army of volunteers who function as instructors and carry out the day-to-day teaching activity. Volunteer instructors commit to staying with UoPeople for five years. Many of these volunteers wish to interact with and help students directly. Thus, the university relies heavily on volunteers, and numerous volunteers are involved in every aspect of its activities; however, the university is not wholly dependent on them. Today, in fact, there are many more volunteers than students, and we are still learning how to manage and use the incredible resources they provide. As time passes, the university will be able to formulate policies and practices for working with this volunteer army. In the short time the university has been in existence, a main lesson learned has been that volunteers are useful, and very helpful in the day-to-day activities of the university, and yet a system had to be built so that for every volunteer there is a paid backup to ensure that no part of the university could be vitally hurt.

Implementation Challenges

Creating and implementing an experimental, online university that is affordable and accessible to people around the globe is not without its challenges. One challenge, as just noted, is managing and using efficiently an army of volunteers. A second challenge is getting the word out to our target audience of students. Although we have had publicity in prominent media outlets such as the *New York Times* and through TED Talks, many of our potential students are not consumers of this kind of media. People who stand to benefit from tuition-free education need to know about us, and yet the people who may need us the most may have a hard time finding out about us. As a nonprofit, and to remain tuition-free, UoPeople must operate on a very lean budget. Thus, without a wealth of funds for marketing, the university is largely dependent on word of mouth and media coverage. Though our mission is to ensure that no one is left behind for financial reasons, we need help both making sure that students can find us in the first place and being able to assist them with financial aid, if necessary, once they do. An ongoing challenge, then, is making sure we are visible and accessible, when people who need us are researching their options, and ensuring we have the scholarships to support them if they attend.

A third challenge to implementing this model is facilitating diversity in admissions. For instance, UoPeople often has applicants who want to study at the university, who stand to gain the most from tuition-free higher education, and who fit our mission, but who, for various reasons, do not have the necessary documentation (e.g., refugees, asylum seekers, internally displaced people).To help meet this challenge, as of November 2014 we have been working with the UN Refugee Agency (the UN High Commissioner for Refugees) to establish policies that make the admission process for refugees as easy as possible in cases where official transcripts and documents cannot be obtained. Thus, UoPeople is attempting to tackle one of its biggest challenges, that of reaching out to the least upwardly mobile people, refugees and asylum seekers. Reaching out to this population is an initiative most in line with our mission: to open the gates to higher education to all qualified students and help those most in need of education overcome other barriers. We are hopeful that this model of collaboration with the UN Refugee Agency can be replicated wherever there are refugees and can be scaled up to serve millions of refugees around the world, providing them with access to higher education.

A fourth challenge faced in implementing this model is that some of the students UoPeople seeks to help educate live in areas with unstable electricity or broadband access. Although we could argue that the spread of technology will ultimately bring education and academic studies to every corner of the world, today many of those who have Internet access still don't have broadband, which limits the educational benefits of technology. To help mitigate this situation, we have sought to design courses that use the technology that is available to students, not the broadband we might wish they had. Such efforts have helped increase our outreach to more than one hundred seventy countries across the world. Nonetheless, we recognize that conditions for online education around the world remain less than ideal; some of our students get by through accessing classes as they move around, looking for free wireless Internet; other students, who do not even have running water or electricity in their homes, must go to a lot of effort to reach their classwork by studying from Internet cafés. We remain hopeful that as more people become educated and inspire the desire for education in others, they will advocate for change, and conditions will continue to improve.

Conclusion

University of the People has changed my perception of online education. Since beginning my studies, I have observed a positive change within myself. I have learned so many things during this short period of time which I would have never discovered on my own. University of the People has given me a purpose and I believe it's the best use of my time for the betterment of my own life. I would like to say with all my heart that education at UoPeople is the best thing that has happened to me in 2009 and I wish it would have come a little earlier.

—Akhtar Razi, a UoPeople student, formerly of Pakistan and now residing in Canada, in a 2011 comment

In presenting the case of UoPeople this chapter has summarized the vision, history, and instructional model for a tuition-free and open university powered by social media, including its potential for educating people around the world and the challenges that implementing such a model entails. This model aligns with a growing trend in higher education. According to a 2006 Sloan Consortium survey, 96 percent of large U.S. colleges and universities offered at least some of their courses online.[2] In addition, many respected online universities today are offering accredited degrees to students. A recent meta-analysis study released by the U.S. Department of Education reported that online learning has some advantages over face-to-face instruction.[3] The study found that students who gained all or part of their instruction online performed better, on average, than those who took the same courses through face-to-face instruction only.

The world's educational system is ill-designed to meet the needs of millions of prospective, capable students. Online education now offers an unprecedented opportunity to rectify this lacuna by eliminating the physical constraints of the campus or classroom and reaching out globally to enable access to education for *all*.

The enormous potential of online education lies in reaching the large numbers of individuals who in the past would have been denied their basic right to an education. UoPeople students may be experiencing firsthand the change this university model is bringing to the world. With a few educated students, our students and their families benefit; with more educated students, their environments and communities benefit; and with many more educated students, the whole world benefits.

Notes

1. UNESCO Institute for Statistics figures, ISCED levels 5 and 6; British Council and IDP Australia projections.

2. I. Elaine Allen and Jeff Seaman, *Making the Grade: Online Education in the United States, 2006* (Newburyport, MA: Sloan Consortium, 2007).

3. Barbara Means et al., *Evaluation of Evidence-Based Practices in Online Learning: A Meta-analysis and Review of Online Learning Studies* (Washington, DC: U.S. Department of Education, 2010).

Bibliography

Allen, I. Elaine, and Jeff Seaman. *Making the Grade: Online Education in the United States, 2006*. Newburyport, MA: Sloan Consortium, 2007.

Means, Barbara, Yuki Toyama, Robert Murphy, Marianne Bakia, and Karla Jones. *Evaluation of Evidence-Based Practices in Online Learning: A Meta-analysis and Review of Online Learning Studies*. Washington, DC: U.S. Department of Education, 2010.

12   Technology and the Economics of Education

Daniel J. H. Greenwood

Introduction

Markets for information do not work, and as a result, successful educational institutions must find a way to evade or overcome market failure. The basic problems, if not their jargon, are intuitive: the *sunk cost problem* and the *trust problem*. Historically, successful universities mitigated both by a combination of cross-subsidies and structures designed to preserve reputation. Today, however, intense market pressures threaten both mechanisms.

The Sunk Cost Problem

The sunk cost problem is the technical term for J. P. Morgan's "ruinous competition," his insight that free markets in capital-intensive industries, unless restrained by bankers like himself or monopolistic mergers, lead to crisis and underinvestment. *Sunk costs*—meaning investments that have already been made and cannot be undone—earn no return in competitive markets, which reward only *marginal cost*—the cost of the last unit of production. When marginal costs are lower than average costs, investment earns no return in competitive markets.

Examples abound. It costs a great deal to build a railroad, a sunk cost, but not very much to add an additional, or marginal, passenger. A computer chip factory requires a huge initial investment, but then it can efficiently convert sand and cheap labor into millions of chips. Pharmaceuticals, software, novel financial instruments, e-books, and music tracks cost a great deal of money to design or create but very little to produce.

To revisit the railroad example, once the initial investment in tracks and staff is in place (the sunk cost), railroads make more money running trains than sitting idle so long as they sell enough tickets to cover the cost of fuel (the marginal cost). Once the railroad is committed to running the train, every extra ticket sold is additional income with virtually no extra cost. A railroad vying for that extra income before its competitors take it will force prices down to the cost of carrying an extra passenger—that is, virtually nothing. If prices fall below the cost of maintaining tracks, training engineers, and developing next-generation infrastructure, the system is doomed to fail. Worse yet, if this problem is obvious in advance, producers, realizing that profits are unlikely, will never enter the market in the first place. Left to itself, even with willing sellers and buyers, the market described in this example effectively and efficiently generates nothing at all. Thus, some way must be found to escape the market's invisible hand.

Universities exist because of the sunk cost problem. Philosophy, the arts, and sciences—useful information in general—are extremely costly to create: researchers and artists must be trained, experiments must be run, data must be analyzed, and thoughtful people must be paid while they think, compose, tinker, or struggle with sentence formation. In contrast to the high costs of creation, the knowledge, ideas, or writing that result are often cheap to reproduce and distribute. If prices reflected marginal costs, books would sell for little more than the cost of paper and retailing; ideas would be priced as so much hot air.

The Internet makes this problem worse. The marginal cost of distributing and consuming lectures, books, newspapers, photographs, research, formulas, music, and movies is approaching zero. Moreover, the artificial monopolies of copyright and patent—intended to free producers from competition and, therefore, marginal pricing—are increasingly easy to evade. Left unchecked, competition will press prices down well below the point at which it is possible to cover the fixed costs of people thinking, creating, researching, collecting, analyzing, and writing. If they can't make a living doing those things, they are likely to do them less. Adam Smith's invisible hand will ensure that individual actors pursuing their individual interests will leave us collectively worse off.

The Trust Problem

Furthermore, markets for information suffer from a trust problem. In any market, reasonable buyers demand assurance that sellers will actually deliver what they have promised. Ordinarily, the best way to demonstrate that a product is as valuable as the seller contends is to let the buyer try it out—take it for a test drive, use it at a friend's, or see the product demonstrated. However, many purchases or experiences are essentially one-shot. By the time you can evaluate most movies or exotic vacations, you are not a customer anymore. Similarly, to show a prospective buyer how good or useful an idea is, the seller must disclose it; but once the buyer has it, why pay for it? Conversely, if buyers are willing to pay before knowing whether the concept is worthwhile, why should the seller deliver? The free market result is a *market for lemons,* in which willing buyers and willing sellers fail to make a deal.[1]

Universities, especially tuition-driven institutions that attempt to pay for the production of knowledge by selling education, are organized in response to the trust problem. In order to know, firsthand, the quality of education an institution offers, the consumer has to actually live an educated life. That is, consumers must themselves be educated to see how well their education has prepared them and to be in a position to evaluate the quality of education an institution offers. An institution that deferred charging until then would run into a free-rider problem.[2] Conversely, and more commonly, schools can charge in advance, but this merely shifts the free-rider problem to the other side: how are consumers to know that the institution will provide the education or status that entices them to enroll?

Reputation can solve the trust issue when buyers believe past performance predicts future quality, so that students and their future employers believe the university has the ability and incentive to produce future education and graduates commensurate with its past. But the end game always poses a problem to reputation-based systems: especially near the end of their careers, sellers may be tempted to mine their reputation by cutting quality and overcharging until buyers catch on. If buyers worry about this kind of defection, sellers may instead defect in the penultimate period— and so on, until the entire reputational gambit fails.

Reputation can create trust only if institutions (individuals can never do it on their own) can credibly deter defection. In universities, faculty governance, peer review, and alumni influence all help reduce the likelihood of defection: alumni and faculty may have personal reputations tied to the institution and, as groups, overlapping time frames with no end point, or penultimate period. Still, administrators may be sorely tempted to win quick reputational gains by shifting resources from long to short term—the academic equivalent of killing the R&D department in favor of better advertising—on the assumption that they, the administrators, will be able to move on before the price comes due. At successful institutions—Harvard, for example—such short-termism would be quickly discovered and harshly condemned by powerful actors with longer-term commitments. For younger alumni and faculty, the long term is far more important than momentary gains. At less prestigious institutions, by contrast, there may be no countervailing forces powerful and committed enough to resist. Then, as potential students, employers, and mobile faculty become aware that reputations are ephemeral, or easily manipulated and exploited, the trust problem might quickly create self-fulfilling pressures to short-termism or churning.

Today's Universities: Navigating Sunk Cost and Trust Problems

American colleges and universities have mitigated the sunk cost problem by cross-subsidization, that is, by depending on alternative sources of income. This allows them to give away their chief products, as market competition would pressure them to do anyway.

Private schools sell a package of undergraduate education, status markers of the type Veblen made famous,[3] and services to help adolescents transition to adulthood at handcraft rates reflecting both the high cost of unmechanized services and the conspicuous consumption value of prestige. Prestigious private institutions supplement tuition with a good deal of begging, or the selling of potlatch prestige (or whatever it is that motivates donors to want their names on educational real estate); endowed and land grant schools also add profits from their real estate, investing, and hedge fund activities. State institutions, like most European schools, traditionally depend on state budgets; research universities are heavily supported by federal grants. Until fairly recently, medical schools were able to use the medical insurance system to charge more than the marginal costs of care, thus cross-subsidizing the costs of educating doctors. Professional schools can charge more than cost because they offer students admission to restricted professions, and students pay the price because the same restrictions limit competition after graduation and allow them to charge a higher price for their own expertise (a sunk cost itself). These partial monopolies, traditionally accompanied by professional norms that limited price competition, protect schools and professionals alike from the corrosive effects of marginal cost pricing.

But cross-subsidization is always unstable. Cross-subsidies depend on excess profits somewhere else. In turn, excess profits invite competitors attempting to seize some of them by reducing price. Thus, competition always threatens to reduce prices to marginal cost and eliminate the profits on which a cross-subsidy depends. Thus, hospitals that are subsidizing medical education must charge more than ones that do not; in competitive markets, nonteaching hospitals will drive them out of business or force them to reduce prices until the subsidy is gone. Professional schools that profit from limits to entry also face enormous temptations to cheat: each additional student represents immediate income, while the costs are nearly all borne by future professionals, who will face more competition and a lower lifetime income, or by customers, who will face reduced services if the profession becomes unprofitable.

Universities charge students more than the cost of teaching alone. Besides teaching, faculty are paid to research, write, think, educate themselves, supervise each other, and police the institution's quality. Specialized teachers, who would pass on existing knowledge without being paid to create new knowledge or even maintain their own expertise, would be cheaper. Often, costs could be cut even further by automation: for example, by replacing the hand grading of papers with multiple-choice tests. To be sure, teaching quality drops when faculty are no longer paid to maintain or increase their knowledge, or when the handwork of guiding an apprentice is replaced with automated sorting systems. Nonetheless, in a fully competitive market, the university as we know it would quickly become an endangered species.

An Entrepreneurial Model for Educational Institutions

An innovative institutional model could, in theory, survive these market pressures. An entrepreneurial profit-maximizer could simply eliminate the cross-subsidies and cut prices closer to the marginal cost of education alone. Rather than paying to support training the next generation of faculty, to maintain the skills of existing teachers, or to support research or scholarship, an entrepreneurial institution would seek to limit itself to the sale of teaching.

Teaching, if done right, will always be expensive; there is a certain amount of handwork involved in explanations and editing that is difficult to automate. Nonetheless, the marginal cost of adding one more student to an existing teacher's portfolio is quite low. It can be lower still if the teacher lectures via movie, grading is shifted to lower-paid piece workers, and the most difficult to automate aspects of apprenticeship and mentoring are simply abandoned. More radical innovators could apply Taylor's principles of scientific management, trying to work out the components of effective teaching and using them to train low-wage replacements for the skilled guild.[4]

This is, of course, precisely the model of test prep and bar review courses, much of the online and for-profit education industry, and our community colleges. Existing academic stars and experts are used for headline teaching, while explanations and grading are automated or shifted to cheap labor, reducing prices dramatically. This route, then, may be highly attractive to consumers and producers alike for a brief period. Students could get cheaper education from better-known faculty; the best teachers would be paid more and—more attractive still—would be able to teach larger numbers of students.

Less radically, the aforementioned entrepreneur could simply hire more adjuncts, post-docs, and similar academic migrant workers. Trained PhDs or engineers have already made their investment in training; their own education is a sunk cost. Without the cross-subsidies and limits on the market of traditional universities, competitive markets will drive them, like railroads, to charge no more than marginal cost—not enough to earn a decent return on the time, effort, and tuition in obtaining the skill or to attract informed newcomers into the field, but just enough to be more attractive on any given day than driving a taxi.

The costs reductions are not from increased efficiency. Instead, students are no longer being asked to pay for the education of the faculty, research, or the creation of new knowledge and cultural artifacts. They are not even paying for maintaining the reputation of the institution, which instead buys existing reputations on the cheap (in the form of its headline teachers). The cheap price results from eliminating the cross-subsidy. But this means that a university system based on marginal cost pricing is self-destructive. The end of the cross-subsidy means that developing expertise and advancing human knowledge will not earn returns. As in any industry where average costs exceed marginal costs and competitive markets price at the margin, the message to those who might enter the field is clear: don't. There are easier ways to earn the living of an adjunct professor.

Even if the professoriate disappears as a middle-class profession, some individuals may be willing to do it as an avocation—living the romantic life of La Bohème or the privileged life of Victorian aristocratic amateurs. A handful of institutions—like Harvard and Yale—may have large enough endowments to support graduate education and creative research work on their own, although even the wealthiest schools would be hard-pressed to support modern scientific research and advanced medical training on endowments alone. The potential number of amateur physicists (for instance) is small, and few American universities and colleges have large enough endowments to pay the fixed costs of education, let alone research, without tuition support.

Much of U.S. productivity, in the crudest sense, freeloads on the university system. For a century, the cross-subsidies of the academy have provided shelter from market pressures that would destroy productive research, by hiring artists, musicians, writers, mathematicians, biologists, economists, physicists, and critical critics to teach and leaving them time for their other work. The wisdom and research that these scholars contribute to the world for free is then available for others to use—for their pleasure, for the social good, or, if they can figure out a way to monetize it, for profit. For example, fundamental research in biology is done in the universities, not in the pharmaceutical companies, because the universities can support it and the companies cannot. To be sure, Bell Labs did great work, and Google pays for undirected creativity today, but these firms cross-subsidize from their monopoly profits, and the former exists no more and the latter might, presumably, succumb either to competition or to the temptation to use its profits otherwise. The core of research and creative work in our economy occurs in universities; if we let them go, we have no reason to expect that their task will be taken up magically by a new, or as yet nonexistent, institution.

Reenvisioning Economics of Education in the Age of Social Media

In short, new information technologies and social media present massive challenges to the economics of education, and to the future of our institutions. These challenges are also playing out in other industries. Journalism, for instance, is a core part of our system of democratic government. If we no longer have a way to pay professional journalists, we have lost something essential. But journalism is relatively cheap; perhaps we will be able to endow research foundations, or shift investigative journalism into the universities. If we lose the universities, we will endanger the soul and brain of our civilization.

To be sure, the world will not end if the academy downsizes to a handful of great institutions able to survive because of endowments or government support, accompanied by a larger number of teaching schools, looking more like community colleges than today's state or private colleges. But shrinking the academy will have important losses: less range of discussion, more inbreeding, fewer graduate students, smaller audiences for the few who remain, and, most important, more aspects of our governing institutions and cultural mores with no critics watching them at all.

Next, I consider one innovative model for the modern university: University of the People (UoPeople), which was introduced in chapter 11. In one sense, it is the People's Express of the academic world: the wild efflorescence of new opportunity possible as the old system collapses. At the beginning of airline deregulation, People's Express reduced airfares and enormously expanded access to travel before succumbing itself to the inevitable pressures of marginal cost pricing. The UoPeople model similarly offers opportunities to everyone that formerly were restricted to the rich. It does this by stripping the service, education, down to its bare core, transforming it in the process. The UoPeople experiment is one to watch. Will it be a harbinger of a new era, or it will destroy itself in its Samson-like declaration of independence?

I am hopeful that UoPeople will survive and prosper, that it will be a transformative experience in the lives of many students, and that it will prove a footnote in our march toward a new system of financing education or a successful rebuilding of the old one. Information wants to be free, said the Internet ideologues. UoPeople is trying to make it so.

Challenge: Infrastructure

Despite the extraordinary potential for transforming the economics of education described above, the case of UoPeople, operating as a nonprofit, tuition-free, accredited online university, is not without its challenges. While information wants to be free at the margin, it is quite expensive to set up. UoPeople needs an infrastructure: coders to design and maintain its websites, people to read and verify applications, others to coordinate volunteers and pinch hit when they punt, as volunteers often do. To work, the model needs lawyers to press for accreditation and to navigate education laws all over the world, staffers to consider novel issues of student discipline online, and so on. Even seemingly simple issues become expensive, especially when its administrators are seeking to keep the budget minimal— expensive and frequently personally painful. What is to be done about the rural student who is four days' journey from a notary who could certify an English-language translation of his high school diploma, the war refugee who cannot possibly obtain a copy, or the student who fills a classroom's online forum with racist rantings? UoPeople cannot shift entirely to the automated "customer service" of some computer companies, where a software program attempts to guess what the problem is and matches it to a canned solution. Someone needs to do the work to find the relevant information.

Challenge: Need for Expertise

More than infrastructure, though, nonprofit, tuition-free, online universities such as UoPeople need expertise and information. Courses can only be created, evaluated, updated, and maintained by experts who know the materials they seek to teach. The UoPeople's plan is for these experts to be volunteers—that is, professors paid by some other university, or retirees living on the proceeds of a career at another university. As a unique or highly unusual service to the poorest sectors of the potential student population, this university hopes it can attract qualified people willing to donate enormous amounts of time.

It is not yet clear whether this is a realistic expectation: preparing a course is a huge amount of work, doing it well is even more work, and doing it in an unfamiliar medium and format without ongoing student feedback is likely to prove more than most volunteers are able to take on. It is already clear that every course must be edited, formatted, and monitored by a paid staffer. It may yet turn out that many also need to be written and peer-reviewed by paid experts; if we reach the stage where distributing existing information is free, it will only be after quite a bit of expense.

Challenge: Scale and Sustainability

Moreover, it is still unclear whether UoPeople can represent a sustainable model for more than the niche of the education market it has currently carved out (i.e., business and computer science education). Its volunteers need to eat, pay rent, and educate their own children. They can do this only if they have jobs elsewhere. They need to be qualified to teach, which means they must have the time to develop their own knowledge and keep it up, and they need to have studied with someone else, who similarly must have been educated.

UoPeople anticipates enormous returns to scale. It anticipates that the same web staff will be able to handle a website for thousands of students as for dozens. Developing courses is major work, but once developed, courses may have a long life span and not require inordinate numbers of volunteers to create new ones and update old ones. The UoPeople's plans for grading and discussion rely largely on peer-to-peer networks—that is, advanced students assist beginners in the system. Such an apprenticeship model becomes more plausible as the UoPeople community grows larger. With tens of thousands of students, some may be interested and competent enough to run the discussions and maintain a wiki-like self-ordering community. One assumption built into this model is that size will create something new and different that does not exist today and cannot exist in a smaller environment.

But ultimately, the model is not socially self-sustaining. It requires and expects continuing, ongoing support from better funded professionals. Those professionals can only be sustained by fully funded universities and can only be sustained by the larger ecosystem gathered around the universities—the opportunities for students, the expectation that reasonably good students will be able to pursue careers in subjects without immediately salable marginal product, the critical mass of scholars and students and teachers to sustain an intellectual discussion and prevent it from turning inward and sterile.

Conclusion

In the end, the question is not one of markets but of politics. If we—collectively, the people of the rich countries—value our cultures and if our political institutions are functional enough to instantiate that value into real support, we will find ways to pay for our core educational institutions, including traditional universities that take the production of knowledge, not just its dissemination, as their mission. In that event, nonprofit, tuition-free, online universities such as UoPeople could be an extraordinary monument to the power of entrepreneurial vision and volunteerism. But UoPeople depends on the wealth of knowledge and skill those core institutions create; it cannot replace them.

We could accept that information is not going to be produced adequately by the market—and is essential for markets to function successfully. Thus, we could simply agree that we need government-financed universities as badly as we need government-financed prisons, wars, and highways. It is simply unfair to our youngsters to require them to pay for the production of the knowledge we all need. Perhaps we will try radically shortened patent and copyright terms, allowing information to flow more freely and avoiding the side effects of governmentally created monopolies, much as we did for physical infrastructure in the early nineteenth century (see the Charles River Bridge controversy).[5] We could instead finance discovery and innovation more efficiently and cheaply with a prize system, financed by taxes and administered by the NIH/NSF or delegated in part to relevant university and industry research departments. Perhaps the process of finding new ways to pay for the creation of knowledge and skill would be eased if we changed governmental accounting norms to reflect that these expenses are investments, so that much of current year "deficits" ought instead to be recorded as "saving for the future."

Notes

1. George A. Akerlof, "The Market for Lemons: Quality Uncertainty and the Market Mechanism," *Quarterly Journal of Economics* 84, no. 3 (1970): 488–500.

2. For an explanation of alumni contributions as repayment of an implicit loan, see Henry. B. Hansmann, "The Role of Nonprofit Enterprise," *Yale Law Journal* 89, no. 5 (1980): 835–901; for the suggestion that alumni and students might view endowment as "insurance against loss of reputational capital," see Henry Hansmann, "Why Do Universities Have Endowments?," *Journal of Legal Studies* 19, no. 1 (1990): 3–42.

3. Thorstein Veblen, *The Theory of the Leisure Class* (New York: A. M, Kelley, 1965 [1899]).

4. Frederick Winslow Taylor, *The Principles of Scientific Management* (New York: Harper, 1914).

5. *Proprietors of Charles River Bridge v. Proprietors of Warren Bridge,* 1837 (overturning a government grant of monopoly to finance a bridge, and thus forcing governments to find different ways to finance such infrastructure).

Bibliography

Akerlof, George A. "The Market for Lemons: Quality Uncertainty and the Market Mechanism." *Quarterly Journal of Economics* 84, no. 3 (1970): 488–500.

Hansmann, Henry B. "The Role of Nonprofit Enterprise." *Yale Law Journal* 89, no. 5 (1980): 835–901.

Hansmann, Henry. "Why Do Universities Have Endowments?" *Journal of Legal Studies* 19, no. 1 (1990): 3–42.

Proprietors of Charles River Bridge v. Proprietors of Warren Bridge, 36 U.S. 420, 9 L. Ed. 773 (1837).

Taylor, Frederick Winslow. *The Principles of Scientific Management*. New York: Harper, 1914.

Veblen, Thorstein. *The Theory of the Leisure Class*. New York: A. M. Kelley, 1965 (1899).

13 Social Media and Education on a Massive Scale: The Case of MOOCs

Minhtuyen Mai, Adam Poppe, and Christine Greenhow

Introduction

Access to postsecondary education is essential to gaining skills in a competitive job market. Massive open online courses (MOOCs) offer one example of education made accessible and from which new knowledge of teaching might be generated. In MOOCs, scholars deliver content to masses of online students across states and countries and incentivize peer-to-peer sharing and feedback, largely through social media. MOOCs are typically characterized by large-scale interactive student participation, open access via the Internet, and interorganizational collaboration. They can open up access to instruction, enabling anyone with Internet access to take classes offered by instructors from across disciplines for free or at a low cost. Such courses seek to gather a wide range of students and foster information sharing and participatory learning. For instance, MOOC enrollment size may range from hundreds to thousands of students. Also, MOOCs vary with regard to the degree of social media used; connectivist MOOCs (cMOOCs) often utilize social media to maximize student-student interaction. In contrast, behaviorist MOOCs (xMOOCs), which seek mainly to deliver content with minimal interaction, utilize technological tools that resemble those typically used in traditional online courses, such as online video-recorded lectures and automatically graded exams.[1]

Definition

The term MOOC was coined in 2008 by David Cormier, an educational activist, while he was discussing an open online class taught by Stephen Downes and George Siemens.[2] Cormier believed that information was everywhere, and that MOOCs could organize and direct that information. According to Cormier, a MOOC is open, participatory, distributed, and establishes a foundation for lifelong, networked learning. MOOCs offer a way to connect and collaborate, engage in the learning process, and most importantly, to connect people who care about a topic. With the use of social media, these courses can connect together to build a networked MOOC curriculum.

History

The first MOOC emerged in 2008, followed soon after by other cMOOCs, as well as many xMOOCs. Many of the current xMOOCs are the product of pairings of various nonprofit organizations and many top-level universities, such as Stanford, Harvard, and MIT. Stanford University, for instance, offered open enrollment to three engineering courses: Artificial Intelligence, Machine Learning, and Databases. On December 19, 2011, MIT offered its version of MOOCs, called MITx. In 2012, Andrew Ng and Daphne Koller from Stanford University launched Coursera. Harvard and MIT soon teamed up to launch their version of MOOCs, called edX. The idea that people with a computer and sufficient bandwidth could take courses offered by top-tier professors seemed revolutionary, as indicated by rising enrollment numbers; quickly, more than 150,000 students had enrolled in MOOCs.

By 2012, MOOCs had gained significant popularity on social media platforms such as Facebook, Twitter, and Tumblr. More universities, both public and private, started offering these classes, perhaps seeking to attract attention from their wealthy alumni, who might then give back to their alma mater. There were both benefits from and challenges to implementing MOOCs in education.

Benefits

Proponents argue that MOOCs offer several benefits, such as opening access to educational opportunities, personalizing curricula, producing insights from research on learning at scale, cost benefits and productive partnerships. First, MOOCs may strengthen education by making it more accessible, affordable, and efficient. Theoretically, MOOCs can provide access to educational opportunities for everyone with Internet access. Supporters claim that MOOCs can also help bridge the equity gap in higher education and make college and university attendance more affordable by offering courses mostly for free. MOOCs can target students who are not in college but who want to gain the skills they need to be competitive in the job market, without charging exorbitant tuitions and fees. For instance, many students seek credentials that indicate they have necessary job skills but cannot afford expensive degree programs. Social media sites like *Degreed* allow learners to connect to their Facebook accounts and acquire "experience points" for the courses they have taken, including formal and informal classes. Moreover, MOOCs could make education more efficient by educating more people at lower costs. For instance, the Georgia Institute of Technology is working with Udacity to offer the first all-MOOC master's degree.[3] The tuition will be approximately $7,000, a more affordable price point than the standard master's degree. In these ways, MOOCs may provide a promising approach to closing the achievement gap for students traditionally underrepresented in higher education, such as students from low-income families.

Second, MOOCs can generate large data sets—through both the content people upload and the behavioral traces (such as log files) they leave behind—which can be mined for patterns and used to test learning and teaching theories at scale. Analysis of these learning patterns has the potential to fuel discovery, integration, and interdisciplinary work as well as build future scholarship.[4] Current projects are harnessing MOOC data, comparing "thousands of records to see where activities rise and fall in online classes" in order to "discover patterns" in both teaching and learning.[5] Thus, MOOCs could allow for the development of learning analytics that could be used for adaptation and personalization of curriculum through predictive modeling and forecasting of learner behavior or achievement or that apply social network analysis techniques to optimize learner interactions.[6] Insights generated from such studies may contribute to new theoretical models, such as models of self- and peer assessment, as well as to the design of automated mechanisms that support students' learning goals and processes.

Third, there are potential cost benefits to MOOCs. While the start-up costs of some MOOCs can be $100,000, once created, MOOCs can be reusable.[7] The cost of taking a MOOC is mostly free, since often there are no classroom or materials' fees. It is important to note that the universities themselves and the companies with which they partner typically pay for MOOC development up-front. In turn, MOOCs can also become profitable by using the *freemium* model, that is, charging premium users more, for more features, while still maintaining a free or low-cost model for other users. In addition, universities have utilized this model to serve their alumni and other people who want to take a class but not necessarily in a formal undergraduate or graduate degree program. By offering MOOCs, universities can cater to these populations who show eagerness for learning.

Furthermore, MOOCs may offer governments a promising way to reenvision their national education models. For instance, Coursera is working with the Education Ministry in Trinidad to build the first national MOOC-based educational system. This effort is designed to give the country's students the necessary skills to compete in the global business job market. In an interview with BBC news, Lila Ibrahim at Coursera stated that this was a "world-leading and unique" scheme, and that locating it in Trinidad was a reflection of the country's willingness to experiment with the idea of online learning.[8] Trinidad's minister of yertiary education, Fazal Karim, also remarked that this approach to reenvisioning the national system is promising because any geographic distance or isolation can be removed with massively open and online learning.[9]

Challenges

If proponents argue that MOOCs can allow anyone who has a high-speed Internet connection to learn from and contribute to course materials anywhere in the world, others claim that MOOCs are perpetuating more educational inequality than they solve. The idea of access, they argue, cannot be realistically accomplished simply by offering these free online courses. Audrey Watters, an education technology blogger at HackEducation.com, has dissected the functionality and effectiveness of MOOCs. Watters cautions that MOOCs do more harm than good. She cites many issues involving MOOCs, such as the dangers of outsourcing public education to for-profit companies, student cheating, labor issues, intellectual property issues, specious credit offers, and curriculum licensing issues.[10]

Many scholars cite empirical evidence to critique the quality and spread of educational opportunities in MOOCs. For instance, they argue that students much prefer and learn better from hands-on activities than from passively watching videos, a practice fostered in many xMOOCs.[11] Others suggest that MOOCs seem to attract a mostly niche population: men who already have a college degree.[12] Recent data suggest that MOOCs have low completion rates and still do not demonstrate any meaningful progress in closing the achievement gap separating low-income students from their high-income peers. In fact, many students from the lowest income quartile do not benefit from online education in general, since many still do not have Internet access in their homes.[13] Examining the dark side of MOOCs and neoliberal ideals, Markus Deimann wrote that by constructing the vision that everyone is a "self-responsible" learner who is in charge of his or her own processes, MOOCs turn learning into a means of achieving economic goals, rather than educational goals.[14]

In a recent turn of events, the founder of Udacity, Sebastian Thurn, announced that his company is no longer adopting traditional xMOOCs and their emphasis on content delivery as the overarching model for massively open and online education. In an interview with *PandoDaily*'s Carmel Deamicis, Thurn remarked, "It's very simple. The MOOC that we created at Udacity was our first attempt to democratize education and we learned from it. Like everyone, we made mistakes. We learned we can drastically boost learning outcomes by adding a service layer around MOOCs. It has a large impact on completion rates and learning outcomes. Many people in the industry would say, 'We told you so.'"[15]

In *Disruptor, Distraction, or What? A Policymaker's Guide to MOOCs*, Andrew Kelly proposes four lessons to take away from this early wave of MOOCs.[16] The first lesson is that educators cannot expect MOOCs to be a substitute for college courses, since obtaining college credits by completing MOOCs is rare. The second lesson is that MOOCs may not be well equipped to replace college-readiness courses in helping reduce the college enrollment and achievement gap. A third lesson is that a hybrid model of online education may offer the ideal solution because it would combine MOOCs and interactive, face-to-face instruction, which could boost course retention and completion rates. Kelly's final lesson is that MOOCs are best designed to help solve a skills gap, such as skills in computer programming.

Implications for the Educational Community

Several implications for teachers, administrators, and others in the educational community follow. First, social media and education on a massive scale, in the form of MOOCs, currently offer an exciting vision for educational innovation, but evidence of a positive impact on valued educational outcomes is lacking. Like many educational interventions, MOOCs require sustained evaluation across multiple contexts and types of learners to document and demonstrate their effects. Second, to foster evidence-based practices in future MOOCs, educators, MOOC developers, and evaluators will need to work together over time to determine which types of MOOCs are most beneficial for which types of learners, educational contexts, and educational or economic goals. Some predict that MOOCs will evolve in much the same way that fast food has, contributing to the "spread of junk education."[17] Others assert that a "MOOC Spring" is taking place that will lead to a fundamental change in how we view education.[18] Some take a more conservative approach.[19] Perhaps after all dust settles from the arrival of MOOCs, we will understand how to utilize them efficiently in ways that complement traditional content-delivery models of education, as well as in ways that are truly revolutionary.[20]

Notes

1. Osvaldo Rodriguez, "The Concept of Openness behind c and x-MOOCs (Massive Open Online Courses)," *Open Praxis* 5, no. 1 (2013): 67–73.

2. D[ave] Comier, "Why Teach MOOCs—MOOCs as a Selfish Enterprise," talk at MIT (video file), March 17, 2014, https://www.youtube.com/watch?v=Smt8lsPU _Mo.

3. Steve Kolowich, "The MOOC 'Revolution' May Not Be as Disruptive as Some Had Imagined," *Chronicle of Higher Education*, August 8, 2013, http://chronicle.com/ article/MOOCs-May-Not-Be-So-Disruptive/140965.

4. Tom P. Abeles, "The University: The Shifting Past," *On the Horizon* 22, no. 2 (2014): 101–109.

5. Frank B. McCluskey and Melanie L. Winter, "Academic Freedom in the Digital Age," *On the Horizon* 22, no. 2 (2014): 136–146.

6. Jennifer DeBoer, Andrew D. Ho, Glenda S. Stump, and Lori Breslow, "Changing 'Course': Reconceptualizing Educational Variables for Massive Open Online Courses," *Educational Researcher* 43, no. 2 (2014): 74–84.

7. John Swope, "How MOOCs Can Be Free and Profitable at the Same Time: A Look at the Economics of MOOCs," *Ed Tech Magazine*, December 16, 2013, http://www .edtechmagazine.com/higher/article/2013/12/how-moocs-can-be-free-and -profitable-same-time.

8. Sean Coughlan, "Trinidad Pioneers Online 'Knowledge Network,'" BBC, May 28, 2014, www.bbc.com/news/education-27610828.

9. Ibid.

10. Audrey Watters, "Top Ed-Tech Trends of 2013: MOOCs and Anti-MOOCs," *Hacked Education: The History and Future of Education Technology*, November 29, 2013, http://hackeducation.com/2013/11/29/top-ed-tech-trends-2013-moocs.

11. Kenneth R. Koedinger et al., "Learning Is Not a Spectator Sport: Doing Is Better Than Watching for Learning from a MOOC," in *Proceedings of the Second (2015) ACM Conference on Learning @ Scale,* ACM (Association for Computing Machinery), March 2015, 111–120.

12. Jonah Newman and Soo Oh, "8 Things You Should Know about MOOCs," *Chronicle of Higher Education,* June 13, 2014, http://chronicle.com/article/8-Things -You-Should-Know-About/146901/

13. Shanna Smith Jaggars, "Online Learning: Does It Help Low-Income and Under-prepared Students?," CCRC Working Paper 26, Assessment of Evidence Series (New York: Community College Research Center, Columbia University, 2011).

14. Markus Deimann, "The Dark Side of the MOOC: A Critical Inquiry on Their Claims and Realities," *Current Issues in Emerging eLearning* 2, no. 1 (2015): 3.

15. Carmel Deamicis, "A Q&A with 'Godfather of MOOCs' Sebastian Thrun after He Disavowed His Godchild," *PandoDaily*, May 12, 2014, http://pando.com/2014/05/12/a-qa-with-godfather-of-moocs-sebastian-thrun-after-he-disavowed-his-godchild.

16. Andrew P. Kelly, *Disruptor, Distracter, or What? A Policymaker's Guide to Massive Open Online Courses (MOOCs)* (Bellwether Education Partners, May 2014), http://bellwethereducation.org/sites/default/files/BW_MOOC_Final.pdf.

17. Jon Baggaley, "MOOCS: Digesting the Facts," *Distance Education* 35, no. 2 (2014): 159–163.

18. Fred Siff, "The MOOC Spring: MOOCs and Technology to Advance Learning and Learning Research (Ubiquity Symposium)," ACEM (Association for Computing Machinery), *Ubiquity*, August 2014, 1–7, http://ubiquity.acm.org/article.cfm?id=2591686.

19. Kevin Carey, *The End of College: Creating the Future of Learning and the University of Everywhere* (New York: Riverhead Books/Penguin, 2015).

20. Rachelle DeJong Peterson, "MOOC Fizzles," *Academic Questions* 27, no. 3 (2014): 316–319.

Bibliography

Abeles, Tom P. "The University: The Shifting Past." *On the Horizon* 22, no. 2 (2014): 101–119.

Baggaley, Jon. "MOOCs: Digesting the Facts." *Distance Education* 35, no. 2 (2014): 159–163.

Carey, Kevin. *The End of College: Creating the Future of Learning and the University of Everywhere.* New York: Riverhead Books/Penguin, 2015.

Comier, D[ave]. "Why Teach MOOCs—MOOCs as a Selfish Enterprise." Talk at MIT, March 17, 2014 (video file). https://www.youtube.com/watch?v=Smt8lsPU_Mo.

Coughlan, Sean. "Trinidad Pioneers Online 'Knowledge Network.'" BBC, May 28, 2014. www.bbc.com/news/education-27610828.

Deamicis, Carmel. "A Q&A with 'Godfather of MOOCs' Sebastian Thrun after He Disavowed His Godchild." *PandoDaily*, May 12, 2014. http://pando.com/2014/05/12/a-qa-with-godfather-of-moocs-sebastian-thrun-after-he-disavowed-his-godchild.

DeBoer, Jennifer, Andrew D. Ho, Glenda S. Stump, and Lori Breslow. "Changing 'Course': Reconceptualizing Educational Variables for Massive Open Online Courses." *Educational Researcher* 43, no. 2 (2014): 74–84.

Deimann, Markus. "The Dark Side of the MOOC: A Critical Inquiry on Their Claims and Realities." *Current Issues in Emerging eLearning* 2, no. 1 (2015): 3.

Jaggars, Shanna Smith. "Online Learning: Does It Help Low-Income and Underprepared Students?" CCRC Working Paper 26. Assessment of Evidence Series. New York: Community College Research Center, Columbia University, 2011.

Kelly, Andrew P. "Disruptor, Distracter, or What? A Policymaker's Guide to Massive Open Online Courses (MOOCs)." Bellwether Education Partners, May 2014. http://bellwethereducation.org/sites/default/files/BW_MOOC_Final.pdf.

Koedinger, Kenneth R., Jihee Kim, Julianna Zhuxin Jia, Elizabeth A. McLaughlin, and Norman L. Bier. "Learning Is Not a Spectator Sport: Doing Is Better Than Watching for Learning from a MOOC." In *Proceedings of the Second (2015) ACM Conference on Learning @ Scale*, ACM (Association for Computing Machinery), March 2015, 111–120.

Kolowich, Steve. "The MOOC 'Revolution' May Not Be As Disruptive As Some Had Imagined." *Chronicle of Higher Education*, August 8, 2013. http://chronicle.com/article/MOOCs-May-Not-Be-So-Disruptive/140965/.

McCluskey, Frank B., and Melanie L. Winter. "Academic Freedom in the Digital Age." *On the Horizon* 22, no. 2 (2014): 136–146.

Newman, Jonah, and Soo Oh. "8 Things You Should Know about MOOCs." *Chronicle of Higher Education*, June 13, 2014. http://chronicle.com/article/8-Things-You-Should-Know-About/146901.

Peterson, Rachelle DeJong. "MOOC Fizzles." *Academic Questions* 27, no. 3 (2014): 316–319.

Rodriguez, Osvaldo. "The Concept of Openness behind c and x-MOOCs (Massive Open Online Courses)." *Open Praxis* 5, no. 1 (2013): 67–73.

Siff, Fred. "The MOOC Spring: MOOCs and Technology to Advance Learning and Learning Research (Ubiquity Symposium)." ACM (Association for Computing Machinery), *Ubiquity*, August 2014, 1–7. http://ubiquity.acm.org/article.cfm?id=2591686.

Swope, John. "How MOOCs Can Be Free and Profitable at the Same Time: A Look at the Economics of MOOCs." *Ed Tech Magazine*, December 16, 2013. http://www.edtechmagazine.com/higher/article/2013/12/how-moocs-can-be-free-and-profitable-same-time.

Watters, Audrey. "Top Ed-Tech Trends of 2013: MOOCs and Anti-MOOCs." *Hacked Education: The History and Future of Education Technology*, November 2013. http://hackeducation.com/2013/11/29/top-ed-tech-trends-2013-moocs/.

14 Social Media and Teacher Education: The Case of STARTALK

Jiahang Li

Introduction

According to Joanna Brenner and Aaron Smith, social media usage in the United States has increased noticeably: 72 percent of online adults claim they use social media, such as Facebook or Twitter.[1] Social media encompass social networking sites, microblogs, wikis, video- and photo-sharing sites, and more. The social media adoption rate has increased 5 percent from late 2012 (67 percent) and almost ten times compared with the results reported in 2008 (8 percent). These increasing numbers suggest that social media are becoming part of people's lives globally, which in turn calls for attention from educators and researchers to begin exploring the affordances and challenges of social media used inside and outside classroom settings.

In the field of education, researchers have started to explore how to integrate social media into teaching and learning. Scholars who study social media and learning in education argue that social media practices can facilitate new forms of collaboration,[2] communication,[3] identity work,[4] social capital,[5] and civic participation in the online-offline community.[6]

In light of the changes facilitated by technology and an increasingly connected world, Angel Gurria, secretary-general of the Organisation for Economic Co-operation and Development, has urged that twenty-first-century schools "help young individuals to constantly adapt and grow, to develop their capacity and motivation, to expand their horizons and transfer and apply knowledge in novel settings."[7] Furthermore, teacher education programs need to prepare teachers to obtain the necessary skills and knowledge to be able to educate their students to use twenty-first-century skills at an early age and prepare for related challenges.[8] To this end, scholars of teacher education are exploring and have identified many potential affordances and challenges that social media offer for teacher preparation.

Social Media Affordances for Teaching

The affordances that social media offer for education may be helpful in overcoming the challenges that current educational systems face.[9] Social media allow learners to (1) generate more self-created-content,[10] (2) access information resources in a virtual community, regardless of distance and time, (3) engage in activities not possible in the real world, and (4) become involved in collaborative inquiry mediated through technology.[11] These potential benefits, if embedded in teaching and learning processes, would be expected to enhance learning outcomes by providing more participatory and collaborative ways of learning.

Collaborative learning Theoretically, social media seem to embody sociocultural views of knowledge as decentralized, accessible, and coconstructed by and among a broad base of users.[12] Sociocultural theories of learning value the communication of knowledge through social practices and the opportunity to engage in various communities to learn with and from others.[13] For instance, Andreas Lund conducted a study using a wiki to construct teenage students' collective and multiple perceptions of the United States. Students' responses on a questionnaire about the wiki project revealed that learners appreciated the sharing, cooperation, and multiplicity of opinions that working with a wiki afforded them. The findings suggest that students were engaged in a collective way of learning and transitioned "from local collaboration to collective and networked production."[14] Moreover, Barley Mak and David Coniam used wikis to investigate the development of secondary school students' writing skills. Seventh-year EFL learners used a wiki to create a printed brochure about their new school for their parents. The study results indicated that, by working collaboratively, students produced larger amounts of text than what was expected and also increased the complexity of their writing by expanding and reorganizing their texts.[15]

Building a community of practice Emphasizing the importance of social participation, individuals engage in and became active members of *communities of practice*[16] as they learn behaviors and form beliefs that align with their social groups and eventually act in accordance with the group's or community's norms.[17] For instance, Blanche O'Bannon, Jeffrey Beard, and Virginia Britt, by integrating a Facebook group into a technology teaching methods course, found that using a Facebook group was effective in increasing pre-service teachers' knowledge of core technology topics.[18] Within the community of a Facebook group, pre-service teachers were able to maintain existing relationships, share photographs, and communicate. The pre-service teachers indicated that the Facebook group was beneficial in improving readiness for course assessments, was convenient, provided a good means of communication, and enhanced learning. This example suggests that social media can provide an ideal context for teachers' professional learning where individuals actively engage in the practices of a collaborative global online community.[19] Virtual communities of practice constructed through social media enable learners to connect with each other, construct a shared understanding, engage in discussions, and share resources. As learners participate in the virtual spaces over time, a community of practice forms to take advantage of technological affordances.[20]

Content generation Social media not only provide an online network environment for members to gather information and consume content generated by others in the network, they also facilitate the creation and application of tools for user-generated content, as demonstrated by wiki and Facebook. Robin Mason and Frank Rennie argued for four major benefits of learner-generated content that social media provide: (1) the learners are able to actively participate in the construction of their experience rather than passively absorbing content; (2) the content can be continually refreshed by the learners rather than requiring expert input; (3) many of the social media are collaborative in nature, so that the learners develop team skills; and (4) shared community space and intergroup communications help motivate learners to learn.[21]

By providing opportunities for collaborative learning, for building a community of practice over time, and for content generation, social media have the potential to be integrated into teacher education programs or professional development programs to enhance both pre-service and in-service teachers' learning experience. In practice, many teacher education programs have already incorporated social media into teaching and learning. A national foreign language teacher education program, STARTALK, serves as an example to demonstrate how social media can be used, and with what benefits and challenges, in teacher education.

Foreign Language Teacher Education Program: STARTALK

STARTALK is a widely known foreign language teacher preparation program that provides funding to support the teaching and learning of less commonly taught languages (LCTLs) in the United States. Originating in 2006 as a component of the National Security Language Initiative, by 2012 the STARTALK program was providing professional development opportunities for more than 1,400 language teachers across the United States.[22] Many of the STARTALK-funded foreign language teacher programs reported integrating social media into the training program to enhance learning. According to a recent survey, more than half of instructors who participated in STARTALK summer teacher training programs claimed they had used websites designed for language learning, nearly one-third used computer software designed for language learning, almost a fifth used video conferencing (e.g., Skype), and almost a quarter used virtual learning environments such as Moodle or Blackboard in their programs.[23]

The format of STARTALK teacher programs ranges from traditional face-to-face professional development courses to hybrid or blended programs (which blend online and face-to-face instruction) to fully online programs for teachers from novice to veteran levels. Various models of teacher training, especially the hybrid or blended and online programs, provide teacher participants with multiple opportunities to work collaboratively to generate content and learn new knowledge through a community of practice. Currently STARTALK programs are offered in eleven languages, Chinese, Arabic, Hindi, Korean, Russian, Urdu, Persian, Portuguese, Swahili, Turkish, and Dari, with participants coming from all over the United States. In the summer of 2012, there were 6,239 students and 1,433 teacher participants enrolled in STARTALK programs nationwide. The mission of STARTALK is to increase the number of Americans learning, speaking, and teaching LCTLs by offering students in grades K–16 and teachers of these languages creative and engaging summer experiences that strive to exemplify best practices in language education and in language teacher development, in this way forming an extensive community of practice that seeks continuous improvement through outcomes-driven program design, standards-based curriculum planning, learner-centered approaches, excellence in the selection and development of materials, and a meaningful assessment of outcomes.[24] Program A is offered as an example to better illustrate the affordances and challenges of using social media in STARTALK teacher programs.

Program A, one of the 2013 STARTALK summer teacher programs, incorporates social media (e.g., wikis) into its teacher training, and it is the wikis with which this discussion is most concerned. Program A was designed to provide a professional development program for cooperating master teachers and world language teacher educators. The program recruited twelve participants, who were teachers, administrators, and teacher educators from Arabic-, Chinese-, Russian-, and Turkish-speaking countries.[25] The program was unique in that the instructional team employed the wiki as an online platform for lesson and project development, communication and collaboration, and to create a professional learning community in which participants could continue to share and support each other after the summer program ended. All the reading materials, PowerPoint slides, assignments, and tasks were uploaded to the wiki (see figure 14.1). The wiki was organized in a way that participants could easily find the relevant information based on each individual topic. Participants were also encouraged to share their ideas through the discussion function embedded in the wiki, which provided opportunities for participants to collaboratively engage in the learning process.

Affordances Interviews with the lead instructor of Program A showed that the instructor believed the wiki was an "essential" component of the program. The lead instructor said she tried to incorporate more collaborative wiki features, such as a discussion forum, to encourage the

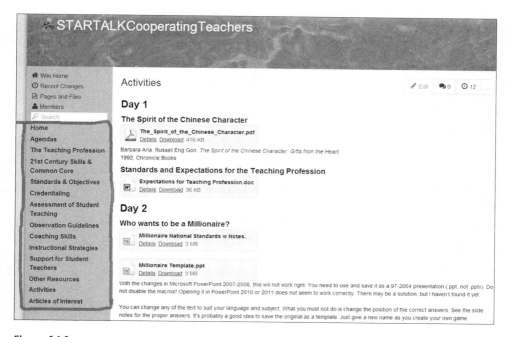

Figure 14.1
Wiki Navigation Panel

participants to connect and share. She explained that the wiki served mainly as a virtual resource center for teacher participants to download materials. The instructor also reported that participants were satisfied with the wiki as a resource center because they could access materials anytime they wanted. In addition, the data indicated that one major benefit of the wiki was that it provided a virtual space teachers and students alike could access to share information.[26]

Moreover, wikis offered a social media form allowing collaborators to add, delete, and modify informational articles in a virtual community. Many researchers have praised the benefits of wikis in foreign language education. For instance, a wiki can be particularly useful in increasing students' motivation and accountability when it is integrated into writing assignments.[27] Using the wiki, students had access to each other's texts from the first draft through the final product; thus, students were constructing the content of the course while serving as their peers' audience. In the case of STARTALK, the wiki allowed teacher participants to "edit" the content and to upload material they thought would be helpful to the program. During this collaborative process, social media were beneficial for communication and interaction, which allowed participants to co-construct knowledge and share what they learned. This example from STARTALK provides evidence that social media such as wikis can encourage a collaborative way of learning in teacher education by allowing adult learners to generate content as part of a practice-driven community.

Challenges   On the other hand, the instructor identified several challenges to integrating the wiki in Program A. First, the discussion forum that was introduced through the wiki did not generate as much discussion and sharing among participants as the instructor had expected. Since the discussion was not a mandatory component, many participants did not pay much attention to this activity. Moreover, it was difficult for the individual instructor to actively encourage participants to engage in the discussion while she was teaching all the program content. Second, the instructor reported in interviews that participants' prior expertise and experience with technology was another factor that influenced their use of social media in the foreign language teacher education program. Because Program A was designed to provide intensive training in just six days, it was difficult for the instructor to both model and scaffold pre-service teachers' use of social media, especially for those with varying levels of expertise in using social media. Third, the instructor believed that contextual factors, such as school constraints on the use of social media, restricted teachers from introducing—or wanting to introduce—social media in their classrooms. Therefore, it was difficult at times to meaningfully integrate social media into the foreign language teacher education program because of the hurdles that foreign language teachers had faced in their home classrooms and would have to surmount in their professional development experience.[28]

The case study data suggested additional challenges that this and similar STARTALK teacher education programs might have to deal with when integrating social media–enabled components. Among these were lack of necessary training and support, individual differences among teachers in accepting and incorporating social media, and contextual factors surrounding both K–12 schools and STARTALK programs in higher education, such as restrictive school or institutional technology policies, lack of time and access to technology, and technical difficulties. The lack of necessary training and K–12 school policy restrictions were the two major barriers identified in STARTALK foreign language teacher education programs. For example, in Program A, without appropriate training in how to use wikis in the classroom, teacher participants did not understand the collaborative nature of wikis and their potentially powerful results for learning. More specifically, teacher educators in Program A not only needed to model how the wiki could be used to generate content, provide comments, and exchange ideas; they also needed to model how it could facilitate and build the community of practice to encourage teachers' participation.

Conclusions and Implications

Social media can be beneficial in encouraging content generation, in building a community of practice, and in enhancing collaborative learning. The integration of social media into teacher education faces many challenges, such as difficulty in engaging participants, teachers' limited prior experiences and expertise in using social media, school policies restricting the use of social media in the classroom, lack of training and technical support, and lack of time and technology access.

The STARTALK program examined in this chapter has several implications for teacher education practices. First, the integration of social media should be carefully planned and implemented, with consideration given to influential factors, including but not limited to program requirements, the type and length of the program, participants' prior experience and achieved expertise in using social media, and the guidance and technical support infrastructure surrounding the professional development. To take full advantage of social media's affordances for language teacher education (e.g., for purposes of collaborative learning, community building, and content generation), program administrators and teacher educators should adopt a flexible approach whereby participants have time to experience and experiment with social media and reflect on how they can be used for teaching and learning. Furthermore, differentiated instruction, or instruction tailored to individual participants and their needs and interests, is more beneficial than teacher-centered, direct instruction because the former honors adult learners' varying expertise, experiences, and interests in using social media. In addition, it is reasonable and beneficial to design the program with the requirement that teacher participants actually use social media to complete learning tasks and assignments, which in turn may help them better understand the possibilities and challenges of using specific social media in their teaching and with their own students.

Finally, the STARTALK example has several implications for future research. For instance, current studies that examine the relationship between social media and teacher education are investigating the strengths and weaknesses of various learning environments, such as distance, online, and blended learning models,[29] different learning management systems (e.g., Blackboard, Desire2Learn), and online professional development.[30] More research is needed to identify the affordances and challenges of social media when integrated into various teacher education environments. Because of the short-term, intensive nature of STARTALK teacher programs, research on this and similar programs provides only a snapshot of teacher participants' perceptions and practices. More longitudinal studies are needed to investigate whether and how social media can be integrated differently and flexibly in various settings, with all types of teachers and with what impacts.

Notes

1. Joanna Brenner and Aaron Smith, "72% of Online Adults Are Social Networking Site Users," Pew Internet & American Life Project (Washington, DC: Pew Research Center, 2013), http://www.pewinternet.org/2013/08/05/72-of-online-adults-are-social-networking-site-users.

2. Ulrike Cress and Joachim Kimmerle, "A Systemic and Cognitive View on Collaborative Knowledge Building with Wikis," *International Journal of Computer-Supported Collaborative Learning* 3, no. 2 (2008), 105–122; Christine Greenhow and Jiahang Li, "Like, Comment, Share: Collaboration and Civic Engagement within Social Network

Sites," in *Emerging Technologies for the Classroom: A Learning Sciences Perspective,* ed. Chrystalla Mouza and Nancy Lavigne (New York: Springer, 2012).

3. Christine Greenhow and Elizabeth Robelia, "Old Communication, New Literacies: Social Network Sites as Social Learning Resources," *Journal of Computer-mediated Communication* 14 (2009): 1130–1161.

4. Christine Greenhow and Elizabeth Robelia, "Informal Learning and Identity Formation in Online Social Networks," *Learning, Media and Technology* 34, no. 2 (2009): 119–140.

5. Christine Greenhow and Lisa Burton, "Help from My 'Friends': Social Capital in the Social Network Sites of Low-Income High School Students," *Journal of Educational Computing Research* 45, no. 2 (2011): 223–245; Nicole B. Ellison, Charles Steinfield, and Cliff Lampe, "The Benefits of Facebook 'Friends': Exploring the Relationship between College Students' Use of Online Social Networks and Social Capital," *Journal of Computer-Mediated Communication* 12, no. 3 (2007), article 1, http://jcmc.indiana.edu/vol12/issue4/ellison.html (accessed July 30, 2014); Sebastián Valenzuela, Namsu Park, and Kerk F. Kee, "Is There Social Capital in a Social Network Site? Facebook Use and College Students' Life Satisfaction, Trust, and Participation," *Journal of Computer-Mediated Communication* 14, no 4 (2009): 875–901.

6. Beth Robelia, Christine Greenhow, and Lisa Burton, "Adopting Environmentally Responsible Behaviors: How Learning within a social Networking Application Motivated Students to Act for the Environment," *Environmental Education Research* 17, no. 4 (2011): 553–575.

7. Angel Gurria, "Education for the Future: Promoting Changes in policies and Practices: The Way Forward," remarks delivered at the Education Ministerial Round Table, UNESCO, Paris, October 10, 2009, http://www.oecd.org/document/34/0,3343, en_2649_37455_43880354_1_1_1_1,00.html(accessed July 29, 2014);

8. Chris Dede et al., "A Research Agenda for Online Teacher Professional Development," *Journal of Teacher Education* 60, no. 1 (2009): 8–19; Mary Hatwood Futrell, "Transforming Teacher Education to Reform America's P–20 Education System," *Journal of Teacher Education* 61, no. 5 (2010): 432–440.

9. Glynda Hull and Katherine Schultz, eds., *School's Out! Bridging Out-of-School Literacies with Classroom Practice* (New York: Teachers College Press, 2002); K. W. Lai, Ferial Khaddage, and Gerald Knezek, "Blending Student Technology Experiences in Formal and Informal Learning," *Journal of Computer Assisted Learning* 29, no. 5 (2013): 414–425.

10. Lawrence Lessig, *Remix: Making Art and Commerce Thrive in the Hybrid Economy* (New York: Penguin Press 2008).

11. Chris Dede, "Technological Supports for Acquiring 21st Century Skills," in *International Encyclopedia of Education,* ed. Eva Baker, Barry McGaw, and Penelope

Peterson, 3rd ed. (Oxford: Elsevier, 2010), http://learningcenter.nsta.org/products/ symposia_seminars/iste/files/Technological_Support_for_21stCentury_Encyclo _dede.pdf (accessed June 8, 2014)

12. Chris Dede, "Reinventing the Role of Information and Communication Technologies in Education," in *Information and Communication Technologies: Considerations of Current Practices for Teachers and Teacher Educators: 106th Yearbook of the National Society for the Study of Education, Part 2,* ed. Louanne Smolin, Kimberly Lawless, and Nicholas C. Burbules, 11–38 (Malden, MA: Blackwell, 2007).

13. Lev S. Vygotsky, *Mind in Society* (Cambridge, MA: Harvard University Press, 1978).

14. Andreas Lund, "Wikis: A Collective Approach to Language Production," *ReCALL* 20, no. 1 (2008): 35–54.

15. Barley Mak and David Coniam, "Using Wikis to Enhance and Develop Writing Skills among Secondary School Students in Hong Kong," *System* 36 (2008), 437–455.

16. Jean Lave and Etienne Wenger, *Situated Learning: Legitimate Peripheral Participation* (Cambridge: Cambridge University Press, 1991).

17. John Seely Brown, Allan Collins, and Paul Duguid, "Situated Cognition and the Culture of Learning," *Educational Researcher* 18, no. 1 (1989), 32–42.

18. Blanche W. O'Bannon, Jeffrey L. Beard, and Virginia G. Britt, "Using a Facebook Group as an Educational Tool: Effects on Student Achievement," *Computers in the Schools: Interdisciplinary Journal of Practice, Theory, and Applied Research* 30, no. 3 (2013): 229–247, doi:10.1080/07380569.2013.805972.

19. Pamela M. Wesely, "Investigating the Community of Practice of World Language Educators on Twitter," *Journal of Teacher Education* 64, no. 4 (2013): 305–318.

20. Kimble Handyside McCann, "Virtual Communities for Educators: An Overview of Supports and Best Practices," in *Technology, Colleges & Community Proceedings, 2009,* http://etec.hawaii.edu/proceedings/2009/McCann.pdf.

21. Robin Mason and Frank Rennie, *E-learning and Social Networking Handbook* (London: Routledge, 2008).

22. See the STARTALK website at http://startalk.umd.edu.

23. Julie Sugarman, Francesca DiSilvio, and Meg E. Malone, *2012 STARTALK Participant Survey Report: Teacher Trainees* (Washington DC: Center for Applied Linguistics, 2012).

24. See the STARTALK website at http://startalk.umd.edu.

25. Cited in Jiahang Li, "Instructors' Beliefs about the Integration of Social Media in STARTALK Teacher Programs: A Collective Case Study" (PhD diss., University of Maryland, 2014).

26. Instructor of Program A, interview, July 12, 2013.

27. Nike Arnold, Lara Ducate, and Claudia Kost, "Collaborative Writing in Wikis: Insights from Culture Projects in German Classes," in *The Next Generation: Social Networking and online Collaboration in Foreign Language Learning,* ed. Lara Lomicka and Gillian Lord (San Marcos, TX: CALICO, 2009), 115–144.

28. Instructor of Program A, interview, July 31, 2013.

29. Yu-chu Yeh, "Integrating Collaborative PBL with Blended Learning to Explore Preservice Teachers' Development of Online Learning Communities," *Teaching and Teacher Education* 26 (2010): 1630–1640.

30. Cynthia Carter Ching and Anthony W. Hursh, "Peer Modeling and Innovation Adoption among Teachers in Online Professional Development," *Computers & Education* 73 (2014): 72–82.

Bibliography

Arnold, Nike, Lara Ducate, and Claudia Kost. "Collaborative Writing in Wikis: Insights from Culture Projects in German Classes." In *The Next Generation: Social Networking and Online Collaboration in foreign Language Learning,* ed. Lara Lomicka and Gillian Lord, 115–144. San Marcos, TX: CALICO, 2009.

Brenner, Joanna, and Aaron Smith. "72% of Online Adults Are Social Networking Site Users." Pew Internet & American Life Project. Washington, DC: Pew Research Center, August 5, 2013. http://www.pewinternet.org/2013/08/05/72-of-online-adults-are-social-networking-site-users.

Brown, John Seely, Allan Collins, and Paul Duguid. "Situated Cognition and the Culture of Learning." *Educational Researcher* 18, no. 1 (1989): 32–42.

Ching, Cynthia Carter, and Anthony W. Hursh. "Peer Modeling and Innovation Adoption among Teachers in Online Professional Development." *Computers & Education* 73 (2014): 72–82.

Cress, Ulrike, and Joachim Kimmerle. "A Systemic and Cognitive View on Collaborative Knowledge Building with Wikis." *International Journal of Computer-Supported Collaborative Learning* 3, no. 2 (2008): 105–122.

Dede, Chris. "Reinventing the Role of Information and Communication Technologies in Education." In *Information and Communication Technologies: Considerations of Current Practices for Teachers and Teacher Educators: 106th Yearbook of the National Society for the Study of Education, Part 2,* ed. Louanne Smolin, Kimberly Lawless and Nicholas C. Burbules, 11–38. Malden, MA: Blackwell, 2007.

Dede, Chris. "Technological Supports for Acquiring 21st Century Skills." In *International Encyclopedia of Education,* ed. E. Baker, B. McGaw, and P. Peterson, 3rd ed.,

1–22. Oxford: Elsevier, 2010. http://learningcenter.nsta.org/products/symposia
_seminars/iste/files/Technological_Support_for_21stCentury_Encyclo_dede.pdf
(accessed June 8, 2013).

Dede, Chris, Diane Jass Ketelhut, Pamela Whitehouse, Lisa Breit, and Erin M.
McCloskey. "A Research Agenda for Online Teacher Professional Development."
Journal of Teacher Education 60, no. 1 (2009): 8–19.

Ellison, Nicole B., Charles Steinfield, and Cliff Lampe. "The Benefits of Facebook
'Friends': Exploring the Relationship between College Students' Use of Online Social
Networks and Social Capital." *Journal of Computer-Mediated Communication* 12, no. 3
(2007), article 1. http://jcmc.indiana.edu/vol12/issue4/ellison.html (accessed July
30, 2007).

Futrell, Mary Hatwood. "Transforming Teacher Education to Reform America's P–20
Education System." *Journal of Teacher Education* 61, no. 5 (2010): 432–440.

Greenhow, Christine, and Lisa Burton. "Help from My 'Friends': Social Capital in
the Social Network Sites of Low-Income High School Students." *Journal of Educational Computing Research* 45, no. 2 (2011): 223–245.

Greenhow, Christine, and Jiahang Li. "Like, Comment, Share: Collaboration and
Civic Engagement within Social Network Sites." In *Emerging Technologies for the
Classroom: A Learning Sciences Perspective*, ed. Chrystalla Mouza and Nancy Lavigne.
New York: Springer, 2012.

Greenhow, Christine, and Elizabeth Robelia. "Informal Learning and Identity Formation in Online Social Networks." *Learning, Media and Technology* 34, no 2 (2009):
119–140.

Greenhow, Christine, and Elizabeth. Robelia. "Old Communication, New literacies:
Social Network Sites as Social Learning Resources." *Journal of Computer-Mediated
Communication* 14 (2009): 1130–1161.

Gurria, Angel. "Education for the Future: Promoting Changes in Policies and Practices. The Way Forward." Remarks delivered at the Education Ministerial Round
Table, UNESCO, Paris, October 10, 2009. http://www.oecd.org/edu/educationforthe
future-promotingchangesinpoliciesandpracticesthewayforward.htm (accessed July
29, 2014).

Hull, Glynda, and Katherine Schultz, eds. *School's Out! Bridging Out-of-School Literacies with Classroom Practice*. New York: Teachers College Press, 2002.

Lai, K. W., Ferial Khaddage, and Gerald Knezek. "Blending Student Technology
Experiences in Formal and Informal Learning." *Journal of Computer Assisted Learning*
29, no. 5 (2013): 414–425.

Lave, Jean, and Etienne Wenger. *Situated Learning: Legitimate Peripheral Participation.*
Cambridge: Cambridge University Press, 1991.

Lessig, L. *Remix: Making Art and Commerce Thrive in the Hybrid Economy.* New York: Penguin Press, 2008.

Li, Jiahang. "Instructors' Beliefs about the Integration of Social Media in STARTALK Teacher Programs: A Collective Case Study." PhD diss., University of Maryland College Park, 2014.

Lund, Andreas. "Wikis: A Collective Approach to Language Production." *ReCALL* 20, no. 1 (2008): 35–54.

Mak, Barley, and David Coniam. "Using Wikis to Enhance and Develop Writing Skills among Secondary School Students in Hong Kong." *System* 36 (2008): 437–455.

Mason, Robin, and Frank Rennie. *E-learning and Social Networking Handbook.* London: Routledge, 2008.

McCann, Kimble Handyside. "Virtual Communities for Educators: An Overview of Supports and Best Practices." In *Technology, Colleges & Community Proceedings, 2009.* http://etec.hawaii.edu/proceedings/2009/McCann.pdf.

O'Bannon, Blanche W., Jeffrey L. Beard, and Virginia G. Britt. "Using a Facebook Group as an Educational Tool: Effects on Student Achievement." *Computers in the Schools: Interdisciplinary Journal of Practice, Theory, and Applied Research* 30, no. 3 (2013): 229–247. doi:.10.1080/07380569.2013.805972

Robelia, Beth, Christine Greenhow, and Lisa Burton. "Adopting Environmentally Responsible Behaviors: How Learning within a Social Networking Application Motivated Students to Act for the Environment." *Environmental Education Research* 17, no. 4 (2011): 553–575.

Sugarman, Julie, Francesca DiSilvio, and Meg E. Malone. *2012 STARTALK Participant Survey Report: Teacher Trainees.* Washington, DC: Center for Applied Linguistics, 2012.

Valenzuela, Sebastián, Namsu Park, and Kerk F. Kee. "Is There Social Capital in a Social Network Site? Facebook Use and College Students' Life Satisfaction, Trust, and Participation." *Journal of Computer-Mediated Communication* 14, no. 4 (2009): 875–901.

Vygotsky, Lev S. *Mind in Society.* Cambridge, MA: Harvard University Press, 1978.

Wesely, Pamela M. "Investigating the Community of Practice of World Language Educators on Twitter." *Journal of Teacher Education* 64, no. 4 (2013): 305–318.

Yeh, Yu-chu. "Integrating Collaborative PBL with Blended Learning to Explore Preservice Teachers' Development of Online Learning Communities." *Teaching and Teacher Education* 26 (2010): 1630–1640.

15 Teens' Participatory Play: Digital Media Learning through Civic Engagement

Benjamin Gleason

Introduction

While nearly 90 percent of adolescents have Internet access both inside and outside school,[1] an emerging problem is the lack of opportunities for teens to become involved in digital media projects that support teenagers' social, cultural, and political participation in the world. Even as some are troubled by the lack of young people's involvement in traditional civic activities such as voting,[2] others have seen civic engagement differently, drawing attention to teenagers' interest in projects that are more personally meaningful, such as volunteering, activism, or consumerism.[3] A new model of citizenship is taking shape in which young people use the affordances of the Internet to pursue interests through loosely based social networks.[4] Informed by a broad conception of civic engagement, projects such as World's Fair 2064 and Mouse offer the kind of participatory learning that can occur through the use of digital (and social) media. In both World's Fair 2064 and Mouse, young people use digital media to address pressing community problems with peers and trusted adults. Each project is explored in more detail below.

Mouse

Mouse is an organization based in New York City designed to "empower underserved youth to learn, lead, and create with technology."[5] The primary objective of the Mouse programs is to train student participants to become technological experts. Since 2000, more than 23,000 students have participated in Mouse and, through their expertise, have served 1.8 million students. Mouse consists of two projects, Mouse Squad and Mouse Corps. The Mouse Squad project trains educators, who in turn train students at their schools to become digital media and technology experts. The educators learn and pass on a number of skills, including how to remix videos using an open-access tool Mouse designed, create appealing websites, and develop new skills in areas such as robotics. By empowering underserved young people to become competent technological leaders while also supporting their academic goals, Mouse has advanced the creation of a national network of technology-focused teaching and learning. Meanwhile, for those with an advanced interest in design and technology, the Mouse Design League encourages young people to work alongside scientists, artists, engineers, computer scientists, and other technological experts as they create innovative projects. One current project, recently presented at the digital media and learning convention Emoti-Con, is an assistive technology product for artists with cerebral palsy. Named Omni Palette, the device allows artists with muscular challenges to swap paintbrushes and change paint. With the aid of a mechanical Arduino, an electronic open-source prototyping platform, the electronic palette encourages painters to continue their craft through assistive technology.

The key innovation of Mouse lies in creating a network of trained teen experts who use their technological expertise to provide a valuable service to the community. Mouse inverts the traditional model of education in which adults with knowledge attempt to transfer it to students by lecture. Mouse supports participatory, youth-led projects that develop the capacity of young people to address pressing community problems with a well-trained cadre of technological experts. Though educational technology has been a major priority for schools, as illustrated by the federal E-rate program, which funds hardware and software purchases, a major challenge has been maintaining technology in heavy-use areas such as schools.

Mouse has shown other community-based organizations and youth-serving networks how to build community capacity while providing necessary career development for underserved youth. However, the program also faces challenges. For instance, though Mouse's program evaluation demonstrated that more than 90 percent of its students gained valuable technology, communication, and problem-solving skills, the program also faces sustainability issues. Programs such as Mouse can be expensive and labor-intensive to implement. If Mouse is able to maintain diverse funding sources, staffing, and organizational capacity, it may be able to meet some of the challenges associated with running a community-focused organization.

The primary revolutionary aspect of Mouse lies in the scale of its outcomes. With 23,000 student participants, the organization was able to reach almost two million students. This suggests that the power of projects

like Mouse lies in their effect not only on the actual students who participate but also on groups, communities, and networks. The technological
expertise that students gain will likely continue to develop the professional
capacity of each community served by Mouse. The students, meanwhile,
benefit from gaining lifelong technological competencies that are highly
valued on the job market.

While Mouse seeks to train a cadre of talented young people to address
New York City's pressing technological needs, across the city another
program is building awareness about the dangers of climate change. The
next section details that program's story.

World's Fair 2064

The goal of World's Fair 2064, an educational and visionary project contemplating the look of a 2064 world fair in New York's Flushing Meadows
Corona Park and comparing it with the current status quo, is to facilitate
creative activism through community service projects based on scientific
issues.[6] Led by the Queens (New York) Zoo, the project was devised as a
way to teach high school students about climate change while building on
students' unique resources, such as knowledge of community, their inven-
tion of characters, and their developing scientific knowledge. The World's
Fair 2064 project uses an innovative approach known as *transmedia storytelling* to tell the story of a community's response to proposed urban
redevelopment.

For instance, to tell the story of climate change, student participants
created a fictitious scenario drawing attention to the central role of the park
in the community. The group imagined the effects of a 2064 proposal to
raze Flushing Meadows Corona Park and replace it with high-rise condo-
miniums, luxury retail outlets, and a sports complex. Flushing Meadows
Corona Park, created for the 1964 New York World's Fair, is a much-loved
home to city residents, different varieties of wildlife (including many kinds
of birds and farm animals), and large recreational spaces. One of the characters created by the young people is Perry Donald, an avid birdwatcher,
who, the students decided, would spearhead the opposition to razing the
park. Through the use of different media—photographs, video, artwork—in
conjunction with social media such as Facebook, Twitter, and YouTube,
World's Fair 2064 encourages young people to participate in the movement
against the redevelopment. Moreover, as a way to bridge the fictive, future
scenario and participants' lived experiences, World's Fair 2064 organizes
real-life bird counts that illustrate the effects of destroying a large, urban

park. The falling numbers of birds suggest the local consequences of a global problem.

The key innovation of World's Fair 2064 is using the most popular social media space with teenagers, Facebook, to detail the negative consequences of eliminating an important park in New York City. And because issues are handled through story format, young people can draw on their creativity and capacity to make large, complex stories (e.g., about climate change) accessible and engaging. Through transmedia storytelling, young people can create captivating learning experiences that help develop their scientific knowledge, technological expertise, and communicative competence.

World's Fair 2064 in action further suggests the powerful relationships that can form as young people use social media to address a critical issue such as climate change: youth involved in the program worked alongside adult mentors, including technology experts, wildlife biologists, and artists, to create multimedia stories that demonstrate their science learning. Though Donald Perry and his fellow activists are fictitious, the factors affecting the real and imagined park are very much the same: climate change will have a serious effect on New York City, affecting people, wildlife, businesses, and beyond. Framing the story of climate change as a local issue allows New Yorkers to see how the loss of Corona Park would lead to immediate follow-on consequences, such as the loss of birds and other wildlife.

Both World's Fair 2064 and Mouse are part of a larger educational approach, called *connected learning,* that builds on young people's particular interests and desires to learn with peers to support economic, social, or political participation.[7] Connected learning projects rely on digital media to lower barriers to participation, offer social supports for learning, and develop identities through the use of online literacy practices such as reading and writing. These projects seem to offer a bridge between youth-initiated activities and interests, such as social media activities, and traditionally defined models of civic engagement, such as community service, voting, and participation in the political process. Henry Jenkins, a scholar of new media and popular culture, has written extensively on how technological, social, and cultural changes support young people's participation in the world around them.[8] As young people post original artwork, photography, or stories online using digital media, Jenkins argues, they gain valuable technological, social, political, and artistic skills that enable community participation. This kind of participation in a peer-driven, low-stakes environment (in contrast to many formal classroom settings) may help develop young people's abilities to use multiple forms of media to tell stories, build worlds, become activists, and represent themselves. Interestingly, Jenkins noted that participation in these digital cultures is not limited to white, suburban males; 40 percent of urban young people surveyed were considered media creators (versus 28 percent of suburban youth), and 27 percent of older girls are involved in participatory activities (versus 17 percent of boys).[9]

While a number of benefits result from these types of learning spaces, there are particular limitations as well. First, while the learning outcomes that occur are exciting, they require significant investment of time, labor, and funding to achieve the sort of high-quality results seen with World's Fair 2064. Though these constraints are significant, fortunately, they are usually distributed among multiple stakeholders, such as learning organizations, community members, adult volunteers, and students. Second, the current educational model offers significant barriers to promoting, recognizing, and validating the learning that happens in this type of environment. While science researchers have found that students typically increase their content knowledge through connected learning projects of this sort,[10] schools may be hesitant to take part in innovative projects. Third, these types of connected learning projects often require the development of new assessment models to evaluate the learning-related outcomes. These challenges, while not insurmountable, draw attention to the capacity of the community (including schools) to develop resources to respond to them.

Recommendations for Policy and Pedagogy

Mouse and World's Fair 2064 model ways in which young people can develop the practices of civic engagement through participatory play. Mouse trains young people to become technological experts in their school community, empowering them to solve technical computing problems; World's Fair 2064 develops the capacity of young people to tell imaginative, multimedia stories about climate change. Both programs encourage youth to transform themselves and their communities by using interactive digital media to build capacity, create powerful narratives, and connect with peers and adult mentors. One link between the projects is an element of play: young people have fun as they take part in activities that serve their communities.

To fully realize the transformative power of digital media to support civic engagement, schools, public libraries, and after-school programs should reverse existing bans on (social) media use, as New York City has done recently. Though schools face particular pressures toward standardized education in a milieu of neoliberal, corporate education reform, they can also be a space of tremendous opportunity to develop educational innovation. Schools serve as an important bastion of democracy (e.g., through educating all students, including those marginalized in larger society; by providing nutrition; and by providing access to mental and reproductive health services) and nurture within the ecology of public participation. As World's Fair 2064 and Mouse show, the use of social media may encourage students to develop important literacy, technological, and artistic competencies. As students develop engaging narratives about the negative consequences of critical global events such as climate change, they add much-needed voices to a conversation often dominated by adults. Thus, a relatively modest policy recommendation has the potential to open up important avenues for learning, participatory play, and community change.

Once the ban on social media use in schools is lifted, teachers and students should take advantage of opportunities to develop collaboration, creativity, and technological expertise through the use of low-cost or free platforms. In this model, exemplified by Mouse, students are seen not as empty vessels that require knowledge to be poured in but as competent experts who can train peers, teachers, and community members in appropriate uses of technology. Empowering students to plan, lead, and participate in learning opportunities will go a long way toward the development of vibrant educational communities. This kind of collaboration counteracts the tendency of schools to focus on autonomous, individual learners.

Digital media can be integrated into schools relatively easily. Rather than replacing or detracting from traditional academic curricula, digital media complement and deepen opportunities for learning. For example, students tasked with writing a persuasive composition, a common requirement in many public schools, might use digital media to create a brief video about the role of justice and equality in their community. The traditional literacy skills of persuasive writing are complemented with the digital media skills of video creation and editing, while the entire project demands negotiation, problem solving, and playfulness.

To that end, teachers, after-school program coordinators, community members, and administrators should develop meaningful curricula that speak to young people's need for creative, artistic practices. A promising educational innovation is the inclusion of the arts in traditional "hard science" practices. These so-called STEAM initiatives use arts to develop and nurture creativity, collaboration, and cross-disciplinary thinking. Like World's Fair 2064, these projects rely on the power of the arts to tell valuable stories through music, photography, video, dance, and sound. Using art acknowledges our humanity and the importance of artistic creation to build community and strengthen ourselves.

Finally, the use of digital media can serve as a meaningful lever to get young people involved in community participation. By encouraging playful, humane learning opportunities—such as becoming a tech expert or using video to tell the story of a local park—young people follow their interests to facilitate positive societal change.

Notes

1. See Mary Madden et al., "Teens and Technology 2013," Pew Internet & America Life Project (Washington, DC: Pew Research Center, March 13, 2013), http://www .pewinternet.org/2013/03/13/teens-and-technology-2013/.

2. Robert D. Putnam, *Bowling Alone: The Collapse and Revival of American Community* (New York: Simon & Schuster, 2000).

3. See W. Lance Bennett, *Civic Learning in Changing Democracies: Challenges for Citizenship and Civic Education* (London: Routledge, 2007).

4. W. Lance Bennett, Chris Wells, and Deen G. Freelon, "Communicating Civic Engagement: Contrasting Models of Citizenship in the Youth Web Sphere," *Journal of Communication* 61, no. 5 (2011): 835–856, http://dfreelon.org/wp-content/ uploads/2008/06/bennettwellsfreelon2011.pdf.

5. Available at http://mouse.org.

6. Available at http://worldsfair2064.wordpress.com.

7. Mizuko Ito et al., *Connected Learning: An Agenda for Research and Design* (Irving, CA: Digital Media and Learning Research Hub, 2013), http://dmlhub.net/wp -content/uploads/files/Connected_Learning_report.pdf.

8. Henry Jenkins, *Confronting the Challenges of Participatory Culture: Media Education for the 21st Century* (Cambridge, MA: MIT Press, 2009).

9. Henry Jenkins and Vanessa Bertozzi, "Artistic Expression in the Age of Participatory Culture: How and Why Young People Create," in *Engaging Art: The Next Great Transformation of America's Cultural Life*, ed. Stephen J. Tepper and Bill Ivey (New York: Routledge, 2008), 171–195.

10. Angela Calabrese Barton et al., "Crafting a Future in Science: Tracing Middle School Girls' Identity Work over Time and Space," *American Educational Research Journal* 50, no. 1 (2012): 37–75, doi:0002831212458142.

Bibliography

Barton, Angela Calabrese, Hosun Kang, Edna Tan, Tara B. O'Neill, Juanita Bautista-Guerra, and Caitlin Brecklin. "Crafting a Future in Science: Tracing Middle School Girls' Identity Work over Time and Space." *American Educational Research Journal* 50, no. 1 (2012): 37–75. doi:.0002831212458142

Bennett, W. Lance. *Civic Learning in Changing Democracies: Challenges for Citizenship and Civic Education.* Young Citizens and New Media. London: Routledge, 2007.

Bennett, W. Lance, Chris Wells, and Deen G. Freelon. "Communicating Civic Engagement: Contrasting Models of Citizenship in the Youth Web Sphere." *Journal of Communication* 61, no. 5 (2011): 835–856. http://dfreelon.org/wp-content/uploads/2008/06/bennettwellsfreelon2011.pdf.

Ito, Mizuko, Kris Gutiérrez, Sonia Livingstone, Bill Penuel, Jean Rhodes, Katie Salen, Juliet Schor, Julian Sefton-Green, and S. Craig Watkins. *Connected Learning: An Agenda for Research and Design.* Irving, CA: Digital Media and Learning Research Hub, 2013. http://dmlhub.net/wp-content/uploads/files/Connected_Learning_report.pdf.

Jenkins, Henry. 2009. *Confronting the Challenges of Participatory Culture: Media Education for the 21st Century.* Cambridge, MA: MIT Press, 2009.

Jenkins, Henry, and Vanessa Bertozzi. "Artistic Expression in the Age of Participatory Culture: How and Why Young People Create." In *Engaging Art: The Next Great Transformation of America's Cultural Life*, ed.Stephen J. Tepper and Bill Ivey, 171–195. New York: Routledge, 2008.

Madden, Mary, Amanda Lenhart, Maeve Duggan, Sandra Cortesi, and Urs Gasser. "Teens and Technology 2013." Pew Internet & American Life Project. Washington, DC: Pew Research Center, March 13, 2013. http://www.pewinternet.org/2013/03/13/teens-and-technology-2013.

Putnam, Robert D. *Bowling Alone: The Collapse and Revival of American Community.* New York: Simon & Schuster, 2000.

Conclusion: Making the New Status Quo: Social Media in Education

Ri Pierce-Grove

Introduction

Tailoring what we say and how we say it to our audience is fundamental to human communication. It extends even to the syntax of our speech. When we converse, we adapt our accent, pitch, syntax, vocabulary, and content to match our conversational partner. Doing so makes us better liked and better communicators.[1] When a practice so deeply rooted is shaken, and our ability to predict our audience is disrupted, considerable social effort is expended to adapt and stabilize. Like politicians, we want to get our messages across without being quoted out of context.

In recent decades, the widespread adoption of successive communications technologies has put pressure on our ability to match our speech to our audience. Email felt private, but it could be forwarded, archived, and subpoenaed. Mobile phones made it possible to call home on the street, but doing so irritated people around us with conversation not addressed to them.

As each technology was adopted by new groups, social abrasions, misunderstandings, and scandals were followed by a negotiation of new norms. This negotiation was encoded in institutional policies. After high-profile court cases showed the damage emails taken out of context could do, companies adopted new document retention policies.[2] Public transit systems banned mobile phones as they had banned radios before them, or offered "quiet cars." These policies both expressed newly negotiated norms and structured future communications.

The essays in this book took shape after the initial creativity, instability. and abrasions of social media's widespread adoption. They are published in a moment in which norms for social media in education are still pliable, but are being codified and institutionalized. Each makes a case for what accommodations should be made as etiquette, business practices, regulations, and institutions settle into the new normal.

The Contributions Made by This Volume

Jack Balkin and Julia Sonnevend opened this volume with a panoramic view of digital education, drawing parallels with other industries to illustrate the forces at work. They laid out a future in which digital technologies would allow education to merge more seamlessly with other forms of knowledge creation, such as journalism, political opinion, and entertainment. In this environment, online education may prove most useful for cooperative projects between students, and in areas where there is a well-established body of knowledge that is not subject to interpretation. Offline education may continue to be superior in areas where the search for meaning, guided by knowledgeable experts, is what is being taught. Online education faces barriers of technology access and language. Resistance from governments and established educational providers give institutions with well-known brands regulatory and funding advantages. Finally, copyright reform will be necessary to enable global sharing and use of information in education.

In his contribution to this book, Mark Warschauer focused on the impact of digital media on equity in education. He looked at the degrees of access diverse groups have to digital media, and how that is influenced by technological and social factors. He then examined the ways in which young people use social media for education, social interaction, and entertainment. Finally, he commented on the educational outcomes of groups that use digital media. The success of digital media in education, which can be significant, depends on the availability of social support and on integration with the educational curriculum.

Many of the essays in this volume are oriented, implicitly or explicitly, toward education and social media in the developed world. Colin Agur helpfully reminded us that the future of social media will be shaped and defined in developing countries, whose populations are much greater. His case study on the distinct infrastructural challenges and complex socioeconomic conditions affecting ICT use for education in India offers insights both for ICT theorists and for educational practitioners.

danah boyd explored the potential for conflict when adults interpret young people's speech on social media as "public" and take it out of context. She argues that adults should adopt Goffman's "civil inattention" in their approach to young people's communication on social media. Adults should politely ignore young people's online conversation unless they hear a cry for help, just as they politely ignore conversations on public streets unless they see someone in trouble.

Valerie Belair-Gagnon related the BBC's reinvention of itself as a leader in the use of social media in journalism, and its education of its staff on the use and benefits of social media both for sourcing stories and as new channels for disseminating them. The BBC did so in response to several challenges: the London Underground bombings and the convolutions of the 'Arab Spring,' when it was often difficult to source stories through traditional reporters, and a scandal involving the on-air revelation of a confidential source. Her research is useful to existing and emerging institutions that are looking to social media for a solution to some of their current problems of outreach and student engagement.

Chris Dede sees a disjunct between classical and contemporary epistemology. In the classical view, knowledge is authenticated, produced by experts, and characterized by a single right answer. The contemporary epistemology valorizes consensus and collaboration. The classroom, he suggested, is an arena in which these two perspectives clash as students bring this newer view into conflict with teachers adhering to the classical view. Dede advocates bringing together diffuse stakeholders in education, distributing the responsibility for education outside the classroom.

Nicholas Bramble and Yite John Lu proposed that accrediting agencies can provide a crucial language to new institutions, through which they can communicate with old institutions, the public, and employers. By developing a system of accreditation that includes new, peer-based, online institutions, education departments can offer prospective students new ways to assess whether the education they are buying is worth their money and time.

Bramble showed us a world in which uncertainty about fair use is combining with opportunistic, overly broad claims by rights holders to constrict the educational uses of media in the very moment in which potentially benevolent uses are able to expand. He recommended a number of alternatives to restore the creative freedom and flexibility that educators and students need. Bramble emphasized two points. First, older norms of fair use are eroding; uses that were commonly seen as fair use are now considered too risky. Second, educators and students, frustrated in their desire to explore the full potential of new media, need copyright reform.

John Palfrey helps us understand the divergent views of online privacy held by adults and young people. Adults are concerned that young people do not care about their own privacy online and that they expose too much personal information. Research, however, shows that young people do care about their online privacy and image, just in a different way than adults imagine. Palfrey encourages us to see young peoples' online activity as an expression of their growing identities. He is, in particular, concerned that social media in education encourage exploration and development rather than stifle or exploit it.

David Buckingham is concerned with the content of education about media, rather than with digital media as a tool for education. He critiqued techno-utopian visions of digital media as radically new and inherently liberating and argued that the need to equip students with critical thinking skills in the context of media education is urgent.

Several case studies looked at concrete examples of education through digital media.

Shai Reshef and Daniel Greenwood provided two distinct views of the University of the People, a tuition-free online university, from the perspectives of founder and adviser, respectively. Reshef offered a snapshot of the University of the People in its early stages. He outlined a plan to scale up from a few hundred students to thousands while remaining tuition-free by relying on online peer interaction and volunteer faculty. Obstacles include many prospective students' inability to meet the requirement of a high school degree and the need for paid staff to supplement volunteers for essential functions. Greenwood described a threatening economic climate for middle-tier educational institutions and praised the University of the People as a philanthropic achievement, but not as a model for the future of education.

Minhtuyen Mai, Adam Poppe, and Christine Greenhow discussed the development of massive open online courses, primarily focusing on the top tier of universities that Balkin and Sonnevend identified as having a competitive advantage. Should these courses prove successful, the proffering institutions could acquire a large and potentially useful set of data on students' behavior with online educational materials.

Jiahang Li offered a survey of literature on the use of social media in teacher education and looked at the uses and pitfalls of a wiki in a summer program for educating language teachers.

Finally, Benjamin Gleason discussed the affordances of social media for participatory play in a connected learning model. His two case studies, Mouse and World's Fair 2064, serve as examples of young people developing digital media skills through projects that support both their personal interests and the needs of their communities.

A Model for Social Media in Education

danah boyd opened her essay by observing that, although social media offer an almost infinite diversity of expression, most people turn to it to connect with the familiar. Like adults, young people go online not primarily to encounter new people and ideas but to replicate and extend their existing connections. Seeking out difference is uncomfortable and takes conscious effort. But the purpose of education is explicitly to go beyond the familiar and learn what we do not know. Perhaps, then, a conscious goal of media education should be to develop students' abilities to engage with and learn from different communities.

The peer-to-peer learning institutions discussed by several of the authors in this volume depend on students' ability to build expertise from one another online. But as some of the other authors point out, this is a skill that is not evenly distributed.

Mark Warschauer and John Palfrey value "geeking out," the self-directed pursuit of developing expertise and sharing it on the web. They also noted that a minority of students have the skills to do so. Some institutions may find it useful to use existing communities of interest online as labs in which students can move from "messing around" to "geeking out," while being mentored by teachers.

In doing so, they could develop students' understanding in three distinct areas. First, students and teachers would have a new arena in which to focus on the subject matter of their course. As students did so, teachers could help them develop skills at learning from strangers online, which should serve them well throughout their lives. The study of social media need not be quarantined within media education. Rather, schools should develop a policy of keeping teachers abreast both of the online communities of interest most germane to their fields and of the shifting market for personal information that provides the business model for many of the services that host these communities.

In the years in which these essays were prepared, roughly 2010 to 2014, active communities existed around programming (Github), collaborative story writing (Wattpad), textual analysis (TVtropes, Goodreads), and current affairs (Twitter, many others). Using existing communities of interest may both relieve institutions of some of the burden of facilitating online interaction and equip students with the skills they need to navigate and learn from a broader online public than their own.

Teaching students to adjust the tenor and syntax of their speech so that they become valuable members of online communities might occupy the place in the twenty-first-century curriculum that public speaking did in the culture of oratory. Guiding students to seek out and build expertise in communities in a variety of fields might be seen as part of twenty-first-century library skills. Knowing how to use textbooks and libraries is a skill that crosses disciplines; so is social learning.

Such an approach would harmonize well with Chris Dede's vision of distributed education, in which stakeholders outside the classroom are brought into closer connection with the curriculum. Organizations like the BBC that have developed a mandate in social media education, as described by Valerie Belair-Gagnon, could become resources and engaged partners in such an enterprise.

Using commercial social media as labs to build students' skills is not without its risks. John Palfrey expressed an important concern that marketing and content are increasingly intertwined in students' social spaces online. To use current commercial services as labs puts a burden on educators to be as well informed as possible about a landscape that is often deliberately obscured.

However, if they use the web themselves in their private capacity, that burden is already there. Both students and teachers currently spend much of their online lives in commercial environments. As they do so, their online actions are constantly monitored and recorded by data brokers, companies that partner with virtually every popular website and social media service. According to the FTC, data brokers collect, store, and correlate billions of data elements from both online and offline sources, covering nearly every U.S. consumer.[3] The resulting profiles can have an invisible impact on what articles and ads an individual sees online or, for example, the cost of their insurance. Educators may join the FTC in lobbying for legislation modeled on the 1970 Fair Credit Reporting Act, which would enable consumers to see what information is being aggregated about them and sold. At the same time, they may choose to shoulder the responsibility of helping students understand how to manage their reputations online in the eyes both of people they know and of data brokers.

But we need not view commercial social spaces as adversaries. Google currently offers institutional accounts, which give educational institutions greater protection and control over data generated by students and ads are not shown to users.[4] These features could be attractive to institutions concerned about the privacy of their constituents and their information. A similar approach could be adopted for other social media, whereby institutions would pay subscription fees to a social media service in return for not being subject to data gathering and ads. Commercial social media companies would benefit by having a package they could market directly to educational institutions, government agencies, and commercial businesses worldwide.

Final Thoughts

If learning through social media is to be integral to education rather than a distraction from it, students will need to be taught how to learn from strangers. Finding and interpreting helpful communities may be seen as an extension of library research skills. Learning how to address and participate in communities outside familiar social groups may be seen as the contemporary equivalent of public speaking in the age of oratory.

Tailoring speech to different audiences is deeply embedded in human communication, but expanding students' ability to do so in unfamiliar contexts will take effort. Greater transparency from data brokers will help both teachers and students be aware of the full extent of the audiences they address when they go online.

As we move into the second decade of widespread social media, its place in institutions and the norms surrounding its use in private life are becoming established. The essays compiled in this book offer guidance and scholarship at a time when institutional decisions that will have far-reaching influence are still being made. For scholars, policymakers, and educators, this volume offers a bird's-eye view of the shifting governmental, market, and social pressures shaping education and digital environments.

Notes

1. Agustin Gravano et al., "Acoustic and Prosodic Correlates of Social Behavior," paper presented at a conference, "INTERSPEECH 2011," Florence, Italy , August 28–31, 2011. in *Proceedings INTERSPEECH 2011*, 97–100, http://www1.cs.columbia .edu/~sbenus/Research/Gravano_et_al_Social_behavior_IS11.pdf.

2. Lexis-Nexis, "Elements of a Good Document Retention Policy," White Paper, 2007. http://www.lexisnexis.com/AppliedDiscovery/lawlibrary/whitePapers/ADI_WP _ElementsOfAGoodDocRetentionPolicy.pdf.

3. Edith Ramirez et al., *Data Brokers: A Call for Transparency and Accountability*, Federal Trade Commission Report, May 2014. http://www.ftc.gov/system/files/ documents/reports/data-brokers-call-transparency-accountability-report-federal -trade-commission-may-2014/140527databrokerreport.pdf.

4. Google, "Data Processing Amendment to Google Apps Agreement, Version 1.3, Contract Amendment," 2014. https://www.google.com/intx/en/enterprise/apps/ terms/dpa_terms.html.

Bibliography

Google. "Data Processing Amendment to Google Apps Agreement, Version 1.3. Contract Amendment." 2014. https://www.google.com/intx/en/enterprise/apps/terms/dpa_terms.html (accessed October 12, 2014).

Gravano, Agustin, Rivka Levitan, Laura Willson, Štefan Benuš, Julia Hirschberg, and Ani Nenkova. "Acoustic and Prosodic Correlates of Social Behavior." Paper presented at a conference, "INTERSPEECH 2011," Florence, Italy, August 28–31, 2011. In *Proceedings INTERSPEECH 2011*, 97–100. http://www1.cs.columbia.edu/~sbenus/Research/Gravano_et_al_Social_behavior_IS11.pdf.

Lexis-Nexis. "Elements of a Good Document Retention Policy." White Paper, 2007. http://www.lexisnexis.com/AppliedDiscovery/lawlibrary/whitePapers/ADI_WP_ElementsOfAGoodDocRetentionPolicy.pdf.

Ramirez, Edith, Julie Brill, Maureen Ohlhausen, Joshua Wright, and Terrell McSweeny. *Data Brokers: A Call for Transparency and Accountability*. Federal Trade Commission Report, May 2014. http://www.ftc.gov/system/files/documents/reports/data-brokers-call-transparency-accountability-report-federal-trade-commission-may-2014/140527databrokerreport.pdf.

Contributors

Colin Agur is a Knight Law and Media Fellow, the Information Society Project at Yale Law School.

Jack M. Balkin is the Knight Professor of Constitutional Law and the First Amendment and Director, the Information Society Project at Yale Law School.

Valerie Belair-Gagnon is Executive Director and Research Scholar, the Information Society Project at Yale Law School.

danah boyd is Principal Researcher at Microsoft Research, Research Assistant Professor at New York University, and a Fellow at Harvard's Berkman Center for Internet and Society.

Nicholas Bramble is a former Fellow of the Information Society Project at Yale Law School.

David Buckingham is Professor of Education and Director of the Centre for the Study of Children, Youth and Media, the University of London.

Chris Dede is the Timothy E. Wirth Professor of Learning Technologies at Harvard's Graduate School of Education.

Benjamin Gleason is a PhD candidate in the Educational Psychology and Educational Technology program, Michigan State University.

Christine Greenhow is Assistant Professor in the Department of Counseling, Educational Psychology, and Special Education of the College of Education, Michigan State University, and a former Fellow of the Information Society Project at Yale Law School.

Daniel Greenwood is Professor of Law at Hofstra University and Chief Financial Officer, University of the People.

Jiahang Li is Assistant Professor in the Department of Counseling, Educational Psychology, and Special Education of the College of Education, Michigan State University.

Yite John Lu is an IP Litigation Associate at Irell and Manella LLP.

Mihntuyen Mai is a researcher in the HOPE Lab, the University of Wisconsin–Madison.

John Palfrey is Head of School at Philips Andover Academy.

Ri Pierce-Grove is a PhD candidate in Communications, Columbia University, and a Visiting Fellow, the Information Society Project at Yale Law School.

Adam Poppe is a PhD candidate in the Educational Psychology and Educational Technology program, Michigan State University.

Shai Reshef is CEO of the University of the People.

Julia Sonnevend is Assistant Professor, Department of Communication Studies, the University of Michigan.

Mark Warschauer is Professor of Education and Informatics at the University of California, Irvine, and Associate Dean of the School of Education.

Index